ABOUT THE AUTHOR: Richard S. West, Jr., is a Professor of History and English at the U. S. Naval Academy. He is the author of *Gideon Welles, Lincoln's Navy Department*, *The Second Admiral, A Life of David Dixon Porter*, *American Sea Power since 1775* (in collaboration), and other volumes.

MR. LINCOLN'S NAVY

MR. LINCOLN'S NAVY

by Richard S. West, Jr.

LONGMANS, GREEN AND COMPANY

NEW YORK · LONDON · TORONTO

1957

LONGMANS, GREEN AND CO., INC.
55 FIFTH AVENUE, NEW YORK 3

LONGMANS, GREEN AND CO., LTD.
6 & 7 CLIFFORD STREET, LONDON W 1

LONGMANS, GREEN AND CO.
20 CRANFIELD ROAD, TORONTO 16

MR. LINCOLN'S NAVY

PUBLISHED SIMULTANEOUSLY IN THE DOMINION OF CANADA BY LONGMANS, GREEN AND CO., TORONTO

FIRST EDITION

LIBRARY OF CONGRESS CATALOG CARD NUMBER 57-11989

PRINTED IN THE UNITED STATES OF AMERICA

VAN REES PRESS • NEW YORK

To my father

1872—1951

Acknowledgments

Mr. Lincoln's Navy HAS LONG BEEN IN PROCESS and owes much to many scholars and friends. To all whose information, advice, and encouragement were helpful in the production of *The Second Admiral, a Life of David Dixon Porter, 1813-1893,* and of *Gideon Welles: Lincoln's Navy Department,* the writer is happy again to acknowledge gratitude, for these earlier books were spadework for the present one. Particularly is he grateful to Charles Lee Lewis, Professor Emeritus, U. S. Naval Academy, his first mentor in the field of naval history, and to Professor Louis H. Bolander, librarian of the U. S. Naval Academy, retired, whose wide knowledge and cheerful assistance in research have informed many pages in this book.

To John L. B. Williams, of Longmans, Green, the author is grateful for suggesting the idea and title for *Mr. Lincoln's Navy,* as well as for later criticism and encouragement. For their criticism on certain sections of the manuscript the author is indebted to two of his colleagues—Associate Professor Robert W. Daly, author of *How the Merrimac Won,* and Senior Professor William W. Jeffries, whose doctoral thesis concerned Commodore Charles Wilkes. Mrs. J. P. C. McCarthy was helpful in preparing the manuscript. Finally, to the "best of women and of wives"—in crusty old Gid Welles's phrase—the author is in debt for help in every stage of the adventure.

Contents

Illustrations

List of Maps

MR. LINCOLN'S NAVY

1.

The Overt Acts

WHEN ABRAHAM LINCOLN WAS ELECTED PRESIDENT on November 6, 1860, the House Divided began to fall apart. The standardbearer of the "Black Republican" Party had himself announced his belief that the nation "could not long survive half slave, half free." In the view of Southern extremists his election itself marked the beginning of the war.

South Carolina separatists, three thousand strong in Charleston's Secession Hall, passed an ordinance declaring "that the Union now subsisting between South Carolina and other States under the name of the United States of America is hereby dissolved." The fateful day was Wednesday, December 20, 1860—three months before Lincoln took the oath of office, four months before Fort Sumter.

Governor Pickens of South Carolina at once sent representatives to Washington to negotiate with President James Buchanan's government for the peaceful surrender to South Carolina of all Federal forts, arsenals, customhouses, and lighthouses within its boundaries.

The secession of South Carolina was celebrated at Mobile by the firing of a hundred guns and a military parade. Church bells were rung and citizens in the streets made fiery Secessionist speeches. Alabama passed the Ordinance of Secession. At New Orleans a hundred guns were touched off and the pelican flag of the state was unfurled. Marching Creoles sang the French revolutionary "La Marseillaise," and a bust of John C. Calhoun, patron saint of Secession, was exhibited wearing a revolutionary tricolor cockade. Louisiana, too, enacted the Ordinance of Secession. Other states in the Deep South swung themselves on board the new bandwagon.

In New York City, meanwhile, the New England Society celebrated the 240th anniversary of the landing of the Puritans by a dinner with patriotic toasts and speeches. Andrew Jackson's slogan: "The American Union: it must and shall be preserved," was wildly applauded. In the border state of Virginia certain citizens of Petersburg raised South Carolina's palmetto flag; but during the night pro-Unionist hands chopped down the flagpole and destroyed the offending emblem.[1]

From Secessionist Mississippi a missionary was sent to Baltimore to persuade neutral Marylanders to embrace their cause. "Secession is not intended to break up the present Government," argued this worthy, "but to perpetuate it. We do not propose to go out by way of breaking up or destroying the Union as our fathers gave it to us, but we go out for the purpose of getting further guaranties and security for our rights." The slavery issue, said the Mississippian, "has been a festering sore upon the body politic; and many remedies have failed, we must try amputation, to bring it to a healthy state. We must have amendments to our Constitution, and if we cannot get them we must set up for ourselves." [2]

In Washington, D. C., President James Buchanan shrank from commencing a war which his successor would have to fight. John B. Floyd, his pro-Southern Secretary of War, who had already distributed Federal muskets to arsenals in Southern states, insisted on maintaining forts and navy yards exactly as they then were, without reinforcement. Buchanan went along with this policy, and assured the Governors of South Carolina and Florida that there would be no changes made at the Pensacola Navy Yard or at the forts in Charleston Harbor.

Groups of state militia, however, egged on by zealots and hoodlums, trampled underfoot this "gentlemen's agreement" with Washington. Arsenals were seized in all the seceded states, and great pressure was put upon commandants to surrender Federal forts and navy yards to the Southern states. Among the forts guarding Southern harbors that were seized and occupied by state militia were Castle Pinckney and Fort Moultrie in Charleston Harbor, Fort Pulaski in Georgia, Forts Morgan and Gaines, the sentinels of Mobile Bay, Fort Marion at St. Augustine, Fort Caswell near Wilmington, North Carolina, Forts Barrancas and McRee at Pensacola, and Forts Jackson and St. Philip on the Mississippi below New Orleans. Several were antiquated structures like the Spanish-built Forts Barrancas and Marion. Around others clustered memories of 1812 and their cannon were mostly of early vintage. A number of the mouldering piles of antique masonry, which uniformed state militia now swept out and began living in, had stood vacant for years. But all of these forts, regardless of age and condition would be invaluable to their possessors after civil war, with its great blockade, had begun. The forts and arsenals were just as unprepared for defense against the present civil uprising as were the post offices, customhouses, lighthouses, and so on, so that a standard procedure of peaceful surrender was evolved in which responsible officials, rather than shed the blood of their fellow citizens, simply yielded before overwhelming numbers of local forces.

This benign pattern of peaceful surrender was sidestepped by two nonconformists who managed to transfer their commands to untenanted forts on near-by islands. Major Robert Anderson shifted to Fort Sumter in Charleston Harbor and Major Adam J. Slemmer took refuge in Fort Pickens on Santa Rosa Island at the entrance to Pensacola Harbor.

Although Anderson was in charge of the several forts at Charleston, he had but two companies of soldiers plus a brass band of eight, making a total of eighty-three men. They were billeted in Fort Moultrie. Castle Pinckney was unoccupied. Fort Sumter, a three-tiered masonry fort standing on an island of New England granite chips in the middle of the harbor, was still under construction. Each day some 150 carpenters and masons were ferried to and from Fort Sumter.

Before Lincoln's election, the army engineer in charge of

construction work on Fort Sumter had requisitioned forty muskets from the Charleston arsenal. He had feared an attempt by a mob to interrupt the work in progress, and had planned to issue the arms to certain loyal workmen. Army Engineer J. G. Foster's requisition had been cleared, but since, after the election, the workmen themselves began to show increasing signs of hostility, Foster changed his mind about issuing them muskets. On December 17, however, he made a routine application to the arsenal for two muskets to be issued according to army regulations to the ordnance sergeants at Fort Sumter and Castle Pinckney. The military storekeeper, in view of the now touchy political situation, declined to issue these arms without special authorization. He could, however, give him the old order of forty muskets, whose delivery had been cleared and which were packaged and ready for him. Foster accepted the forty muskets, issued two to the sergeants, and stowed the remainder in the magazines of Castle Pinckney and Fort Sumter.[3]

This special "arming" of the untenanted forts was so vigorously resented by Governor Pickens that Secretary of War Floyd had the forty muskets returned to the arsenal. Fort Sumter and Castle Pinckney were left without defense beyond closed shutters and locked gates.

While Major Anderson was under orders to avoid every act which would needlessly provoke aggression, he was directed to hold possession of the forts in Charleston Harbor and, if attacked, to defend himself "to the last extremity." On the day following South Carolina's secession, Secretary Floyd clarified by annulling these orders: "Under these instructions, you might infer that you are required to make a vain and useless sacrifice of your own life and the lives of the men under your command, upon a mere point of honor. This is far from the President's intentions. You are to exercise a sound military discretion on this subject. It is neither expected nor desired that you should expose your own life or that of your men in a hopeless conflict in defense of these forts. If they are invested or attacked by a force so superior that resistance would, in your judgment, be a useless waste of life, it will be your duty to yield to necessity, and make the best terms in your power." [4]

Fort Moultrie commanded the harbor but had no defense against such a possible enemy as a mob of angry citizens approaching it from the rear. Sand dunes, behind which sharpshooters might take cover, could not be leveled by Major Anderson for fear of arousing the populace. A cow might wander into the fort from the rear. Major Anderson decided that Fort Sumter in the middle of the harbor would be easier to defend.

Quietly, therefore, on the night of December 26, Anderson utilized the boats' going out to get the workmen to shift his tiny garrison from Fort Moultrie out to Fort Sumter. While Anderson was crossing the bay to Fort Sumter, Engineer Foster spiked the guns of Fort Moultrie, burned their gun carriages, and for good measure chopped down the fort's flagstaff.

The next afternoon a steamer landed at Castle Pinckney state troops, who scaled the walls with ladders and took possession. After dark, two steamers bearing a similar force seized Fort Moultrie. In Charleston the palmetto flag was raised over the post office and the customhouse. Two companies of militia set up a guard around the arsenal.

The Charleston *Mercury* fulminated over the Federal government's "gross breach of faith," and accorded to Major Anderson "the unenviable distinction of opening civil war between American citizens." [5] Governor Pickens dispatched commissioners to Washington to protest Anderson's dismantling of Fort Moultrie and occupation of Fort Sumter, and to urge immediate withdrawal of the troops from the harbor of Charleston. President Buchanan refused.

Secretary of War Floyd supported the South Carolinian commissioners, and, when the President still declined to abandon the precarious Federal hold on Charleston Harbor, Floyd resigned.

Major Anderson had a food supply barely sufficient to last

four months, and he would have to survive without such conveniences as soap and candles and coal. Moreover, he was compelled by the Charleston authorities to retain the 150-odd workmen within the fort so that their subsistence would the more quickly deplete his provisions and force him to surrender.

Winfield Scott, the seventy-five-year-old general-in-chief of the Army, recommended to President Buchanan that Fort Sumter be reinforced and held. "It is Sunday; the weather is bad, and General Scott is not well enough to go to church. But matters of the highest national importance seem to forbid a moment's delay, and if misled by zeal he hopes for the President's forgiveness. Will the President permit General Scott without reference to the War Department and otherwise, as secret as possible to send two hundred and fifty recruits from New York Harbor to reinforce Fort Sumter, together with some extra muskets or rifles, ammunition, and subsistence stores?" [6]

With the President's approval, Scott dispatched Lorenzo Thomas, an aide, to New York to organize a secret relief expedition. From M. O. Roberts the steamer *Star of the West* was chartered at twelve hundred dollars per day. She was loaded with provisions and cleared on the afternoon of January 5 as for a normal run to New Orleans. Outside New York Harbor after nightfall she was met by several steam tugs belonging to A. H. Schultz, which brought off to her from Governor's Island two hundred soldiers and three hundred muskets. As a further precaution to preserve secrecy, Lieutenant Colonel Thomas cut off all communication between Governor's Island and the city for the next four days.

In Washington, meanwhile, General Scott obtained from the Navy Department the assignment of the sloop of war *Brooklyn,* then lying at Norfolk, to accompany the *Star of the West* to afford aid in case she should be "shattered or injured," and to bring back the troops in case they should be unable to land at Fort Sumter.[7]

A War Department telegram to New York ordering the

Star of the West to stop at Old Point Comfort did not arrive until after the ship had sailed for Fort Sumter, but this bungling attempt to modify the original sailing order caused information of the expedition to leak out and Charleston was forewarned by notices in the press of the coming attempt to reinforce and provision Fort Sumter.

The relief ship arrived off Charleston Harbor at midnight of January 8 to find coast lights extinguished and channel buoys removed. Near daylight the *Star of the West* sighted a steamer lying in the main ship channel but was unable to answer her recognition signals. The *Star of the West,* flying the American ensign, followed this steamer into the bay as close to Morris Island as possible to avoid coming within range of Fort Moultrie. When less than two miles from her goal, she was fired upon by a new masked battery near the north end of Morris Island. Although a full-sized United States flag was now displayed at the fore, she continued to be fired on by the South Carolina battery. Most of the balls passed overhead. One just missed her machinery. Another landed a few feet from her rudder. A ricochet shot struck in her forechains two feet above the water line and just below where the leadsman was standing to sound the channel. With long-range fire from Fort Moultrie now opening upon her, the ship reluctantly came about and returned to New York.

Three days later, as the *Star of the West* nosed into New York, the U.S.S. *Brooklyn* arrived off Charleston Harbor to learn that the Secessionists had sunk five vessels to obstruct the passages over the bar to the harbor, that the Charleston lights were put out, that pilots had been forbidden to go on board armed vessels, and that batteries had been planted all along the shores.

From Fort Sumter Major Anderson enquired of South Carolina's governor whether the firing "upon an unarmed vessel bearing the flag of my Government" had had the governor's sanction or authority and was informed that it had. No further efforts being made either to reinforce the garrison or more clearly to define their hostile relationship to the Secession government, Fort Sumter's garrison retained its tenuous footing in Charleston Harbor on a sort of "wait and see" basis—wait and see what Mr. Lincoln would do.

General Scott's directive to prevent the seizure of the Pensacola forts reached Lieutenant Slemmer on January 9, the day the *Star of the West* was fired upon at Charleston and just twenty-four hours before Florida passed her own ordinance of secession.

There were three forts at Pensacola: Barrancas, McRee, and Pickens. The first two were on the mainland, while Fort Pickens, ungarrisoned, stood like a gatepost at the harbor mouth on the western tip of Santa Rosa Island. The major prize for which these forts were the shield was the navy yard near Warrington village, some seven miles down the bay from the city of Pensacola. The commandant of the navy yard was Commodore James Armstrong, aged sixty-seven, with fifty years of service in the Navy behind him. To defend the three forts, Lieutenant Slemmer had forty-six men. These were billeted in Barrancas barracks, a building separate from the antiquated little Spanish-built Fort Barrancas and entirely without means of defense if confronted with civil disturbance. The navy yard, too, was defenseless, except for its low wall and its battery of two dozen salute guns with rotten guncarriages.

For the past week, because of rumors of attack, Lieutenant Slemmer had kept in touch with Commodore Armstrong. But the superannuated naval officer, in the absence of orders from Washington and surrounded by actively pro-Secessionist officers on his staff, judged it inexpedient to take action on the basis of mere rumor.

On the morning of the ninth, however, Armstrong received from the Navy Department instructions similar to Slemmer's. The artillery lieutenant and the naval commandant now decided that, with their limited means, they could hold but one of these forts and that that should be Fort Pickens; as it commanded the harbor, it could be reinforced from outside in the Gulf, and, being situated on an island, would be most easily defended. Armstrong, believing defense of the navy yard not feasible, agreed to give Slemmer all the ordinary seamen he could spare from the yard (he had eighty) and to send the screw steamer *Wyandotte* (five guns) and the naval storeship *Supply* (four guns) to help shift Slemmer's garrison from Fort Barrancas across the bay.[8]

These arrangements were repeatedly interfered with by two pro-Secessionists of the commodore's staff, Commander Ebenezer Farrand and Lieutenant F. B. Renshaw. Slemmer had to make several trips back to Armstrong's office to beat down the opposition of the hostile aides.

Lieutenant Henry Erben, a junior officer on the *Supply,* tried in vain to persuade Armstrong to let him blow up the powder magazine that lay outside the walls of the yard. A forthright individual, Erben became involved in a political argument, clinched with a pro-Secessionist officer, and rolled down the commandant's stair like a bulldog without releasing his hold on the man until he reached the bottom.

At 8:00 A.M. on January 10 a barge and a number of small boats from the navy yard were brought to the wharf at Fort Barrancas and loaded with troops and ammunition. Kegs of powder which could not be carried on this first trip were rolled to the beach to be later transported over to Fort Pickens or else destroyed. All the guns in Barrancas were spiked and the ammunition at Fort McRee was blown up, as Slemmer had neither the means nor the time to save them.

The next day Slemmer received from Commodore Armstrong only thirty of the eighty seamen he had hoped for, and on the twelfth the *Supply* dumped on the beach near Fort Pickens the food stores for its garrison.

The twelfth was a day dark with occasional showers. Commodore Armstrong learned that Alabama had seceded and that her militia had seized the gateway forts at Mobile Bay. Definite information reached him that an armed force was gathering to capture his own Pensacola Navy Yard, and he was depressed by the futile, all-is-lost advice of his pro-Secessionist aides. Should he make "a bloody and bootless" resistance? "Great God," agonized the old commodore, "what can I do with the means that I have?" [9] The President's messages and public opinion spoke with one voice: civil war should be avoided at all costs. Into the commandant's befuddled ears Commander Farrand and Lieutenant Renshaw continually dinned that resistance would shed the blood of kinsmen and brother, that a surrender would not be to a foreign enemy but to fellow Americans.

The day of April 12 was so wet that the gate sentries could not charge their muzzle-loader muskets. During the morning uniformed militia from Alabama joined with Florida militiamen in citizen's dress in the seven-mile march from Pensacola to the navy yard. Their number was reported to the commodore as between five hundred and eight hundred. A half mile from the yard they halted and peacefully seized the naval magazine.

At noon two commissioners appointed by Governor Perry of Florida were escorted into Commodore Armstrong's office. They were Captain Victor M. Randolph, late of the U. S. Navy and designated by the governor to take charge of the Pensacola Navy Yard, and Richard L. Campbell.

"Although I have served under the flag of the United States in sunshine and in storm for fifty years," groaned the commodore, "loving and cherishing it as my heart's blood, I will strike it now, together with the blue pennant, the insignia of my present command, rather than fire a gun or raise my sword against my countrymen, especially in circumstances like the present, when I am without the means of defending my position and when an attempt to do so would result in a useless loss of life and destruction of property." [10]

So saying, he signed a capitulation turning over public property in the yard to the State of Florida and guaranteeing to the United States officers and citizens attached to the station the freedom to remove their families and property or to remain on parole.

There were sharp and bitter conflicts of loyalties. William Conway, seaman, who was directed by Lieutenant Renshaw to haul down the United States flag, indignantly refused to obey the order. The squad of thirty-nine marines, who early in the morning had been formed under arms, were now commanded to stack their pieces. "It was an order," testified the marine sergeant, "that all of the men seemed very reluctant to obey. They were very much affected, some of them to tears, and said they would not obey; they would not suffer the humiliation; they would sooner be shot." [11] Some of them held on to their muskets as long as an hour after the direction was given before relinquishing them. The muskets were not loaded. It was a wet day. Later in the afternoon, three hundred Florida and Alabama militiamen marched into the navy yard and occupied the barracks. Captain Randolph, the Florida-appointed commandant, chose Commander Farrand to be his executive officer. Commodore Armstrong, doddering in a daze about the yard, declined to give any further orders when his puzzled seamen requested them, mumbling that he was himself a prisoner of war on parole.

Just before the disturbance began at Pensacola Navy Yard, the storeship *Supply* had received orders to carry coal and provisions to the American vessels stationed off Vera Cruz, Mexico. Not having been able to load on these supplies, Commander Henry Walke, her skipper, now risked a general courtmartial by employing his vessel to carry north the Unionist personnel of the navy yard and their families. Among the ninety-nine persons on Walke's passenger list, ironically enough, were eleven mechanics, four warrant officers, twenty-seven ordinary seamen, and thirty-four marines —"paroled prisoners of war," who, save for Commodore Armstrong's dilatoriness, might at this moment have been doing essential duty in Fort Pickens.[12]

The *Brooklyn,* after her return from Fort Sumter, was sent with a company of soldiers from Fortress Monroe to reinforce Slemmer at Fort Pickens, and Secretary of the Navy Isaac Toucey ordered the *Sabine,* under Captain H. A. Adams, and the *St. Louis,* under Captain C. H. Poor, from the Home Squadron off Vera Cruz to proceed at once off Pensacola Harbor.

From Washington by train to Pensacola naval Secretary Isaac Toucey dispatched Captain Samuel Barron on January 21 with instructions to warn the vessels not to enter Pensacola Harbor, but to remain outside, landing their troops and marines as near to Fort Pickens as possible, and, having done so, to stand by to use their broadsides to defend the fort from attackers. Captain Barron found the situation in the harbor tense but friendly. Authorities on shore were allowing the *Wyandotte* to carry out mails and fresh provisions to Fort Pickens. Barron stationed Lieutenant Berryman of the *Wyandotte* outside the harbor to warn naval ships not to enter. Barron's effort to prevent a collision seemed, he reported, "to have given great satisfaction and comfort to all." [13] As a matter of fact, a group of Southern politicians, including Colonel W. H. Chase, head of the armed forces of Florida, and Senators S. R. Mallory and John Slidell were busy negotiating an "armistice" to freeze the situation in Pensacola Harbor as it now stood.

Assured by the Florida politicians that Fort Pickens, with its garrison of eighty men, would not be assaulted by their fifteen hundred militiamen if Pickens were not reinforced, the Secretaries of War and of the Navy in Washington sent a joint order to Lieutenant Slemmer and the captains of the several naval ships en route to Pensacola that the troops on the *Brooklyn* were not to be put on land "unless said fort shall be attacked or preparations shall be made for its attack." Provisions were to be landed and the warships were to remain on the station, exercising utmost vigilance and prepared at a moment's notice to disembark the troops.

This armistice arrangement lasted until Lincoln's inauguration. The company of soldiers under Captain Israel Vodges, U. S. Army, remained uncomfortably billeted afloat. The *Brooklyn,* the *Macedonia,* the *Sabine,* and the *St. Louis* remained off the entrance to the harbor, their glasses trained across the flat sand island to the bay beyond, over which an invading force would have to come. Captain Barron, the Federal emissary, who was comfortably housed at the navy yard, reported that some of the militia from other states were to be sent home, and that as a result of the armistice the *Wyandotte* was being permitted under flag of truce to carry coal and provisions to the fort. Lieutenant O. H. Berryman, the skipper of the *Wyandotte,* managed even to bring fresh water to the menacing ships outside the harbor, despite personal friction between himself and Commander Farrand at the navy yard. "Things look—if not brighter," reported Berryman, "at least we have some scintillations of light." [14]

But the ability of the Federal ships outside the protected harbor to reinforce Fort Pickens on short notice was, to say the least, doubtful. They had to lie two miles off shore, and they possessed no steam tugs to tow their launches. A southwester on February 10 dispersed and drove some of them almost down to Mobile. A norther on the twenty-fifth blew them straight out into the Gulf. Moreover, as senior Captain, H. A. Adams of the *Brooklyn* pointed out, should the armistice agreement break down, the people on shore would have the advantage of prior knowledge of it.

While uncertainty beclouded the situation at Pensacola, there was none of this at the remoter Federal outposts in Florida, Fort Jefferson at Dry Tortugas and Fort Taylor at Key West. In answer to rumors that five hundred hot Secessionists from New Orleans were about to embark to seize these important posts, Lieutenant T. A. M. Craven of the U.S.S. *Mohawk* and Lieutenant J. N. Maffitt of the U.S.S. *Crusader* put gangs of blue jackets ashore to carry supplies into Fort Taylor and to help mount cannon in Fort Jefferson. Both of these officers won praise from the Navy Department, although Maffitt himself soon after resigned to join the Navy of the Confederate States.

As Mr. Lincoln's inauguration drew near, President James Buchanan's inertia seemed to stiffen a bit in response to public opinion in the Northern states.

Throughout the North, certainly, most men were ready to

respond favorably when Abraham Lincoln announced in his inaugural address: ". . . the Union of these States is perpetual . . . that no state, upon its own mere motion, can lawfully get out of the Union . . . and that the acts of violence within any State or States against the authority of the United States, are insurrectionary or revolutionary . . . the Union is unbroken, and to the extent of my ability, I shall take care, as the Constitution itself expressly enjoins upon me, that the laws of the Union shall be faithfully executed in all the States. . . . The power confided to me will be used to hold, occupy, and possess the property and places belonging to the Government. . . . We are not enemies, but friends. We must not be enemies. Though passion may have strained, it must not break our bonds of affection. . . ." [15]

2.

Fort Sumter and Fort Pickens

When a lanky youth of nineteen, Abraham Lincoln, the future Commander-in-Chief of the United States Navy, had worked as deckhand on a flatboat floating down the Mississippi River to New Orleans. During this trip there was etched upon his memory the silhouette of the town of Vicksburg as viewed from the river, a scene that he recalled when that hilly village became a chief military and naval objective during the Civil War. At romantic New Orleans, the young man in butternut-colored homespun saw flatbottomed, architecturally boxlike river steamers mingle on the river with deep-hulled, streamlined ocean vessels having graceful, towering masts. As a congressman from Illinois in 1847-49, during the War with Mexico, he probably visited the navy yard at Washington, D. C. But such fleeting tourist glimpses constituted the sum of President Lincoln's prior experience with things maritime or naval.

Gideon Welles, Lincoln's Secretary of the Navy, was a Hartford editor and postmaster who had come to Washington more than half expecting to be appointed postmaster general. Fortunately, in view of his surprise assignment to the Navy Department, he had been chief of the naval Bureau of Provisions and Clothing in 1846-48, when Lincoln was a congressman. Welles had a core of stubborn righteousness and hard-bitten practicality, and an unusual flair for economy in government spending. It is likely, however, that President Lincoln valued Welles as an ex-Democrat in his politically heterogeneous Cabinet and as an editor with demonstrated capacity to evaluate and to mold public opinion.

When Lincoln took stock of the country's situation soon after his inauguration, the problems of Fort Sumter and Fort Pickens loomed larger than others because by March of 1861 those two precariously held military outposts had come to symbolize and encompass almost all of the main issues confronting the nation. Could a solution be found which would win back to their allegiance the seven seceded states? If not, how might one prevent the remaining slaveholding states—North Carolina, Virginia, Maryland, Tennessee, Kentucky, Arkansas, and Missouri—from leaving the Union?

Lincoln's statement of policy in his inaugural address, praised in the North, was interpreted in the South as "coercive" in character. The Confederate States Government, organized at Montgomery in February with Jefferson Davis as president, actively took over and coordinated the scattered efforts of the militia in the seceded states. Confederate General Braxton Bragg, ordered to Pensacola on March 5, strictly forbade the citizens there to supply water, fuel, and provisions to either Fort Pickens or the naval ships "now occupying a threatening appearance off this harbor." [1] General P. G. T. Beauregard, the new Confederate commander at Charleston, was busy coordinating the build-up of forts and batteries around Fort Sumter. The Charleston *Mercury,* convinced that the fate of the Southern Confederacy hung "by the ensign halliards of Fort Sumter," reiterated its demand that the menacing handful of "foreign" soldiers be evicted from their harbor.[2]

Lincoln turned first to General Scott as one who should know how to deal with Charleston, inasmuch as Scott himself had been sent there by Jackson in 1833 in a similar situation. But Scott was not reassuring. Last January he had strongly advised Buchanan to reinforce Forts Sumter and Pickens. At that time he had believed that skeleton garrisons could hold the forts against armed mobs. Now the old general shook his head and counseled Lincoln to try persuasion. In effect his advice was: "Conjure back the seceded states by any concessions which will induce their return, but if all your offers and your promises will not entice them, then, in the last resort, you must let them go. Wayward sisters, go in peace." [3]

Not satisfied with this negative answer, Lincoln put before his Cabinet and other military advisers the question: "Assuming it to be possible to now provision Fort Sumter, under all the circumstances is it wise to attempt it?" [4] Professional soldiers fell into line alongside General Scott. Extensive Confederate preparations in Charleston Harbor had made necessary (in Scott's estimate) a force of five thousand regulars and twenty thousand volunteers. To recruit, organize, and train such a force would require from six to eight months. The time for relieving Fort Sumter had run out. Sumter's food supply would be exhausted by April 15. As evacuation of Fort Sumter appeared "an inevitable necessity," Secretary of War Cameron suggested that the sooner it was abandoned the better.

Secretary Welles saw no reason to "impeach the conclusions" of the military. "In a political view," reads his memorandum to the President, "an impression has gone abroad that Sumter is to be evacuated and the shock caused by that announcement has done its work." [5] Abandonment of the position would be attributed to the previous administration, Welles argued. Hence, under all the circumstances it would be unwise to provision Fort Sumter. Secretary of State Seward thought it best to let the cotton states go.

The one Cabinet member who was so antagonistic to General Scott's view that he offered to resign if an attempt were not made to provision Sumter was Montgomery Blair, the postmaster general. Blair was the brother-in-law of a dynamic and furiously energetic former naval officer who had proposed to Buchanan's government a plan for relieving Fort Sumter and who now through Blair himself renewed his offer to the Lincoln government.

This former naval officer, Gustavus Vasa Fox, believed that the *Star of the West* might have reached Fort Sumter in

January if she had held determinedly to her course and ignored the really inefficient fire from the rebel batteries. Fox's plan called for one large passenger liner to carry troops and stores, several small gunboats to move into the mouth of the harbor to fend off enemy naval craft, and one large war vessel to supply small boats and seamen to man them, with which the supplies and troop reinforcements were to be run in to the fort. "Arriving off the bar, I propose to examine by day the naval preparations and obstructions. If their vessels determine to oppose our entrance, and a feint or flag of truce would ascertain this, the armed ships must approach the bar and destroy or drive them on shore. Major Anderson would do the same upon any vessels within range of his guns, and would also prevent any naval succor being sent down from the city." [6] With surface opposition dispersed, Fox's small boats on a full tide at night would race for Fort Sumter. Fox was willing to gamble that if the Confederate land batteries around the harbor sank one or two, they could not knock out all of the small moving targets. Enough would get through.

On the nineteenth of March Lincoln sent Fox by train to Charleston to obtain accurate information from Major Anderson. In order to obtain permission to go out to the fort, Fox was forced to pledge his word to Governor Pickens that his visit was "by authority, for pacific purposes entirely." [7] He was thus unable to communicate freely with Anderson. His plan, to be sure, had not yet been adopted. Anderson's men, he found, had been working feverishly to ready the fort for defense. Fox understood that if Anderson put his men on half rations he could hold out until April 15. Apparently Fox did not understand that Anderson expected Washington to order him to go on half rations. The optimistic Fox returned to Washington more convinced than ever of his project's feasibility. General Scott argued with irrefragable logic that, even should Fox succeed once in throwing in a few men and provisions, the necessity of replenishing supplies would return again and again, and *that* during the approaching season for yellow fever.

Lincoln, yet wavering, sent his former law partner, Ward Lamon, to Charleston. In Charleston Lawyer Lamon, basking in momentary fame as "authorized agent of the President," advised Governor Pickens that Anderson would soon be transferred to another post. Whether his word to Pickens had been authorized, it is difficult to say. If so, Lincoln repudiated it when he issued the following order to the Secretary of the Navy: [8]

Executive Mansion
March 29, 1861

Sir: I desire that an expedition, to move by sea, be got ready to sail as early as the 6th of April next, the whole according to memorandum attached; and that you cooperate with the Secretary of War for that object.

Your obedient servant,
A. Lincoln

Hon. Secretary Navy.

Gideon Welles now ordered the only vessels available to be immediately fitted for sea. These were the *Pocahontas* at Norfolk, the *Pawnee* at Washington, and the revenue cutter *Harriet Lane* at New York. To this list on April 1 Welles added the powerful side-wheel battleship *Powhatan,* which had just arrived from the coast of Mexico. Two hundred troops were to be brought from New York on the chartered steamer *Baltic*. Ex-naval officer Fox, a civilian, was placed in charge of the expedition.

While the relief expedition was being prepared, a report received in Washington from Major Anderson revealed that he was expecting orders to vacate Fort Sumter, as Colonel Lamon had indicated, and that his food supply was desperately short. Wrote Anderson: "I told Mr. Fox that if I placed the command on short allowance I could make the provisions last until after the 10th of this month; but as I have received no instructions from the Department that it was desirable I should do so, it has not been done. If the governor permits me to send off the laborers we will have rations enough to last us about one week longer." [9] This report, dated April 1 and received on the fourth, caused Lincoln so much anxiety that he immediately modified his plan for the relief of the fort. Anderson was notified that it was not the President's intention to subject his command "to any danger or hardship" beyond what in Anderson's judgment would be "usual in military life." Lincoln's new plan was simply to provision Fort Sumter and—only in case the attempt were resisted—to reinforce also with men and arms.[10]

With modified instructions, Fox departed from New York in the *Baltic* on April 8 to rendezvous with the naval craft off Charleston Harbor on the eleventh. The day the expedition sailed from New York, Robert S. Chew, an employee of the State Department, arrived by train in Charleston to read to Governor Pickens an official notification: "I am directed by the President of the United States to notify you to expect an attempt will be made to supply Fort Sumter with provisions only, and that if such attempt be not resisted no effort to throw in men, arms, or ammunition will be made without further notice, or in case of an attack upon the fort." [11] Mr. Chew's identity and the authenticity of his message were vouched for by Captain Theodore Talbot, Assistant Adjutant General, who had been sent with Chew to bear the identical message to Governor Pickens.

Captain Talbot now asked permission to go out to Fort Sumter. General Beauregard, C. S. Army, denied his request. From the Confederate States Government in Montgomery, Beauregard explained, had come instructions that no further communications with Major Anderson would be permitted, except to convey an order for the evacuation of the fort. The Federal emissaries, accordingly, departed on the 11:00 P.M. train for Washington.

Fort Pickens was in some respects easier to relieve than Sumter. This fort's military reinforcements of two hundred men were already there, just off the harbor on the U.S.S.

Brooklyn, impatiently awaiting release from the "armistice" which had held them idle since January. Lieutenant Slemmer's eighty-two men within the fort had marked time by mounting cannon and standing many extra false-alarm watches. Although General Bragg had cut off the supply of fresh provisions from the mainland as of March 5, there was crude justice in this, since Fort Pickens had not paid its grocers' bills for six months. The January "armistice" was still being observed. The mails, albeit with Confederate surveillance, were still suffered to go through, and couriers could still travel overland between the fort and Washington. The long strain was beginning to tell, however, on both Slemmer and his men. A case or two of scurvy had developed, and everyone was jittery for fear that on some dark night the Confederates would land on Santa Rosa Island, set up batteries to fend off the ships, and lay siege to their fort.

Gideon Welles, with all available naval craft allocated to the relief of Sumter, sent Lieutenant John L. Worden by train to Pensacola with positive verbal instructions to Captain Adams of the *Brooklyn* to land the relief force at once, regardless of the armistice.[12] Worden assured Bragg that his message was "of pacific nature," and thus got through to the ships. On the night of April 12, accordingly, the troops were put ashore, along with enough marines to bring the total in Fort Pickens to five hundred men. Worden (later commander of the *Monitor* in her famed fight with the *Merrimack*) had the poor judgment to attempt to return north by train through the enraged South and was arrested and imprisoned in the Confederate capitol at Montgomery.

Meanwhile, in Washington, Secretary of State Seward was sponsoring an effort to relieve Fort Pickens, which, being secret and behind the back of the Secretary of the Navy, created administrative snarls that involved Fox's expedition to Fort Sumter, as well as Seward's own expedition to Fort Pickens.[13]

Seward coralled two fast talking officers with plausible ideas and took them to the White House. They were Captain

Montgomery C. Meigs, U. S. Army, and Lieutenant David D. Porter, U. S. Navy. To Lincoln the three men proposed that a military Department of Florida be established under Colonel Harvey Brown, U. S. A., whose purpose would be to reinforce and securely hold Fort Taylor at Key West, Fort Jefferson at Dry Tortugas, and Fort Pickens at Pensacola. With Europe in view, Seward was particularly interested in holding the forts on the Florida keys, which he regarded as a sort of American Gibraltar, capable of controlling ocean traffic in the Gulf. Porter impressed on the President what was already painfully clear, that routine orders could not emanate from Navy or War Departments without news leaks, so honeycombed were the government departments with Southerners resigning, or about to resign, to join the Confederacy. Meigs argued that an expedition setting sail from New York to an unknown destination—Sumter, Pickens, wherever—would create such consternation in the South as to discourage even South Carolina in her rebellious efforts!

Lincoln saw some truth in each of these points of view and fell in with their plan to mount a secret expedition to carry troops to Forts Taylor, Jefferson, and Pickens. In the President's anteroom Porter and Meigs, the professional ringleaders in the plot, wrote out the necessary orders and Lincoln signed them.

"Seward," jested the President, "see that I don't burn my fingers." The Secretary of State's excursion into naval affairs reminded Lincoln of the preacher who was induced by a gambler to play poker and won all the gambler's money. "It's all because we've mistaken our trades," said the gambler. "You ought to have been a gambler and I a preacher, and, by ginger I intend to turn the tables on you next Sunday and preach in your church." [14] And he did.

Among the sheaf of Seward-Meigs-Porter orders which Lincoln signed were two that particularly infuriated the austere Secretary of the Navy when he learned about this undercover business.

The first was an executive order directing a change in the Office of Detail. As his detailing officer, his own right hand, so to speak, a man who knew the officers of the Navy from intimate lifelong association with them and upon whom the Secretary could rely for advice in making out assignments to duty—for this all-important billet Gideon Welles had chosen Captain Silas H. Stringham, like Welles, a native of Connecticut. At noon on April 1, while having luncheon at Willard's, Welles was handed the order by John Nicolay, one of Lincoln's clerks. The order directed Welles to send Captain Stringham to Pensacola and to assign the job of detailing officer to Captain Samuel Barron, unquestionably an able man but a native of South Carolina and notoriously friendly toward Secessionists. In short, Barron was suspect, as indeed were all Southerners in Gideon Welles's rigorous view.[15]

Abandoning the rest of his meal, Welles went at once to the White House and read the document to Lincoln. Lincoln seemed surprised, as the Barron matter had no apparent relation to the Fort Pickens affair. Lincoln explained that he had signed without reading the paper, that Seward and two young men, Meigs and Porter, had a project which the President was unable to disclose at this time. Welles expressed surprise that the Secretary of State should trespass so cavalierly upon the navy secretary's domain. Lincoln agreed with Welles and promised that he would not allow this sort of thing to happen again.

The second of the Seward-Meigs-Porter documents (Welles did not learn about this one for nearly a week) diverted the *Powhatan* from the Sumter expedition (which Welles had ordered) to the Fort Pickens expedition (that Seward had arranged). The order read: [16]

Executive Mansion, April 1, 1861.

Sir: You will fit out the *Powhatan* without delay. Lieutenant Porter will relieve Captain Mercer in command of her. She is bound on secret service, and you will under no circumstances communicate to the Navy Department the fact that she is fitting out.

Abraham Lincoln.

Commandant Navy Yard
New York

Secretary Welles's order, bearing the same date and received at the Brooklyn Navy Yard at the same hour, did not specify to whom the command of the ship would be given. It read simply: [17]

Washington, April 1, 1861.

Fit out *Powhatan* to go to sea at earliest possible moment.

Gideon Welles,
Secretary Navy

Commandant Navy Yard
Brooklyn, N. Y.

Since both orders required him to prepare the *Powhatan* for sea, Captain Andrew H. Foote, the commandant, proceded to fit her out. Meigs and Porter arrived in New York to push their preparations, and all went well until the fifth, when an order from Secretary Welles assigned the *Powhatan* to Captain Mercer to participate in the Sumter relief expedition. For forty years Captain Foote had been accustomed to report his every action to the Secretary of the Navy. And now more than ever, with old friends capitulating and going over to the Southern Confederacy, he feared trickery and itched to report the situation to the Secretary. Porter restrained him, emphasizing the President's injunction of secrecy.

The *modus operandi* agreed upon by Porter and Mercer called for the latter to take the vessel out beyond Staten Island and there turn it over to Porter whose order signed by the President had priority. This procedure having been executed, the *Powhatan* under Lieutenant Porter set sail from New York at 2:45 P.M. on April 6.

Back at the navy yard, Captain Foote was in the act of

writing a full account for the Secretary when a telegram came for Porter: [18]

> GIVE UP THE POWHATAN TO CAPTAIN MERCER.
>
> SEWARD

Foote relayed this message on a fast tug chartered for the purpose, but Lieutenant David D. Porter returned to Captain Foote his regrets that the dispatch had come to his hands too late for him to change his plans, his colleague Captain Meigs having already sailed with the cooperating troopship *Atlantic*. To Seward the preposterous young officer retorted by telegram: "I received my orders from the President and shall proceed and execute them."

Seward trudged to Willard's to make his peace with Welles; and, although it was late, the two set out for the White House. Describing the scene in his journal, Welles noted that, as naval secretary, he "questioned whether the President would detach and send away an officer without at least informing the Department, certainly not to take command of a ship that was in commission, that such irregular proceedings would throw the departments and government into confusion, and were wholly inconsistent with correct and systematic administration." On the way to the White House Welles routed out of bed his detailing officer, Captain Stringham, to accompany them. "On our way thither," records Welles, "Mr. Seward remarked to me that, old as he was, he had learned a lesson from this experience, which was that he had better attend to his own business, not interfere with others, and confine his labors to his proper Department. To all of which I assented." [19]

Lincoln, who had not yet retired, was "astonished and perplexed" over the confusion of orders that had come about. On points where his memory was hazy, Welles supplied the official record and Captain Stringham backed him up. Lincoln, like Seward, was made to realize that outside interference was not welcome in Gideon Welles's department. The Seward-Meigs-Porter affair, as Welles later stated, served in some degree to "define the province of the different departments of the Government under President Lincoln." [20]

When Charleston received prior notice of an attempt to provision Sumter, it was already on a war footing. By the Confederate War Department at Montgomery, General Beauregard had been directed to stop all concessions to Major Anderson, since his own and Anderson's men had assumed "the status of hostile forces . . . who may at any moment be in actual conflict." [21] On April 10 Beauregard was ordered to demand that the fort be evacuated, and, if that were refused, "to proceed, in such manner as you may determine, to reduce it." At 2:00 P.M. on the eleventh Beauregard's messengers delivered this demand. Major Anderson penned a courteous refusal, which he presented to the South Carolinian emissaries with the remark: "I will await the first shot, and if you do not batter us to pieces we will be starved out in a few days." [22]

Beauregard, after relaying this latter comment to Montgomery, received authority to delay the attack if Anderson would name the day when he would evacuate.

Anderson agreed to evacuate if not otherwise instructed by his government, and fixed the hour of his evacuation at noon April 15.

At 3:00 A.M. on Friday April 12, Gustavus Fox arrived at the rendezvous off Charleston Harbor. Beauregard at 3:20 A.M. notified Anderson that he would fire on his batteries in one hour.

At 4:30 on this fateful Friday morning Confederate guns opened upon Fort Sumter from all sides.

From his position ten miles off the harbor, Gustavus Fox heard the cannonading and was mortified to find that only one of the naval vessels of his expedition, the *Pawnee,* had yet appeared at the rendezvous. Fox boarded the *Pawnee* at 6:00 A.M., told Captain Rowan that in spite of the Confederate bombardment he was going in to offer to land provisions, and asked him to accompany him. To the civilian leader of the expedition, Rowan replied stiffly that his orders were to remain ten miles east of the light and await the *Powhatan.* Fox, with the revenue cutter *Harriet Lane* as escort, drew in close enough to see that Fort Sumter was "replying gallantly."

The next morning Fox rowed into the mouth of the harbor and "saw, with horror, black volumes of smoke issuing from Sumter." [23] Fox now learned from Captain Rowan that the *Powhatan,* which Rowan had been ordered to await, had been detached from Fox's expedition and sent elsewhere. Around 2 P.M. the *Pocahontas* appeared, just in time to witness the surrender of the fort.

Not only had Fox himself arrived too late, but his major support, the *Powhatan,* had failed him, and the other naval ships had been bound by their orders to await the *Powhatan*'s arrival ten miles east of the harbor!

Under a flag of truce the frustrated Fox offered a passage north to Major Anderson and his men. General Beauregard assented. Before leaving, Anderson was permitted to salute his flag with fifty guns.

The only loss of life inside Fort Sumter had been one soldier, killed by premature explosion when charging a salute gun. After this unfortunate casualty had been buried inside the fort, the powder-grimy, weary garrison marched out and were transported to New York on board Fox's chartered liner *Baltic.*

Meanwhile, the Meigs-Porter expedition arrived in the Gulf. Meigs, on board the fast transport *Atlantic,* stopped at Key West to reinforce Fort Taylor. Meigs interviewed the loyal officials of the town and assured them that the commander of the fort was under orders to support them against any Secessionist opposition. Supplies and men were also put ashore at Fort Jefferson on lonely Dry Tortugas.

The *Atlantic,* bearing Colonel Harvey Brown, the commander of the new Department of Florida, arrived off Fort Pickens on April 17 and by 2:00 A.M. the next day Brown had landed and assumed command of Fort Pickens.[24]

According to plan, Lieutenant Porter, who had not yet arrived in the slower *Powhatan,* would attempt to force an entrance into Pensacola Bay. Colonel Brown feared that such an event would precipitate a collision, and the state of Fort Pickens's defenses was so bad, in Brown's opinion, as to force him to postpone offering the Confederates any unnecessary provocation.

Porter, in the *Powhatan,* delayed by heavy gales, head winds, and defective boilers, arrived off the mouth of the harbor a few hours behind the transport. Meigs, in the *Wyandotte,* flagged him down with imperative orders from Brown, and Porter dropped anchor outside.

As events turned, Fort Pickens made small headlines, but, since it could be easily reinforced from outside the enemy's harbor, it proved in the long run more valuable than Fort Sumter might have been to Mr. Lincoln's Navy. It nullified the usefulness to the enemy of the most important navy yard south of Norfolk.

3.

Loss of the Norfolk Navy Yard

A FEW DAYS BEFORE FORT SUMTER WAS FIRED upon, the Virginia State Convention meeting in Richmond voted to remain in the Union and a Unionist politician was elected mayor of Portsmouth, Virginia, hard by the country's largest and most important naval base, the Norfolk Navy Yard. Not that the old Dominion's Secessionist party was inactive or lacking in vision. They were, on the contrary, infused with virile energy and were rapidly increasing in numbers. Their ambitious goals included the seizures of the Norfolk Navy Yard, Harper's Ferry Arsenal, Fortress Monroe, commanding the lower Chesapeake Bay, and, with aid from Maryland, they hoped to seize the Federal capital itself.

From the first, Lincoln had proceeded warily. Normal patronage practice would have been to sweep out of the Norfolk Navy Yard the jobholders who had been appointed by the defeated political party. Instead of harvesting the political spoils, the President directed Secretary Welles to refrain from "all unnecessary exercise of political party authority." [1] In short, Lincoln appeased Norfolk's political jobholders, hoping that they in return would hold Virginia in the Union. Thus, for the critical first six weeks of Lincoln's administration, the Norfolk Navy Yard was staffed by civilian officials and workers who were Democratic in politics and Southern in sympathy.

News of Fort Sumter instantly paralyzed business in Virginia. In alarm over the situation, the Richmond Convention requested President Lincoln to define anew his policy toward the Confederate States, now well organized and functioning in Montgomery, Alabama. Lincoln quoted from his inaugural address the passage: "to hold, occupy and possess property and places belonging to the Government," and explained that he chiefly alluded to military posts and property "which were in the possession of the government when it came into my hands." "But if," Mr. Lincoln continued, "as now appears to be true, in pursuit of a purpose to drive the United States authorities from these places, an unprovoked assault has been made upon Fort Sumter, I shall hold myself at liberty to repossess it, if I can . . . and in any event I shall, to the best of my ability, repel force by force. . . . I consider the military posts and property situated within the States which claim to have seceded, as yet belonging to the Government of the United States as much as they did before the supposed secession." [2]

A few hours later, interpreting the firing on Fort Sumter as an unprovoked assault, Lincoln issued a call for seventy-five thousand militia. Most of the border states angrily refused to contribute their quotas of troops. Hitherto neutral North Carolina replied by seizing the Federal forts and arsenals within her bounds and later on passed a Secession ordinance to legalize her acts. Virginia's convention on April 17 voted to secede, and the next day Governor Letcher appointed a general to take command of the militia at Norfolk and Portsmouth, and ordered a naval officer (Captain Robert B. Pegram) to proceed to Norfolk and assume command of the naval station.[3]

The Norfolk Navy Yard lay above the cities of Norfolk and Portsmouth on the Portsmouth side of Elizabeth River. It fronted three quarters of a mile along the river and was a quarter of a mile wide. Its dry dock of granite was constructed in the same manner as the great dry dock at Charlestown, Massachusetts. The yard contained two enormous ship houses, or sheds fully equipped for building ships inside them, and a third ship house was under construction. For building or repairing ships of the old Navy of wood and sail, there were sail lofts, riggers' lofts, gunners' lofts, sawmills, timber sheds, spar houses, carpenter shops. For modern steamers—four screw steamers and one side-wheeler had been built in this yard—there were foundries, machine shops, boiler shops. Back from the shoreline stood marine barracks and homes for officers.

There were 1,198 guns of all calibers scattered around the yard.[4] Some were of vintage familiar in 1812. The best were nine-inch Dahlgren guns, manufactured by the naval gun factory to the rigid specifications of their inventor, Commander John A. Dahlgren. Of these most valuable cannon at Norfolk there were fifty-two.

At a safe distance below the city of Norfolk was located a naval magazine known as Fort Norfolk, which, like the arsenal at Charleston, was unguarded for fear of arousing suspicion among the citizens.

Of the ten ships berthed at the Norfolk yard on March 4, there was only one important capital ship, the steam sloop *Merrimack,* and she, irrespective of her later adventitious fame as a rebuilt ironclad, was worth more than all the rest of the ships together. This 3200-ton screw steamer, built in Boston five years before the Civil War, was 375 feet long and 38½ feet across, with a depth of 27½. She had two gun decks and three masts to carry her auxiliary motive-power sails. The *Merrimack* was at Norfolk awaiting repairs to her engines which the commandant of the yard estimated should take a month. In addition to the *Merrimack,* the only serviceable craft were two sail sloops, the *Germantown* and the *Plymouth,* of twenty-two guns each and the tiny, three-gun brig *Dolphin.* The antique ship of the line *Pennsylvania* was in commission as a station ship; the *New York* was still on the stocks, unfinished some ten years after the laying of her keel. The remaining five vessels were genteel hulks up to forty years of age, and moribund.

The commandant of the Norfolk Navy Yard, Commodore Charles S. McCauley, like his counterpart at Pensacola, was a sixty-eight-year-old naval officer with fifty years' service. Quizzical Gideon Welles scanned his record for blemishes, found none, and, hearing only praise of his "fidelity and patriotism," continued him in his post. The Secretary was aware that a majority of the officers on Commodore McCauley's staff were of Southern descent, but, since the Navy's policy prior to Virginia's seceding was to avoid antagonizing Southerners, there was no way to foresee that three of the four commanders and seven of the twelve officers in lower ranks would resign to go South.[5]

To excite no undue suspicion, when in March the *Pocahontas* and the *Cumberland* returned from Vera Cruz, Secretary Welles ordered them to Norfolk to refit. But later, when the *Pocahontas* was sent with Fox to Charleston, the move infuriated Secessionist sympathizers in Norfolk. Gideon Welles several times in March asked General Scott for troops to defend the Norfolk yard, but the old general, his lame leg swinging in harness suspended from the ceiling of his office, refused to grant any troops. "Norfolk," said he, "lies in enemy country." The Navy's people could defend themselves on shipboard and depart from Norfolk at will; but Army personnel sent to Norfolk would be easily trapped on shore. In Scott's view, Fortress Monroe was the point to be held at all hazards, and this pentagonal masonry fortification he proposed to hold with his few hundred available troops. Let the Navy bring its ships out to anchorages in the Roads under the ample protection of Fortress Monroe.[6]

Finding crews for the ships that were sent to Forts Sumter and Pickens completely cleaned out the receiving ships of the Norfolk, Philadelphia, and New York navy yards, and increased the difficulties of Lincoln's Navy in dealing with the puzzling situation in Norfolk. As early as March 31, Secretary Welles requisitioned from New York a crew of 250 men for the *Merrimack,* and so careful was he to avoid publicity that he sent a special messenger to New York to charter a private steamer to take them to Norfolk. In three weeks the New York Navy Yard managed to recruit 173 seamen, but it was then too late for them to be sent to Norfolk. The Philadelphia yard chartered the *Keystone State* and brought a crew to Hampton Roads just twelve hours after the *Merrimack* had been scuttled. The naval recruiting station in Baltimore rounded up a crew which might have reached Norfolk in time to save the *Merrimack* had not pro-Secessionist officials of the Baltimore Steam Packet Company flatly refused to transport them at a time when there was no other means of transportation available.

On the eve of the firing on Fort Sumter, Welles cautioned Commodore McCauley "that great vigilance should be exercised in guarding and protecting the public interests and property." [7] Welles wanted the *Merrimack* made ready to escape in case of unlawful attempts to seize her; yet, at the same time, he warned McCauley not to give needless alarm. Along with these instructions the Secretary sent Engineer-in-Chief B. F. Isherwood to put the *Merrimack*'s engines in order and Commander James Alden to assume command of the vessel and take her to Philadelphia.

On the sixteenth, with the firing on Sumter officially confirmed, Welles became alarmed about Norfolk and ordered McCauley to "impose additional vigilance and care in protecting the public property." The commandant was to lose no time in putting the *Merrimack*'s armament on board and moving the other vessels (*Plymouth, Dolphin,* and *Germantown*) out of jeopardy. "The vessels and stores under your charge you will defend at any hazard, repelling by force, if necessary, any and all attempts to seize them, whether by mob violence, organized effort, or any assumed authority." [8] Commodore G. J. Pendergrast on the *Cumberland* was directed to aid in defense of the Norfolk Navy Yard in view of the deficiency of men there. These confidential orders were carried to Norfolk by Commodore Hiram Paulding.

While Paulding was in McCauley's office, he was approached by Commander Richard L. Page on behalf of himself and other Southern officers at the yard. They were, explained Page, "painfully situated." Their families and interests were in Norfolk: "there was very great excitement, and apprehensions were entertained of violence from the people outside of the yard." Although these officers believed that Virginia would go out of the Union, Page pledged himself, and was authorized by the other officers to pledge them also, to stand by the commandant and defend the public property with their lives. At the same time Page begged Paulding to "say to the Secretary of the Navy that it was very desirable to them to be relieved." [9]

Upon his return to Washington, Paulding conveyed the officers' statement to the Secretary and to Mr. Lincoln, who directed Mr. Welles to have those officers of the yard replaced by Northern men. But before this action was taken Virginia had seceded and the Southern officers had resigned.

Engineer Isherwood, pushing a double crew of workmen day and night for four days, got the *Merrimack*'s engines to turning over by four o'clock on Wednesday afternoon, April 17.

During the previous night, however, pro-Secessionists of Norfolk had partially obstructed the channel to block the *Merrimack* in.

The sixteenth was foggy and through the mist the lookouts on the flagship *Cumberland,* at anchor five hundred yards off the navy yard, reported that a steam tug towing two lightboats had passed by headed down the river. An hour later a second tug with another lightboat was seen also bound downstream. The captain of the ship dispatched armed boats to observe what was going on, and to prevent the Secessionists from sinking the lightboats in the channel, but the tugs eluded them below Craney Island. "The night was very dark, blowing fresh, with rain." [10]

When Isherwood reported to the commodore that he had loaded on coal and engaged a sufficient number of firemen and coal passers to take the *Merrimack* to sea, Commodore McCauley had just learned that the lightboats had been sunk between Craney Island and Sewell's Point. The masts of the sunken craft were grotesquely thrusting above water for all to see. McCauley, influenced by Southerners on his staff and leaning over backward to avoid alarming the populace, directed Isherwood not to light the boilers until the next morning.

The following morning, April 18, when Isherwood called upon the commodore, the latter was in a quandary. This was the day following Virginia's secession, and McCauley's Southern officers had resigned in a body. Isherwood reported that he had kindled his fires at daybreak and requested McCauley's permission to cast loose and go.

"He then, to my great surprise and dissatisfaction," reads Isherwood's report to the department, "informed me that he had not yet decided to send the vessel, but would let me know further in the course of a few hours." [11] Isherwood called the commodore's attention to the peremptory character of the Navy Department's instructions, and expressed the opinion that the *Merrimack* would be able to pass any obstructions the enemy could have placed in the channel, adding that if he delayed a few hours the vessel would have to remain another day because of the tide and that during the night the obstructions might be increased. About 2:00 A.M., when Isherwood again called upon him, Commodore McCauley said that he had decided to retain the vessel and directed that her fires be withdrawn. Isherwood, frustrated, returned to Washington.

Gideon Welles heard Isherwood's story and his opinion that the aged commodore was "under the influence of liquor and bad men," and a short time later, when Commander Alden arrived from Norfolk, Welles was called out of Cabinet meeting to hear Alden's tale of disappointment.[12] Welles introduced the naval officer to the President and Cabinet, and to them Alden repeated his story "with emotion which he could not entirely suppress." Commodore McCauley had refused to let him take out the *Merrimack*, which was at the wharf, all ready to go. Remarks of some of the younger officers at the yard had left no doubt in Alden's mind that they had control of the Commodore. The old man "seemed stupified, bewildered, and wholly unable to act." [13]

Lincoln and Welles once again approached General Scott. The general-in-chief reiterated his opposition to sending troops to Norfolk, but at the President's insistence agreed to send on temporary loan a battalion of Massachusetts militia that had newly arrived at Fortress Monroe. To this force Welles added one hundred marines from Washington.

Commodore Hiram Paulding was sent with these forces to relieve McCauley of responsibility for "all the naval forces then afloat" and to see that no arms and munitions fell into the hands of the insurrectionists. If necessary, Paulding was to destroy the navy yard and ships.

Paulding's expedition took two days to organize and get to Norfolk. At the Washington Navy Yard, Commander Dahlgren, the gunnery expert, loaded on board Paulding's ship 40 barrels of gunpowder, 11 tanks of turpentine, 12 barrels of cotton waste, and 181 portfires.

Commodore Paulding embarked from Washington the evening of Friday the nineteenth. In addition to one hundred marines, he carried with him on the *Pawnee* a number of officers from the Washington area who had been assigned to assist him, including Captain Charles Wilkes, the Antarctic explorer, and Commanders B. F. Sands, James Alden, and John Rodgers. To supervise the highly specialized task of blowing up the dry dock, should that be found necessary, Paulding had two experts: Captain H. G. Wright, of the U. S. Army Engineers, and Lieutenant Henry A. Wise, of the Navy's Bureau of Ordnance.

The *Pawnee* rounded to off Fortress Monroe at 2:30 P.M. on Saturday, April 20. During the afternoon Colonel David W. Wardrop's battalion of Massachusetts militia was taken on board. These 349 fresh recruits were armed with old-fashioned muskets. As yet undrilled in arms, they were of doubtful value for any military use except heaving powder barrels on shore. At 6:45 P.M. the *Pawnee*, with its additional passengers, set out on the final eighteen-mile lap across Hampton Roads and up the Elizabeth River to the navy yard. They proceeded slowly and were able to steam around the sunken lightboats. As they passed Norfolk, a crowd on the dock sent up a shout in which were mingled both jeers and welcome. The sailing sloop *Cumberland* in midstream cheered from their shrouds and the station ship *Pennsylvania,* berthed in the mud along the sea wall, shouted "with a hurricane of heartiness." [14]

Confusion at the navy yard had increased and the "atmosphere of treason" had thickened. Nine hundred workmen, the entire force, had quit their jobs. Such prowlers as ventured into the yard were suspected of pilfering government arms for use in their militia companies. On the night of the nineteenth the Virginia state militia under General Taliaferro seized the navy's powder magazine at Fort Norfolk. Impressing all the horses and carts in the area, they transferred thirteen hundred barrels of powder to lighters and other vessels to be sent up the James River to Richmond, and the remaining fifteen hundred barrels they carried inland beyond range of guns on shipboard.

On the nineteenth the Secessionist surveyor for the Port of Norfolk with about fifty armed men was foiled in his effort to seize the government tug *Yankee* by the sixty marines of this yard. In Norfolk, trainloads of troops arrived from Richmond and Petersburg. Lieutenant Colonel James Edelin, in charge of the marines, hired a spy to keep him posted on the number of troops in Norfolk, and according to that informant some five thousand had come in before April 20. At St. Helena, a pine-wooded village across the river from the navy yard, it was rumored that Confederate General Taliaferro's militia had mounted batteries that commanded the navy yard itself. Commodore Pendergrast's lookout at the masthead of the *Cumberland* was unable to see any of these rumored batteries, but since there were trees to mask them he could not be certain. Commodore Pendergrast, who lived in Norfolk and had gone home every night while his ship was at the navy yard, had witnessed a good deal of parading by militia companies. He had not himself seen the rumored three to five thousand troops that worried Commodore McCauley. McCauley was his senior. Pendergrast assumed that McCauley had sources of information not available to himself.

A few days previous McCauley had ordered the *Merrimack* under the shears to hoist her guns on board, but he had countermanded this order "upon the representation of certain parties that such a proceeding would certainly bring on a collision with the people outside of the yard." [15] So nothing had been done. The *Merrimack's* broadside guns continued to lie on shore in the gunparks, along with the obsolete armaments of the hulks that were anchored in midstream.

Then, just a few hours before Paulding's arrival, doddering Commodore McCauley, stricken by panic, ordered his seamen and marines to spike the guns on the yard and to scuttle the *Merrimack* and the other ships.

At 8:00 P.M. the *Pawnee* made fast alongside the navy yard wharf to the northward of the first ship house. Commodore Paulding, hearing of conditions on shore, sent his marines to hold the gates of the navy yard and Lieutenant Wise, with an emergency crew, to try to stop the scuttled *Merrimack* from sinking. Wise entered the foundering ship, which had been moored near by, made his way down to her lower decks, and dropped a block into her water-filled hold. Judging by the sound of the splash, the water was now over the vessel's orlop deck. Wise reported that it was too late to save her unless they could send down a diver to plug the hole. There was no diver available.

Commodore McCauley and Commodore Pendergrast came on board the *Pawnee*. McCauley, learning the substance of Paulding's orders, considered himself as having been superseded, turned everything over to Paulding, and returned to his quarters.

After McCauley left the wharf, Paulding inquired of Pendergrast why the ships had been scuttled, and Pendergrast attributed it to apprehension that otherwise the people surrounding the yard would obtain possession of it. He told of the rumor that batteries overlooking the yard had been erected at St. Helena and of the growing number of Secessionists that were collecting under Confederate General Taliaferro.

It was now possible for Paulding with a thousand men under his control to seize and hold the navy yard. With the broadsides of the *Pawnee* and the *Cumberland,* he could demolish Norfolk and Portsmouth. Such became an acceptable practice a year later when Farragut bombarded the river town of Donaldsonville, Louisiana, in retaliation for the firing of guerrillas upon his ships. But on the night of April 20, 1861, the shooting war was only in its second week. Paulding, like his predecessor, took alarm, giving credit to wild rumors "of people then assembling in great numbers to take the yard." With the ships that he had come to save already scuttled and sinking, Paulding found the task of saving them immeasurably magnified, in fact, impossible. He also considered his mission to be a special and temporary one. He was unduly impressed with the fact that the troops loaned by the Army were to be with him only temporarily, and he felt that the *Pawnee,* too, should return at the earliest moment for the possible defense of threatened Washington. In other words Paulding carried out his Norfolk mission with one eye upon Washington.

At 9:00 P.M. he decided to destroy what was left of the Norfolk Navy Yard.

A hundred sailors from the *Cumberland* were detailed to further disable the spiked cannon by pounding off their trunnions. A few blows of a hammer shattered like glass the side projections of old cannon, but not so in the case of the late-model Dahlgren guns. Upon these best naval guns one hundred men hammered for an hour with eighteen-pound sledges without breaking a single trunnion.

Lieutenant Wise, an ordnance expert who had been brought to Norfolk to demolish the dry dock, was ordered instead to lay powder trains and set fire to the ships. "I had a boat manned from the 'Pawnee,' " reads Wise's narrative of this night's doings, "and put in her a number of powder tanks filled with spirits of turpentine and cotton waste. When the boat was ready I reported to Commodore Paulding, who called me down into the cabin of the 'Pawnee' and gave me the names of the ships I was to set fire to, which I took down in pencil on a slip of paper. I then shoved off and came alongside the 'Merrimack;' went on board with an officer and some of the boat's crew, and got together combustible material, such as cordage, rope, ladders and gratings, hawsers, etc., and laid them in the form of the letter V, before her mainmast to one of the offshore gun-deck ports. On the top of this were laid ropes of cotton waste saturated in turpentine. I then flooded the decks, fore and aft, and the beams likewise, with the same liquid, leaving the ends of the waste ropes outside the port. While this was going on the officer whom I had placed on the lookout reported to me that a large crowd of men were about to make a rush and fire into the boat we went to the 'Merrimack' with. When the work was all done we shoved off, and pulled up to the vessels lying alongside the yard, and laid trains on them in the same way." [16]

Captain Wilkes and Commanders Sands and Alden were sent to lay powder trains to the marine barracks, ship houses, and other shore installations, while the mining of the dry dock was put in charge of Commander Rodgers and Captain Wright, of the Engineers. A Federal party of forty Massachusetts volunteers placed a two-thousand-pound mine inside a pumping gallery running back of one of the massive granite sidewalls of the dry dock. The night was dark, their time short, and the fact that there was two feet of water inside this gallery made it necessary for them to forage for scaffolding materials to secure above water the mine and its powder train to the outside.

While these varied preparations were going forward, General Taliaferro, commanding the military forces of Virginia, sent a message to Commodore Paulding under a flag of truce to offer a bargain compromise. To save the letting of blood, the Secessionist general offered to permit the *Cumberland* to leave port unmolested if the Federal commodore would discontinue destruction of public property in the yard! To this overture Paulding returned the threat "that any act of violence on their part would devolve upon them the consequences." [17]

About 2:00 A.M. the marine barracks prematurely burst into flames, which lighted up the yard and caused so much confusion among the Federal wreckers that preparations for burning certain important machine shops were omitted. While the troops and marines were re-embarking, the youngest son of Commodore McCauley, tears running down his cheeks, reported to Commodore Paulding that his father refused to leave his post. Commander Alden was sent to explain to the old man that the rest of the buildings were to be fired and that his life must be lost if he did not yield. This last effort succeeded and with the wretched McCauley safe on board Paulding shoved off.

The steamer *Pawnee* and the tug *Yankee* took in tow the sailing sloop *Cumberland,* flagship of Commodore Pendergrast's Home Squadron, and proceeded down the river. When the ships were beyond danger, a rocket from the *Pawnee* gave the signal to set fire to all powder trains. Captain Wilkes's small boats picked up the men who fired the buildings. "The station I had chosen for the boat," reads Wilkes's account, "was just ahead of the *Germantown* and at the end of the eastern ship-house. The *Merrimack* lay close astern of the *Germantown* and the fire soon reached her rigging and spars. In a few minutes Commander Alden and his men and Commander Sands and his two men joined me. The flames were making rapid progress, and all attention was turned toward the direction [of the dry dock] from whence Commander Rogers and Captain Wright were to come. The conflagration was rapid, in vast sheets of flame, and dense smoke, which enveloped us from the *Merrimack,* soon made it evident that it would be impossible for anyone to pass through it. . . . It was a painful anxiety to see every moment the chances of their escape diminishing. Our own safety was not thought of until all hope or chance of their joining us were at an end. Then, and with great reluctance, I gave the order to shove off." [18]

A reporter for the *New York Times,* who viewed the scene from the *Pawnee,* wrote that the conflagration burst like the day of judgment upon the startled citizens of Norfolk and Portsmouth. "Any one who has seen a ship burn, and knows how like a fiery serpent the flame leaps from pitchy deck to smoking shrouds, and writhes to their very top, around the masts that stood like martyrs doomed, can form some idea of the wonderful display that followed. It was not 30 minutes from the time the trains were fired till the conflagration roared like a hurricane, and the flames from land and water swayed, and met and mingled together, and darted high, and fell, and leaped again, and by their very motion showed their sympathy with the crackling, crashing roar of destruction beneath." [19]

Wilkes's small boats caught up with the *Pawnee* at Craney Island below Norfolk. Commander Rodgers and Captain Wright, marooned by the inferno, were taken prisoners by General Taliaferro's militia who swarmed into the yard. They were billeted in Norfolk's best hotel and later sent to Richmond, where they were courteously treated by the Governor and returned under Confederate military escort to Washington to prevent their being abused by angered Virginians.

The dry dock's mine did not explode. Whether its fuse was defective, whether it was stamped out by a Virginia militiaman, or whether water sufficient to flood the gallery was let in by the newly resigned Lieutenant C. F. M. Spottswood, as one rumor reported, is not known.

The *Merrimack* burned down only through her upper decks. Her sunken hull and machinery were left intact. The marine barracks and the ship houses were totally destroyed. But the true measure of Commodore Paulding's panic is the fact that the following essential shore installations were left unsinged: the dry dock, the ordnance building, the smiths' shops and sheds, carpenters' shops and sheds, timber sheds, boiler shops, foundries, all the machine shops, the saw-mill, spar house, provision house, and all the dwellings.

"At that particular juncture of affairs no greater calamity could have happened to the cause of the Union than the loss of their important station." So concluded the Congressional Committee of Investigation. "Not only was the pecuniary loss to us very considerable, but the acquisition to the enemy was of incalculable value, in putting into their hands a fine yard and harbor wherein to build, arm, equip, and iron-sheath their ships-of-war to be used against the government, and great numbers of ordnance of the heaviest calibre for their coast and inland fortifications." [20]

The *Cumberland* grounded on one of the lightboats sunk in the lower reaches of Elizabeth River. Paulding pushed on in the *Pawnee* to Fortress Monroe, where he found the steamer *Keystone State,* just in from Philadelphia, bearing a crew for the *Merrimack!* The *Keystone State* helped to pull the *Cumberland* through to deep water in Hampton Roads. In the *Pawnee* Paulding now stood up the Potomac to Washington in defiance of rumored Confederate batteries at Alexandria. They passed Alexandria with the crew at general quarters, but discovered no enemy batteries. Near Washington they ran aground on a shoal and were pulled off by a tugboat. The *Pawnee* reached the Washington Navy Yard on April 23, two days after leaving behind her the holocaust at Norfolk.

4.

Gideon Welles Forms a Plan

DURING THE CRITICAL AND EXASPERATING THIRD week in April, all news was bad. The arsenal at Harper's Ferry was blown up and burned by its small Federal garrison, and there were rumors that, when Maryland seceded, Washington would be isolated and captured. The chain bridge west of Washington was jammed by Southerners fleeing the Federal capital. Many Northerners, too, left the city, taking the western rail route via Wheeling rather than attempting to escape through Secession-hot Baltimore. The Sixth Massachusetts, the first militia regiment to rush to the defense of Washington, was mobbed in Baltimore by plug-uglies and "blood tubs" when they marched across the city from the President Station to the Camden Station. Irate Baltimoreans now cut Washington's telegraph wires and burned sections of bridges on railroads leading north. For four days Washington's telegraphic communications were broken.

Lincoln's call on April 15 for seventy-five thousand volunteers to serve for three months brought forth Jefferson Davis's retaliatory proclamation of the seventeenth, offering letters of marque to mariners who wished to prey upon Yankee commerce. Lincoln parried by branding such letters of marque as pirates and proclaiming a formal naval blockade of the Southern coast.

There were two of these blockade proclamations. That of the nineteenth applied to the coast line from South Carolina through Texas, while the supplementary proclamation issued on the twenty-seventh, following the secessions of Virginia and North Carolina, extended the blockade from South Carolina up the Potomac shore opposite Washington itself. All vessels willfully seeking to violate the blockade were declared subject to seizure and condemnation as naval prize. All persons who, under the "pretended authority" of the seceded states, molested United States commerce were declared pirates and held amenable to laws "for the prevention and punishment of piracy." [1] The Southern coast line thus brought under formal naval blockade was 3,549 statute miles in length and included 180 harbors and navigable inlets. At the time this giant undertaking was officially ordered, Mr. Lincoln's Navy contained a total of only forty-two vessels in commission.

On Sunday, April 21, the day the Norfolk yard was destroyed, the Cabinet was in continuous session. The all-absorbing question was how the Federal Government might continue to function in case Maryland should secede. Mayor George W. Brown of Baltimore had been summoned and General Scott was present. Brown contended that the only way to prevent a collision was for the Federal Government not to route any more troops through Baltimore. Lincoln urged the "irresistible necessity" of such a transit for troops to defend Washington. The protection of Washington was the sole military object, he insisted, not hostile action against Maryland. Unable to bring troops up the Potomac—the river being closed by batteries at Alexandria—the government must either transport them through Maryland or abandon the capital.

Lincoln turned to General Scott. The general pointed out that a compromise was possible. Troops might circle around Baltimore, either coming by water from Perryville to Annapolis or marching to the westward through Ellicott City and the Relay House.

With that the Mayor seemed content. Later in the day, however, receiving a dispatch that troops from Pennsylvania were approaching through Cockeysville, a few miles north of

Baltimore, he returned to the White House, angrily brandishing the newly received dispatch. Lincoln, unwilling to incur suspicion of bad faith in calling the mayor to Washington and allowing troops to march on the city during his absence, desired that these troops be sent back at once to York or Harrisburg. Scott, accordingly, arranged to have the troops rerouted via Harrisburg, Philadelphia, Perryville, and the bay steamer to Annapolis and over the Elk Ridge and Annapolis Railroad to Washington.

Throughout these discussions, Gideon Welles became more and more alarmed. Whispering a few words to Seward and Chase and requesting the President to excuse him, he retired to the Navy Department, where he was soon joined by Seward and Chase. While messengers were summoning Commodore Joseph Smith and Chief Clerk Berrien, Welles had a consultation in his office with the other Cabinet members. "There was entire unanimity in the conclusion that vigorous steps must be at once taken," reads Welles's diary, "and the powers of the government exercised and enforced—that the rebellion must be stopped and suppressed without further temporizing with men, or mobs, or organized insurrection against the government.

"Washington was . . . severed from the Northern States, without mail facilities or telegraphic intercourse; and the administration was thwarted by the insurgents whom the Mayor said he could not, and evidently did not wish to control in that respect. The troops which were on their way to the Capital were stopped and denied approach—these troops were, as yet unorganized, and undisciplined—without commanders, and many without arms—the few naval vessels on the Atlantic coast that were available had been sent to Charleston [and Pensacola], and when they returned would be wholly inadequate for the immediate and indispensable wants of the government.

"I had been told by the President after the Proclamation [of the Blockade] was issued, that I must take such means as might seem to me necessary in the emergency to maintain the national authority, and that he would share with me or take upon himself the responsibility of such orders as I in my discretion, should issue. . . . When therefore, the Cabinet officers whom I have named were assembled on that Sunday morning in the Navy Department, I stated the necessity of chartering or purchasing without delay vessels for the naval service—to close the rebel ports, and assert national supremacy. All concurred in my proposition." [2]

Emergency orders were drafted to the commandants of navy yards at New York, Philadelphia, and Boston to charter or purchase at once twenty steamers capable of mounting naval cannon to be used to convoy troops and supplies to the national capital and to keep open the sea route via the Virginia capes and the Potomac River. Horatio Bridge, Chief of the Bureau of Provisions and Clothing, who carried these dispatches, was sent westward through Wheeling in order to bypass Baltimore.

In addition to the emergency conversion of merchant steamers, Gideon Welles did not hesitate to share his own powers as Secretary of the Navy with others and to employ unusual methods to save money in government purchasing. If, in the future, the telegraph lines to Washington should be cut as they were at present, the commandants of the Northern navy yards were authorized to consult with the following lawyers and merchants of New York City: Governor E. D. Morgan, William Evarts, George D. Morgan, R. M. Blatchford, and Moses Grinnell. These men were "empowered to act for the Secretary of the Navy in matters pertaining to forwarding men and supplies" to Washington.

Captain Samuel L. Breese, commandant of the New York Navy Yard, with advice from the "proxies" of the Secretary of the Navy, fitted out merchant steamers to serve as naval convoys. William H. Aspinwall, steamship executive, bought the steamer *Yankee* and put it at Breese's disposal. Breese gave a temporary commission as acting lieutenant to Gustavus V. Fox, newly returned from Fort Sumter, and Fox took the steamer to Annapolis in time to aid with the opening of the route to Washington through Perryville and Annapolis. Captain Samuel F. Du Pont, a popular member of the family of powder manufacturers, who was commandant of the Philadelphia Navy Yard, obtained extraordinary aid from S. M. Felton, president of the Baltimore & Philadelphia Railroad. Felton gave Du Pont and General B. F. Butler of Massachusetts the right to seize and mount howitzers upon the railroad's ferryboat at Perryville.

Within a few weeks the route down Chesapeake Bay avoiding Baltimore was secure. General Butler stamped out Secession activity along the right of way of the railroad to Washington and made Secession impossible in Maryland by seizing Baltimore.

Throughout the summer of 1861, the Navy Department advocated landing troops on the south bank of the Potomac to hold the major promontories, and thus prevent the Confederates from mounting batteries there to interdict commerce. But the War Department—moved by General Scott's phobia that small isolated garrisons would inevitably be captured—declined to risk their troops in that manner. Annapolis, therefore, became the port of Washington. Midshipmen of the Naval Academy—minus Southerners who resigned—were embarked upon the schoolship *Constitution,* "Old Ironsides" of 1812 fame, and sent to wartime quarters at Newport, Rhode Island. The Navy developed a sort of flying squadron for Chesapeake Bay to protect the highways to Washington, the one via Perryville at the head of the bay, the other around by sea and north from the Virginia capes.

Naval officers from Maryland and Virginia, hitherto wavering in their allegiance, now felt compelled to make their decisions. Captain Raphael Semmes of Baltimore resigned to become in the Confederate States Navy the most famed of the Civil War's commerce raiders. In the belief that his native Maryland would secede, Captain Franklin Buchanan, the popular and influential commandant of the Washington Navy Yard, brought his commission to Mr. Welles "and with studied pathos and manner, and feelings not unaffected, laid

National Archives

The Honorable Gideon Welles

Library of Congress

President Abraham Lincoln

FROM THE MESERVE COLLECTION

National Archives

Gustavus V. Fox,
Assistant Secretary of the Navy

Frank Leslie's Illustrated Newspaper

American naval officer going into action—new style invented by Commodore Farragut

Library of Congress

Rear Admiral Samuel Francis Du Pont

National Archives

Commodore Andrew H. Foote

Library of Congress

Admiral David D. Porter

National Archives

Admiral David G. Farragut

Official U.S. Navy Photograph

Commodore Charles Wilkes

Official U.S. Navy Photograph

Rear Admiral John A. Dahlgren

Official U.S. Navy Photograph

The Battle of Hampton Roads, March, 1862

Official U.S. Navy Photograph

U.S.S. Black Hawk

Official U.S. Navy Photograph

U.S.S. Hartford *stripped for battle*

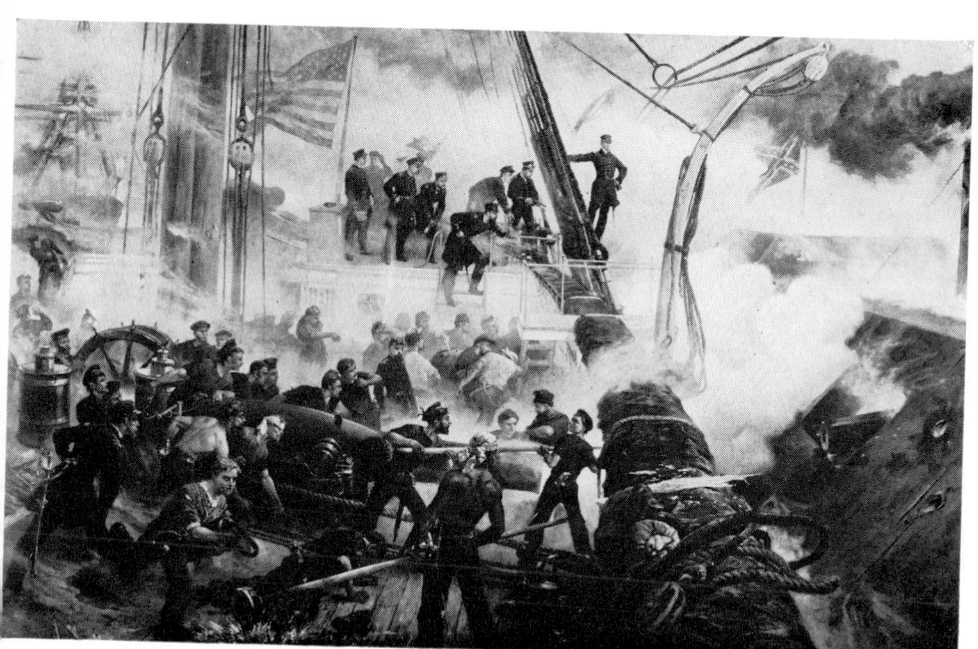

Official U.S. Navy Photograph

The Battle of Mobile Bay

National Archives

Library of Congress

(upper) *Admiral John A. Dahlgren and group*

(lower) *Admiral David D. Porter and officers on board the U.S.S.* Malvern

Official U.S. Navy Photograph

Official U.S. Navy Photograph

(upper) *New Orleans, Farragut's fleet*

(lower) *Crew of the U.S.S.* Monitor

Courtesy of the White House

"The Peacemakers" by G. P. A. Healy

SHERMAN, GRANT, LINCOLN, AND PORTER

it with emotion and tears" upon the Secretary's table. "It was," he said, "tearing out his heart-strings, parting with what was dear as life to him." Welles asked him "if he had spent his years in the service of the State of Maryland or of the United States government—had he been employed and drawn pay from the treasury of the former or the latter—had his honors from boyhood to age been derived from the state or the nation?" [3] Buchanan affirmed that his first duty was to his immediate government, the state. Welles advised him to think it over a few weeks, especially since Maryland had not actually seceded, but Buchanan insisted that his mind was made up. In just a fortnight he was back again, asking leave to recall his commission and resume his duties as commandant of the yard. But Welles had already turned over the navy yard to a younger officer, Commander John A. Dahlgren, and had begun to feel that any officer of Buchanan's age, standing, and intelligence who in such a crisis might "falter, be faithless & doubt his flag" could never again be trusted. Buchanan, thus rebuffed, went South to become commander of the famous *Merrimack* ironclad. The crippled Commander M. F. Maury, Superintendent of the Naval Observatory, and Captain George Magruder, Chief of the Bureau of Ordnance, both Virginians, spent an agonized afternoon with Mr. Welles but gave no indication of intent to resign. That evening, however, Maury deposited his keys on Magruder's doorstep and decamped with his family into Virginia, and a few days later Magruder tendered his own resignation. Welles refused to accept the resignations of these officers but dismissed them from the service. All told, 259 naval officers resigned or were dismissed.

To find replacements for the officers who went South, as well as to procure new officers for an expanding service, became one of Welles's worst problems. Fifteen ex-officers of the Navy who had resigned in peaceful times were welcomed back to active duty. Although Welles could not legally restore them to their former positions in the line of promotion, he gave them temporary commissions as acting lieutenants and a promise that Congress would be approached in their behalf. From the commercial marine he obtained 25 acting volunteer lieutenants, and by December of 1861, when he made his first annual report, he had appointed from the merchant service 433 acting masters and 209 master's mates. Replacements for paymasters and engineers were also obtained from the merchant marine. An aggregate of 993 acting appointments were made during the first year.[4] These officers, selected by examination, met high standards. Those later found "addicted to intemperance" or otherwise unsuited had their appointments promptly revoked.

After several weeks of service in the steamer *Yankee* on the Chesapeake Bay, Gustavus Fox, through his kinsman Postmaster General Blair, let it be known that the diversion of the *Powhatan* to Fort Pickens had made his expedition to Fort Sumter look ridiculous. Lincoln wrote Fox a letter of consolation, assuming blame for his own remissness in the matter. "I most cheerfully and truly declare that the failure of the undertaking has not lowered you a particle, while the qualities you developed in the effort have greatly heightened you in my estimation. For a daring and dangerous enterprize, of a similar character you would today be the man, of all my acquaintances, whom I would select." Lincoln offered Fox a ship in the Navy and a volunteer officer's commission, but Blair advised that Fox take a post in the Navy Department itself, "as the naval war will be only one of blockade." [5] To this latter proposition Fox assented. Lincoln shifted the incumbent chief clerk to another position and on May 8 Secretary Welles appointed Fox to the vacancy. After Congress met in July, the new post of Assistant Secretary of the Navy, carrying the pay of a navy captain on sea duty, was created for Fox.

Fox's appointment infused new blood and a dynamic spirit into Lincoln's Navy Department. After eighteen years in the Navy, Fox had resigned in 1856 because of moribund conditions and stagnation of promotion. An ardent advocate of a new steam-driven Navy, he himself had had unusual experience in command of mail steamers. While out of the Navy from 1856 to 1861, he had learned something about business as an executive of a textile mill in Lawrence, Massachusetts. Fox was as honest, forthright, and daring as Gideon Welles, but without the latter's reticence. Whereas the latter was given to secret speculation, and silent and even crafty analyses of the men who served under him in the Navy, Fox was open, hearty, jovial, ready at all times to let anyone fill his ear with gossip so long as he had patriotic intent and a genuine desire to get the job done. Fox was the ideal liaison officer, able to approach congressmen, officials in other departments, ship-owners, manufacturers, whoever might have business with the Navy.[6] And, speaking the language of naval officers, he was at his best in obtaining their confidence. He was their friend at court, and they in turn—all types of naval officers—made him their confidant, told him their joys, sorrows, problems, difficulties. He was as gay, as bighearted and generous, as Mr. Welles was tightfisted and secretive. The two of them got on perfectly together, the one sitting quietly at the helm holding a steady course, the effervescent assistant forever darting here and yonder to seek out the best channel to steer through.

From the start of the war it was clear that the prime concern of Lincoln's Navy would be to develop and maintain a tight blockade around the coast line of the Confederate states. The Confederacy bore no comparison to the Northern states in development of industry and could not match the North in naval construction. In all the South there were but a few small iron-working establishments, and no factory that could manufacture marine engines. Southerners, therefore, were limited to the vessels they seized in their harbors at the outset of the war, steamboats on the Western rivers, and ships they could procure abroad.

Once the war lines were drawn as they now were, how to proceed became Welles's first problem. What should be his general over-all plan? Prior to the firing upon Fort Sumter, no plans had been drafted for turning the nation's war machinery against the Southern states. At the outbreak of the war Lincoln's Navy Department knew a great deal about the geography of the coast of Mexico, scene of operations for the so-called Home Squadron. The western seaboard of Africa was familiar, for the United States maintained a squadron off Africa to enforce the antislave-trade treaty. The image of the Mediterranean, thanks to service in the Mediterranean Squadron, was etched on every American naval officer's mind. But the character of the coast line of the Southern states and its implications for the Federal blockade were imperfectly understood.

Welles appointed a fact-finding and strategy-forming board to study the littoral of the South Atlantic states. Capain S. F. Du Pont, who had helped to open the route to Washington, was called to the capital to head this board, and with him were associated Professor A. D. Bache, Superintendent of the U. S. Coast Survey, Major J. G. Barnard of the Corps of Engineers, U. S. Army, and Commander C. H. Davis, U. S. Navy.[7]

Meanwhile, Welles recalled ships from foreign stations and set up three squadrons, the Atlantic Blockading Squadron under Stringham, the Gulf Blockading Squadron under Mervine, and the Home Squadron in the West Indies under Pendergrast. The first two put into effect Mr. Lincoln's blockade; the third answered the early hue and cry of New York insurance companies for protection of the California treasure ships from Confederate privateers and commerce raiders.

To procure enough ships to cover the Southern coast, Welles, during the first nine months, repaired and recommissioned from the old Navy 76, purchased 136, and constructed 52, for a total of 264 ships, and during this time the number of seamen jumped from 7,600 to 22,000. "I have shrunk from no responsibilities," reads the Secretary's first report, "and if, in some instances the letter of the law has been transcended, it was because the public necessities required it. To have declined the exercise of any powers but such as were clearly authorized and legally defined . . . would have been an inexcusable wrong and a cowardly omission." [8]

What troubled the Secretary's conscience was that he had given to a single agent the sole power to purchase ships for the Navy in New York, and that that agent, George D. Morgan, was Welles's brother-in-law. In the exercise of his extraordinary power, Morgan, a shrewd New York business man, was able, substantially, to beat down prices in a way that officers at the New York Navy Yard had never been able to do. Welles's situation was complicated because Senator John P. Hale of Maine tried to influence the department to purchase a vessel belonging to some of his friends, and because Welles had the temerity to decline it because her owners valued it much higher than he did.[9] The Senator, after badgering Welles at home and at his office, finally resorted to retaliatory "nuisance resolutions," investigating not only ship purchases by the Navy but the losses of the Norfolk and Pensacola Navy Yards. Newspaper sniping at "Grandfather" Welles, the "Rip Van Winkle of the Navy Department," suggests that the mercantile community of New York disparaged Secretary Welles's economy-mindedness; although a prominent and disinterested shipowner of Boston came to the Secretary's defense:

> The administration of Mr. Welles & Fox together has been a success and . . . it would be a great misfortune to have them disturbed or disheartened by Congressional criticism! Especially so when you pitch into the best things they have done in going out of routine and trying to carry on as *practical men* would do it. You are beginning your reform at the wrong end when you censure a thing that is *well done,* merely because it was not better done, and because it has an unlucky appearance of nepotism which gives a handle for popular complaint.[10]

Welles's board of strategy recommended division of the South Atlantic coast into two sections, the demarcation falling approximately at the line between North and South Carolina, and proposed that separate blockading squadrons be formed to deal with the peculiar geographical characteristics of each section. In the northern sector it was impossible to blockade Richmond and Norfolk simply by stationing ships in the lower Chesapeake Bay, for Virginia's chief cities had backdoor entrances through Albemarle and Pamlico Sounds and the Dismal Swamp Canal. The narrow belts of sand which separate the inland sounds from the ocean are broken at irregular intervals by inlets through which the tides wash to and fro. Some of these inlets, the strategy board believed, might be blocked by sinking in them hulks laden with ballast. The southern sector, including South Carolina and Georgia, consisted largely of a succession of islands that present on the ocean side a moderately straight sea beach with sand hills and woods, the marshy inner edges of these islands outline a series of sounds and harbors that provided good inland channels for vessels of shallow draft. Somewhere near the southern end of the Atlantic coast the board recommended establishment of a coal and supply base—a harbor of refuge within which blockade ships might ride out a storm.

Secretary Welles adopted the essential suggestions made by the strategy board. The Atlantic Squadron was divided into North and South Atlantic Blockading Squadrons.

With the aid of the Army, an amphibian expedition was launched in late July against the Confederate forts at Hatteras Inlet. Major General Benjamin F. Butler, the Massachusetts political general who had seized Annapolis and opened the railroad to Washington, led the troops and Flag Officer Stringham, within whose province the target lay, commanded the naval forces. Hatteras Inlet, just under the cape, was a newly washed-out inlet, so new in fact that it did not appear on the Coast Survey maps used by the strategy board. Although the original plan had been to destroy the Confederate forts and plug the entrance with block ships, Stringham and Butler, when they saw the harbor, decided that it would be best to fortify it and use it as a blockade base.

The South Atlantic Blockading Squadron in November launched a more ambitious combined army and navy assault against Port Royal, midway between Charleston and Savannah, the forces in this case being led by General Thomas W. Sherman and Flag Officer Samuel F. Du Pont. Port Royal Sound, with its ample anchorage and adequate acreage of protected sea islands, was later developed into the most extensive Atlantic base south of Hampton Roads.

Obtaining from the special session of Congress that met on July 4 an appropriation to build ironclad warships, Welles appointed a board to consider this new type of vessel. Commodores Joseph Smith and Hiram Paulding, and Commander C. H. Davis investigated the use of ironclad batteries in the Crimean War and studied the records of the Stevens battery of Philadelphia—an iron-sheathed vessel into which a discouraged Congress over a period of years had sunk over half a million dollars. Present urgency in the matter of ironclads grew out of the fact that the Confederates had raised the sunken hull of the *Merrimack* and were rebuilding her as an ironclad ram to break through the Federal blockade.

In the early months of the war Lincoln's Navy weathered defection of personnel and disastrous losses of navy yards. From only four ships available in home ports at the outset, the Navy had been built up to a substantial blockading force of 264 ships. In the chaos of early reverses, long before there were ships available to make it effective, Lincoln had proclaimed the blockade. He had marked the course for the Navy. Secretary Gideon Welles, by feeling his way at first and by assuming the extraordinary emergency powers of the executive, had gradually conceived the main lines of action which the Navy would attempt to follow through the war.

These lines, as he stated them in his Annual Report for 1861, were as follows:

1. The closing of all the insurgent ports along a coast of nearly three thousand miles, in the form and under the exacting regulations of an international blockade, including the naval occupation and defense of the Potomac river, from its mouth to the federal capital, as the boundary line between Maryland and Virginia, and also the main commercial avenue to the principal base of our military operations.

2. The organization of combined naval and military expeditions to operate in force against various points of the southern coast, rendering efficient naval cooperation with the position and movements of such expeditions when landed, and including also all needful naval aid to the army in cutting intercommunication with the rebels and in its operations on the Mississippi and its tributaries; and

3. The active pursuit of the piratical cruisers which might escape the vigilance of the blockading force and put to sea from the rebel ports.[11]

5.

Beginning the Blockade

LINCOLN'S POLICY WHEN HE INAUGURATED THE blockade in April of 1861 was to be lenient toward the enemy, and both considerate and generous toward foreign powers whose commercial interests were affected. Above all considerations he wished by firm police tactics to persuade the "deluded people" to forget their Secession heresy and return to the Union, and to speed that return he sought to avoid foreign interference.

Lincoln might have made the task easier for his naval watchdogs had he simply closed the ports of the insurrectionary states. In this case all violators would have been subject to capture, like the breakers of any other domestic law. Instead, Lincoln, in effect, conceded belligerent rights to the Confederacy and neutral rights to foreigners by proclaiming a formal "blockade" to be enforced according to the cumbersome rules of international law. Under the system as Lincoln set it up, the blockade of a particular Confederate port could not be established until a naval force had been posted off that port which would be able to prevent the entrance and exit of vessels. The commander of the blockade craft upon arrival would have to notify the authorities on shore that a blockade had been established and to allow foreign vessels already in the port fifteen days in which to put to sea. After this period of grace the port would be closed, and all outgoing vessels would be captured. When a neutral or foreign vessel appeared which had not been warned of the existence of the blockade.

this notification had to be inserted in writing on the muster roll of the vessel by the blockade officer, together with the date and the latitude. A vessel so warned would later be subject to capture if caught attempting to run the blockade.[1]

Thus, the blockade would have to be established piecemeal, one part at a time as naval ships were built, purchased, and converted, or drawn in from foreign stations. It would be several months before the major ports were formally blockaded and years before such important ports as Mobile and Wilmington were completely closed to blockade-runners.

To patrol the Potomac and prevent Virginians from capturing the national capital, the authorities at the Washington Navy Yard had early impressed into service four river steamers belonging to the Acquia Creek Line. To these were added the Hudson River side-wheeler *Freeborn,* and two second-class navy sloops, the *Pawnee* and the *Pocahontas.* This motley group, euphemistically entitled the Potomac Flotilla, wrestled with the difficult sector from Washington down to lower Chesapeake Bay.

Under its first leader, Commander James H. Ward, the Potomac Flotilla replaced the channel markers that had been removed by Virginians, and seized canoes, oyster boats, and other bay and river craft that tried to run supplies across the river from Maryland to Virginia. The river had to be patrolled daily from Washington to its mouth to prevent the enemy from erecting batteries on the wooded Virginia promontories and to convoy transports and supply vessels to Washington.

On May 24 the flotilla assisted the Army in its landings on the Virginia shore from Washington down through Alexandria. When the Confederates erected a series of batteries at Acquia Creek, Commander Ward engaged them with the two thirty-two-pounder guns of his flagship, the *Freeborn.* Next day he brought the *Pawnee* to assist the *Freeborn.* As the ships remained outside the range of the shore batteries, they were not hit. (It was sound naval doctrine in the early summer of 1861 that ships were no match for land-based guns.) But neither did they inflict damage on the Confederate batteries.

Discouraged over his inability to take his fragile steamers close enough to damage the enemy batteries, Ward a month later sent a party on shore at Mathias Point, some fifty-five miles below Washington, to erect a battery of his own. Unfortunately, his work party were surprised and routed by Confederate riflemen. To cover their retreat, Ward brought the *Freeborn* so close inshore that he was himself killed by a musket ball.[2] All in the landing party got off to the ship, thanks to Seaman John Williams, who warned his men that they must all die at the thwarts sooner than leave a single man behind, and who, when the flagstaff of his boat was shot in two, although suffering from a gunshot wound in the thigh, seized the flag and brandished it defiantly.

Much of the work of the Potomac Flotilla was performed at night by small boats rowing up and down the shores on picket duty.[3] During the daytime the ships ceaselessly sounded the channel to replace markers. Often in spite of every precaution they ran aground on bars and shoals. In hourly danger from batteries masked by undergrowth, their quarters uncomfortable, their prizes mere rowboats and small, worthless river craft, the men of the flotilla led a more varied and interesting life than their fellow blockaders stationed down the Atlantic coast. Yet even on the river the blockade, like blockades everywhere, could be dull. "To all appearances everything seems to be deserted," wrote one flotilla captain; "nothing was to be seen on the river save now and then a fishing canoe, with one colored man in [it], who immediately on our approach retreated into shoal water.... The wheat crop is cut and stacked in the fields, and, judging from the number of stacks, I should pronounce the crop to have been very large. The corn crop looks well, and we saw a large number of cattle grazing on the banks of the river. Everything looked so peaceful that it was difficult to imagine that we are at war with the people of Virginia." [4]

Flag Officer Silas H. Stringham, commander of the Atlantic

Blockading Squadron, was a curly-haired Yankee from Connecticut with a V-shaped mouth and humorous twinkle in the eye. Unlike his friend Gideon Welles, also a native of Connecticut, he was not thrifty but lavish in his yearning for more ships. He perhaps understood the facts of the situation better than the Secretary, for every few days he sent in an official request for more ships. Exclusive of the Potomac Flotilla, which was good only for use in the river and Chesapeake Bay, he began his service with only fourteen vessels, and with these he was expected to maintain a strict blockade of some nine hundred to a thousand miles of coast from Hampton Roads to Key West. His insistent pleading for more vessels at a time when Welles had scraped the bottom of the barrel persuaded the Secretary that perhaps the blockade really could not be made as strict as had been called for. "It is possible that some of the lighter craft may in thick weather and at night run the blockade," Welles wrote him, "but your great effort will be to prevent it." [5] Acknowledging the need for more ships for the giant task, Welles merged the four ships of Pendergrast's Home Squadron with Stringham's.

The extra reward or inducement for the Civil War soldier was the bounty money he collected when he enlisted. While the sailor received no bounty, he did look forward to naval prize money, the amount of which would be determined partly by luck, but also to some extent by his own alertness and exertion in sighting and capturing violators of the blockade. At Hampton Roads dozens of prizes fell to the happy blockaders during the first months of the blockade. Tradesmen of Richmond and Baltimore, blindly refusing to accept the reality of war, sought to continue their normal peacetime traffic. The blockaders captured all such "enemy" craft, confiscated for their own, or for Army, use coal, hay, and other commodities, and sent prize vessels laden with tobacco and lumber to the admiralty courts in Philadelphia and New York. Strong objections were raised in Maryland, where such knotty questions could not appear so simple as at Hampton Roads, and Secretary Welles was induced to release some of the bonanza of prize vessels to their "loyal" owners. Stringham's vigorous protest against surrendering prizes that had sailed with Secession state clearances was met by Welles's bland rejoinder: "There will doubtless be many cases involving new questions that you may find it difficult to decide, but the courts of admiralty must dispose of them." [6]

Catching smugglers was like swatting mosquitoes in the lower bay. Schooners would load in Baltimore and clear for Deal's Island or Snow Hill in Maryland, wait for a suitable night, and then cross to York River and discharge in Mobjack Bay. William Bayne, a Baltimore tobacconist, made many fraternal visits to a brother in Westmoreland County, Virginia, until the blockaders discovered that letters and important papers were being hidden on the person of the young girl who invariably accompanied him.

Apart from blockading operations, there were certain political chores to perform at Hampton Roads. Let a group of visiting senators remain too long at Fortress Monroe to catch the bay steamer back to Baltimore and the courteous Stringham would return them to Washington on the flagship of the Potomac Flotilla. Or let a group of Unionists in Norfolk appeal to President Lincoln for transportation north, and Stringham would assign one of his most efficient side-wheelers, the *Keystone State,* to negotiate under flag of truce with the Secessionist mayor and bring out 116 women and children. Only 35 of these refugees were content to be placed on board the Baltimore boat at Old Point Comfort; the other 81 claimed and obtained a presidential favor of transportation all the way to New York City!

Hampton Roads, the most commodious anchorage on the coast and the safest, since it lay under the protection of Fortress Monroe, was the sole base for the Atlantic Blockading Squadron. Key West, though theoretically available, was too distant from important Atlantic coast points. Ships down the coast were continually returning to Hampton Roads for coal, water, and minor repairs. Whatever their purpose at Hampton Roads, their mere presence offered a continual temptation to political generals like Benjamin F. Butler to request naval assistance. After the blockaders had aided in transporting Butler's troops from Baltimore to Fortress Monroe, Butler requested that they cooperate with his troops in the seizure of Newport News and that later they make reconnaissances of various Confederate batteries that had been placed at the mouths of the James and Elizabeth Rivers. Gideon Welles had to remind the blockaders at Hampton Roads that their main task was to blockade.

The most important point on the Atlantic blockade in the early months was Charleston. Apparently Lincoln hoped that to discourage "the cradle of Secession" would be to bring the war to a speedy close. As far as Lincoln's puritanical Secretary of the Navy was concerned, however, the blockade was to be made strict at Charleston as a matter of simple, eye-for-an-eye retaliation.

The plan of Lincoln's Navy Department was to post outside of Charleston one large vessel for offshore cruising and two smaller and swifter craft to operate close in. During the early months only four large vessels were available: the *Niagara,* the *Minnesota,* the *Wabash,* and the *Roanoke*. The day the *Niagara* departed for Charleston the Navy Department received intelligence of a shipment of arms from Europe to Mobile, and dispatched orders for the *Niagara* to proceed to the Gulf. Before she received these orders, however, she established the blockade off Charleston on May 10 and notified eight vessels by officially endorsing their registers. One of these, the *General Parkhill* from Liverpool, which refused to leave the port after being warned off but edged in with signals flying in communication with the shore, was seized as prize and sent to Philadelphia. On the eleventh two armed steamers from Charleston came across the bar, accompanied by launches filled with men. Possibly mistaking the *Niagara* for a merchantman, they made a demonstration as if to attack her. Captain McKean maneuvered his large ship toward them, but before he could come within range they scurried back inside the harbor. McKean promptly dispatched to Washington the first of hundreds of admonitions that light-draft steamers were essential to enforce the blockade.

After the *Niagara's* departure, the three remaining steam frigates took turns at sentinel duty off Charleston, usually with one or two small craft to assist them. It was particularly exasperating to Flag Officer Stringham that many of his lighter vessels, while they had speed, carried so little coal that they could not keep the sea, but had to spend a disproportionate time running to and from Hampton Roads to refuel. The need of a supply base near the southern end of the blockade coast became painfully apparent.

Equally obvious was the need to blockade all of the secondary inlets and harbors. Too often vessels warned off from Charleston simply ran up or down the coast to put in at Savannah, Bull's Bay, or Newbern or Wilmington, North Carolina. Stringham's sense of humor vanished under the exasperations of his many-faceted job. Daily from Washington he received intelligence of foreign arms shipments coming to New Brunswick, the Bermudas, or Nassau to be transferred to Southern vessels and run through the blockade, news of Confederate preparations to send out commerce raiders, frantic pleas from New York insurance companies to stop the activities of the Confederate privateers, *Jefferson Davis, Dixie,* and *Savannah.* At Hatteras Inlet, where the Confederates had removed navigation lights, vessels became stranded. Shallow-draft privateering craft from the sounds would now issue from the inlet to capture or plunder the distressed vessels. The *Roanoke* under Pendergrast, sighting Confederate batteries being erected at Hatteras Inlet, stood in at long range to draw their fire. This Confederate "pirate's nest" had only a few guns mounted, but within a short time its offensive strength might become formidable.

One of the most successful of the Confederate privateers, the *Jefferson Davis,* captured Yankee merchantmen all along the coast. But the untutored prize crews which sought to bring the *Davis'* prizes into Charleston sometimes came to grief. All hands but the Negro steward had been removed from the prize schooner *S. J. Waring,* but about fifty miles south of Charleston this doughty Negro butchered three of his captors with a hatchet and compelled the rest of the prize crew to sail the vessel to New York.[7] The *Enchantress* of Boston was seized off Sandy Hook by the *Davis* and again the prize crew retained on board the Negro cook. Nearing Charleston, when hailed by the blockader *Albatross,* the prize crew replied that they were from Newburyport and bound to Santa Cruz. At that instant the Negro leaped overboard, yelling: "For God's sake, Captain; she's a Secesher, bound for Charleston." [8] The Negro's story tallying with accounts of the capture in the newspapers, the blockader placed the prize crew in irons and sent them with the schooner to Philadelphia.

Rivaling detective fiction, the Carolina coastal schooner *Charles McCees,* two days before the blockade went into effect, cleared from Newbern, North Carolina, with a cargo of turpentine. Learning of the blockade at Nevis in the West Indies, she sailed to Halifax under the same *Susan Jane.* Here she took on an assorted cargo of blankets, cloth, iron, steel, brogans, axes—all of which had been shipped to Halifax by merchants in Boston and New York. She now made the run to Hatteras Inlet, where she was captured by the *Pawnee* and sent to Philadelphia.

The tempo of the naval blockade in the Gulf was more leisurely. In fact, it dragged. For three months after his troops had been landed at Fort Pickens, Colonel Harvey Brown continued to brandish his original orders covering the reinforcement of the fort. Now somewhat wrinkled, the document read: [9]

Executive Mansion
Washington, April 1, 1861.

All officers of the Army and Navy to whom this order may be exhibited will aid by every means in their power the expedition under the command of Colonel Harvey Brown, supplying him with men and material and cooperating with him as he may desire.

Abraham Lincoln

In effect this magic paper gave Brown the power of a unified command. Considering his position inside Fort Pickens as untenable without the stand-by services of *all the ships in the area,* by means of rigorous argument and waving of his orders, he contrived to hold all the Gulf vessels at anchor off Pensacola Harbor for six weeks. The senior naval officer, Captain H. A. Adams, was a senile oldster who complained that the country had fallen on evil times and wished himself in his grave.[10] The U.S.S. *Water Witch* on May 12 brought word of Lincoln's proclamation of a blockade and on the thirteenth Captain Adams sent an official notice of it ashore to General Bragg.

But not until Captain W. W. McKean in the *Niagara* arrived two weeks later were any of the ships dispersed from Pensacola. On this date the *Powhatan,* under Lieutenant D. D. Porter, was sent to establish the blockade at Mobile and to watch for the expected arms shipments from Europe. A week later, the *Powhatan,* being relieved at Mobile, shifted to a new blockade station off the South West Pass of the Mississippi, and Captain Poor in the *Brooklyn* blockaded Pass a l'Outre.

William Mervine, whom Welles appointed to command the Gulf Squadron, proved to be a man of correct deportment and habits who in normal times "would float along the stream with others." He was later judged by the Secretary as wanting not in patriotism, but in executive ability, "is quite as great on little things as on great ones." [11] Mervine was long in getting out to his station, and accomplished nothing after he got there.

Mervine's flagship, the huge and clumsy side-wheeler *Mississippi,* escaped from the repairman of the Boston Navy Yard on May 23. As she steamed down the harbor, a sabotaged delivery pipe, through which water was forced out of the side of the ship, gave way, pouring a flood of water into the ship.[12] The engines were immediately stopped and an anchor thrown out. After making temporary repairs she tried to haul in her cable. It broke and she limped back to the navy yard mourning the loss of a six-thousand pound anchor.

Mervine reached Key West on June 7 and began puttering over details. One matter which doubtless disgusted Gideon Welles was the excessive attention the flag officer paid to a political favor that had been asked of Lincoln. On May 28 the President had written the Secretary a perfunctory note:

My dear Sir: A friend of mine residing at Chicago, Ill., Mr. C. Beckwith, has a lady relative, Miss Elizabeth Smith, at St. Marks, in Florida, whom he much desires to have brought away from there, and he has been induced to think that some of our vessels connected with the blockade could effect this without much trouble. If this is practicable, I shall be obliged if you will direct it to be done.[13]

This note, along with dozens of more important matters, Welles relayed to Mervine to be complied with "if practicable." But Mervine, instead of disregarding it and attending first to the major problems of the blockade in the Gulf—Mobile, New Orleans, and Galveston were at this time wide open—squandered the services of a blockade ship for nearly three weeks off the coastal village of St. Mark's, exchanging letters with the Florida governor, while Miss Smith herself evinced no desire to be "rescued."

After spending two weeks at Key West, Flag Officer Mervine made a leisurely arrival off Fort Pickens on June 23, and was so impressed by Colonel Brown's outdated orders from the President that he employed all the small boats of the flagship *Mississippi* and of the *Niagara* for two solid weeks lightering army stores from transports to the beach. Owing to the almost daily arrival of transports, he began at length to fear that his seamen would never get naval drill and that his ships would be converted into "mere appendages of the Army." "It appears," he explained to the Secretary, "that his Excellency the President issued an order which authorized Colonel Brown, on his assuming command of the Department of Florida, to call upon the Navy for aid, at a time, however, when Fort Pickens was in a defenseless condition. I can not believe that that order was intended to be continued in force when the post was in position to defy attack, well supplied with men, scows, and large launches sufficient, when manned by the soldiers, to afford the means of transportation required." [14] Needless to say, Gideon Welles promptly saw the President and got the old orders cancelled. Henceforth, the naval forces off Pensacola were to act only "in concert with," but not be subordinate to, the Army. Mervine's gigantic task, as the Secretary had spelled it out for him, was to "establish and enforce a blockade at each and all of the ports south of Key West to the Rio Grande. . . . The blockade must be strict and effectual." [15]

Meanwhile, for the first few weeks the blockaders off Mobile, off the Mississippi deltas, and off Galveston did a brisk business in capturing coastal vessels that sailed with Confederate clearances, apparently in ignorance that United States blockaders were their enemy. After the latter fact had been assimilated, Confederate shippers shifted their vessels to foreign registry. The English consul made a special trip from New Orleans to South West Pass to assure Lieutenant Porter of the *Powhatan* that such transfers were "proper" and that the English Government was responsible for his acts.

Only the two most important channels through the Mississippi deltas could be blocked—by the *Brooklyn* off Pass a l'Outre and the *Powhatan* off South West Pass. There were many secondary entrances that could be used by small merchantmen but there were no shallow-draft blockade ships to stand guard over them. The *Powhatan* and the *Brooklyn* were large and deep of draft. When they saw Confederate vessels approaching down the river, they could not enter the river to give chase because of the bars of silt that had partially filled the channels. It was dangerous, moreover, for the Federal craft to leave their stations to chase blockade-runners from the outside, making toward the secondary passes. One had to prevent enemy raiders from getting out to sea. At New Orleans five cruisers were being outfitted as commerce destroy-

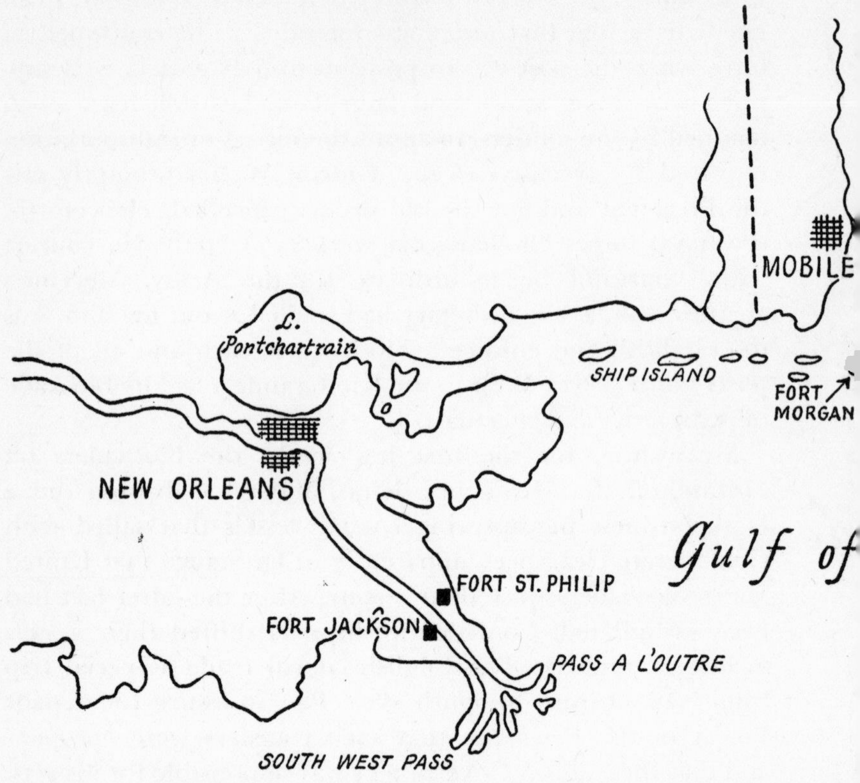

SECTION OF THE GULF BLOCKADE COAST. Off the ports of New gled to prevent Confederate cruisers from getting out and

ers, according to information gathered by Porter. And some of these were being strengthened with iron across the bow for ramming the Federal ships and forcing open the blockade.

In April, when the *Powhatan* had been fitted out for the Fort Sumter expedition and diverted to Fort Pickens, she had taken no more stores than necessary. July found her anchored athwart the South West Pass of the Mississippi, destitute of ordinary materials to keep the ship in order. "We cannot raise a tack, scarcely a nail to repair any damages with," Porter reported to Mervine.[16] "We have not an ounce of paint on board, nor whitewash. The ship is actually going

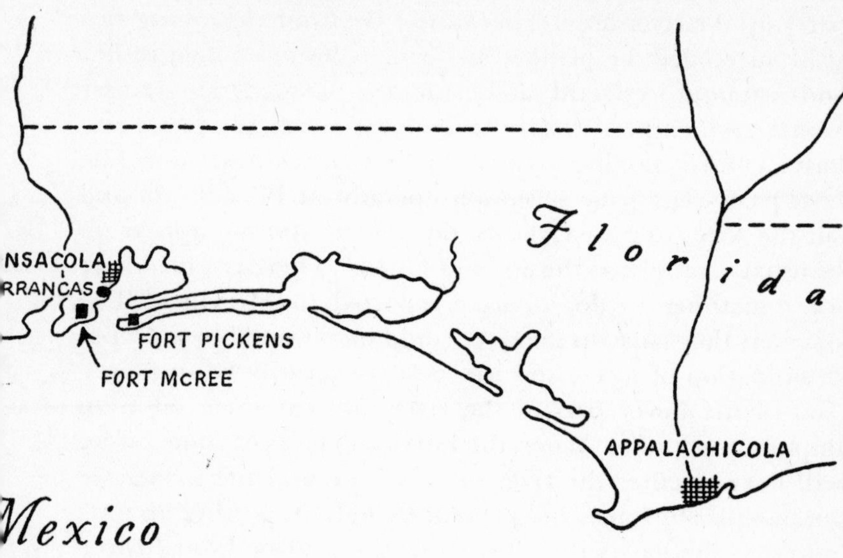

Orleans, Mobile, and Pensacola, Lincoln's blockaders strug-
blockade runners from getting in.

to ruin for want of her wood being covered. It is now over a year since she had any paint put on her. We could not repair a boat for want of a plank, and our machinery having broken down brought to my notice that there was no rope in the ship to make sheets, bowlines, braces, halyards, etc." Porter requested Mervine to send to Havana for certain castings to repair the *Powhatan*'s boilers, and he begged him to send shallow-draft vessels to help seal the blockade of the deltas. Boredom of the blockade vexed the active and energetic Porter. "A man don't associate down here with alligators, sand flies, mosquitoes and rattlesnakes for nothing, he soon gets his eye teeth, and gets wide awake."[17] Porter sent a boat party up the river hoping to capture the Confederate tug *Ivy*. If he succeeded, he planned to put two hundred men in her and attempt to board and seize the Confederate cruiser *Sumter,* which periodically came down South West Pass and Pass a l'Outre, hoping to catch the blockaders off station. The boat party seized the telegraph operator at Pilot Town and cut the wires to New Orleans, but the *Ivy* did not appear on its usual schedule, so the attempt failed. "There is a field here for something to do," Porter reported to Mervine. "The steamers they have up the river could be captured by a proper combination of force, and we could very easily be in possession of the lower part of the river and cut them off from important supplies. When the hurricane months come on we will have to enter the river or go to sea, and the sooner we get in with our forces and prevent them from putting up forts at any of the Passes the sooner this war will be brought to a close. I am an old cruiser in this river, and know every inch of the ground. I assure you that an expedition up the river is an easy thing for vessels not drawing over 16 feet, and I do believe that the people would return to their allegiance if they had any guarantee of protection. I know most of the pilots, light-house keepers, etc., and this is their feeling."[18]

The next day, the same mosquito-bitten blockader wrote his friend Gustavus Fox: "I have written a long letter to the Flag Officer pointing out to him the advantages of coming down here and operating in a manner that will produce results, but I have no great opinion of flag officers generally, especially after they have arrived at the age of one hundred years, it is time then for the government to take care of them and don't let them go abroad, where they eat Uncle Sam's rations without any adequate return."[19]

On June 30, while the *Brooklyn* was chasing a blockade-runner a few miles from her station at Pass a l'Outre, the C.S.S. *Sumter* under Raphael Semmes escaped through the unguarded pass. For this *faux pas* the Gulf Squadron paid dearly in the emergency detachment from time to time of ships to chase the raider. The blockade captains themselves eagerly sought relief from the tedium of the blockade whenever information as to the *Sumter's* whereabouts offered some promise of success. Among those going at various times in chase of the *Sumter* were McKean of the *Niagara,* Poor of the *Brooklyn,* and Porter of the *Powhatan.* Flag Officer Mervine's reputation in the Secretary's office suffered, although Gideon Welles approved of the energy displayed by Mervine's captains in these short emergency cruises after the *Sumter.* Welles prodded Mervine to take his ships inside the Mississippi River and to obstruct as many inlets as possible by sinking in them worthless blockade-runners, but the ineffectual Mervine failed to obtain results.

The most brilliant exploit of Mervine's regime was the cutting out and burning of the rebel commerce raider *Judah* on September 14. This craft, as watchers from Fort Pickens could plainly see, was moored to the wharf at the Pensacola Navy Yard under the protection of guns mounted on shore. In the spirit of Stephen Decatur at Tripoli, a hundred seamen from the *Colorado* in launches and cutters rowed in darkness across the bay. An instant before boarding they were discovered and fired into by a volley of musketry. While the fight raged, Yankee crews set fire to the vessel below decks. A ten-inch columbiad on shore, fired rather than aimed at the attackers, was seized and spiked, and its tampion was brought off as a souvenir. Three Federals were killed and eleven wounded. One of the raiders, having lost his distinguishing mark during the fighting, was killed by a shipmate.

The flaming *Judah,* lighting the way for the retreating boats, burned her mooring ropes, drifted into the middle of the bay, and sank when the flames ate through her hull.

Flag Officer Mervine's good tidings of the destruction of the *Judah* crossed in the mails the Secretary's orders detaching him and assigning command of the Gulf Blockading Squadron to Captain W. W. McKean of the *Niagara.*

To McKean, in giving him the command, Gideon Welles explained that his energy and promptitude had impressed the department. "The condition of public affairs is such that the country demands that the best men in the service should be called upon to command her navies and armies. . . . You have a difficult duty to perform, but this you will meet with alacrity, and, I feel assured, will surmount, to your own and the country's satisfaction. To lock up the outlets of the great central valley of the continent so that her products in that portion of the insurgent States shall not reach the ocean, and so that the craving wants of her population for the products of other lands shall not be supplied while their hands are raised against the Government, will demand your special attention. I need not enlarge upon its importance, and of the embarrassments you will experience in closing the passes and numerous bayous and inlets along the whole coast. These difficulties will present themselves to you, and on the resources of your own mind, with such assistance as the Department can send you, must you rely to remove them." [20]

The burning of the *Judah,* happily, afforded Secretary Welles opportunity to say a few truly gracious words to old William Mervine, now retiring after fifty-three years in the Navy.

6.

Early Amphibian Operations on the Coast

HIS STRATEGY BOARD, HAVING RECOMMENDED seizure of a point on the Atlantic coast suitable for a coaling depot and rendezvous for the blockading squadron, Gideon Welles in late July presented the matter to Lincoln and the Cabinet.[1] The rout of Bull Run had just shaken the capital to its foundations and the Government, yet jittery after the debacle, approved Mr. Welles's plan for a positive strike down the coast "upon the flank of the enemy." The War Department appointed General Thomas West Sherman to lead the military forces, and after many conferences Welles selected Captain Du Pont, chairman of the strategy board, to command the naval contingent. To gain the maximum psychological advantage the point chosen for attack, Port Royal Sound, lay in South Carolina, chief leader of Secession. Port Royal Sound was a beautiful anchorage from one to three miles wide and extending twenty miles inland. It washed the shores of some of the wealthiest of the Sea Island plantations and cut across the important protected waterway between Savannah and Charleston at a point forty-five miles southwest of Charleston and thirty northeast of Savannah. "The importance of this expedition . . .," Welles on August 3 wrote Du Pont, "cannot be overestimated." [2] He ordered Du Pont to proceed to New York as early as practicable, confer with General Sherman, and lose no time in getting afloat.

From the start, the Port Royal expedition encountered exasperating delays. After Bull Run no troops could be removed from the pool of soldiers in the Washington area. T. W. Sherman was directed to interview the governors of New England states with a view to obtaining certain new regiments, but on August 20, as the time approached for the expedition to leave, the New England troops were diverted to Washington because of fresh Confederate threats on the Potomac. A month later Sherman himself was ordered by General Scott to come to Washington, bringing all his troops except the smallest guard necessary to protect his camp in New York. By September 18 the military plans had been shifted so often that Lincoln wrote a directive to the War Department that the "joint expedition of the Army and Navy, agreed upon some time since . . . is in no wise to be abandoned, but must be ready to move by the 1st of or very early in October." [3] Du Pont, promoted to flag officer of the new South Atlantic Blockading Squadron in mid-September, was thus given time to make elaborate preparations for the naval part of the expedition.

Meanwhile, in August the Navy Department also launched an amphibian force to close and lock the back door to Norfolk and Richmond, and this became the first such movement to be carried through during the Civil War. The blockade ships at Hampton Roads cut off Virginia's chief cities from direct commercial intercourse with Maryland and with Europe. Indirect communications, however, were still open via the extensive inland waterways along the Virginia and North Carolina coasts. Vessels drawing no more than eight feet of water could pass from Richmond or Norfolk through the Dismal Swamp Canal into Currituck, Pamlico, and Albemarle Sounds. Over these waters, even in peaceful times, the extent of traffic in cotton, grain, lumber, turpentine, and provisions of all kinds was immense. "The shores of Currituck," wrote a blockade officer with financial interests in the area, "are lined with large and expensive hotels and cottages, where in summer crowds of wealthy resort for summer bathing. . . . The waters are covered with vessels carrying on inland trade, while many steamers ply to and from the many towns and villages. All this being the case . . . the effect of a blockade from the Rip Raps [in Hampton Roads] will to a great extent be evaded." [4]

On the same day that Du Pont was ordered to prepare for Port Royal, Secretary Welles, with the approval of the strategy board, ordered Flag Officer Stringham to close the inlets into the North Carolina sounds by sinking across them hulks loaded with stone.

It was a drastic measure, this destruction of North Carolina's inland ports. Whether the damage would prove permanent none could tell. But after Bull Run, with the enlistments of the three months' volunteers running out and the end of the war farther away than ever, the struggle took on a greater earnestness for Lincoln's Navy. The blockaders themselves, with a few chartered steamers and tugs, could haul the stone hulks down the coast from Baltimore and sink them in undefended inlets. But the "pirates' nest" of Hatteras Inlet, with its two log-and-sand forts, called for a cooperating army. Welles persuaded General Scott to detail temporarily a force of 880 men from Fortress Monroe under General Benjamin F. Butler to aid Stringham.

In a conference on board the flagship, Butler found Stringham cool toward the project. Stringham told Butler that the vessels necessary could not be immediately prepared.[5] Stringham believed that the very nature of the inlets through the sand bar made the idea of block ships absurd, and only a few weeks earlier had written the Secretary that the channels of such inlets were constantly changing: "A single gale often closes up a channel and opens a new one."

Butler, a skillful Massachusetts lawyer and politician, had just been superseded as commander at Fortress Monroe by the superannuated General John E. Wool. He was at the moment smarting under a sense of injustice and anxious to refute the judgment of his detractors by winning a military victory. For Butler, Hatteras Inlet was made to order. Looking over the map with Stringham, the Massachusetts political general became convinced that, rather than destroy Hatteras Inlet, it would be better to place a small garrison there and hold it, saving thereby "the services of one or more blockading vessels, at a very exposed and strong point of the coast during the Autumn, besides furnishing a Depot at which the blockading Steamers could go and get supplies." This being precisely what Stringham wanted, Butler undertook to persuade Washington of its feasibility, and preparations for the expedition went forward smoothly.

Several captains of vessels wrecked at Cape Hatteras came off in rowboats from Hatteras and Ocracoke Inlets to be rescued by blockade ships. Having been held prisoner in Fort Hatteras, they were able to give Stringham valuable information on conditions there. In six weeks these men had seen as many as one hundred vessels pass through Hatteras Inlet. The majority of these were bound to the West Indies, with naval stores, rice, and lumber. Four armed privateers stationed there had captured nine prizes. On signal from a lookout that the coast was clear of blockaders and that a merchantman was in sight, these craft dashed out to seize their hapless victims. The two forts were located on the right-hand side entering Hatteras Inlet and were spaced a mile apart so as to allow a cross fire on vessels negotiating the channel. Fort Hatteras, the largest and furthest to the west, was octagonal in shape. Its walls of sand, five feet high and twenty feet across the top, were covered with heavy turf lifted from a near-by salt marsh. They mounted eight guns. Fort Clark, on the seaward side of the sand beach, was a square structure half the size of Fort Hatteras, with four guns. The forts had been constructed by 180 North Carolina slaves under the supervision of Colonel W. B. Thompson, C. S. A., and were garrisoned by three companies under Major W. S. G. Andrews, C. S. A.

The expedition which cleared from Hampton Roads by 1:00 P.M. on Monday, August 26, consisted of seven naval ships: [6]

Minnesota, flagship, steam frigate, 3,307 tons, 47 guns, Captain Gersholm J. Van Brunt

Wabash, steam frigate, 3,274 tons, 46 guns, Captain Samuel Mercer

Susquehannah, side-wheel sloop, 2,450 tons, 12 guns, Captain John S. Chauncey

Cumberland, sailing sloop, 1,708 tons, 24 guns, Captain John Marston

Monticello, screw steamer, 655 tons, 3 guns, Commander John P. Gillis

Pawnee, steam sloop, 1,289 tons, 10 guns, Commander Stephen C. Rowan

Harriet Lane, side-wheel steamer, 600 tons, 2 guns, Captain John Faunce (U. S. Revenue Marine)

Two chartered vessels were sent for carrying troops: the *Adelaide,* under Commander Henry S. Stellwagen, and the *George Peabody,* under Lieutenant R. B. Lowry; and the "tug" *Fanny,* with one gun, under Lieutenant Pierce Crosby. The *Fanny* was not an ocean-going steam tugboat but a flat-bottomed canalboat for navigating shallow reaches of the sounds. Only a daredevil would have risked his neck in the open sea on such a craft. Each of the troop ships towed a stone-freighted hulk with surf boats lashed topside.

The passage down the coast was rough enough to make the troops seasick and not so bad as to swamp the canalboat. The latter, with her boilers secured to the deck with rope, rolled about like a tub, but she came through. Her skipper, wrote a reporter on the flagship, "deserves much credit for his valor—perhaps less for his discretion." [7]

Tuesday afternoon the armada came to anchor off Hatteras Inlet. Surf boats were hoisted out and preparations were made for landing the troops the next morning. "Our plan," General Butler at this moment wrote Mrs. Butler, "is to land the troops under cover of the guns of the 'Harriet Lane' and 'Monticello' while the 'Minnesota' and 'Wabash' try to shell them out of the forts. We are then to attack on the land side, and my intention is to carry them with the bayonet." [8]

Early the next day the *Minnesota,* flying Stringham's flag at the fore, stood in toward the outer bar, followed by the *Wabash* and the *Cumberland.* The *Minnesota* (47 guns) and the *Wabash* (46 guns) were powerful screw steamers with guns on two decks and rated as frigates. The *Cumberland* (24 guns) was a sailing ship of the old wood-and-sail Navy which had had to leave Hampton Roads ahead of the other ships and now had to be towed into action by the *Wabash.* As Stringham's ponderous vessels moved toward the channel, Forts Hatteras and Clark became visible, along with the little village of wooden shacks used as barracks for soldiers and Negro laborers. In Pamlico Sound, beyond the narrow neck of land, at the tip of which lay the forts, Stringham could see three steamers, several schooners under sail, and a brig at anchor under the guns of the forts.

At ten o'clock the *Wabash* and the *Cumberland* opened fire on Fort Clark, which was nearer. The fort replied promptly, but its shot fell short by half the distance, raising a shout of derision on the Federal gun decks. A stray shot from the ships landed in a herd of cows behind the forts and set the animals loping to the other side of the point. The *Minnesota* at 10:10 passed inside of the *Wabash* and the *Cumberland,* and a quarter of a mile nearer the shore, and the firing was kept up steadily and rapidly. These heavy vessels, since they drew from twenty-one to twenty-three feet of water, could not enter the channel, but had to move back and forth along the outer edge of the bar. Confederate shot fell near but did not quite reach them. The Southern cannon were antiquated smoothbores, chiefly thirty-two's, and were placed to command the channel immediately in their front. Stringham's big ships were beyond the range of the forts.

In the excitement on board the flagship, the chaplain forgot himself and cheered a well-aimed shot, then covered his embarrassment by pouring coffee for the gunners. One of the *Minnesota*'s guns was manned by a crew of fugitive slaves. The sweating blacks, whose legal status as "contraband of war" had been recently established by General Butler, worked with a will. In all hands the fighting spirit ran high. Seaman J. D. Kraigbaum, while sponging a gun, dropped his hot sponger overboard. Instantly he dived into the water to retrieve it and was pulled back on board through a porthole by his comrades. He tried to explain that he had not wanted his gun to be disgraced.[9]

By 11:30 A.M. the troops commenced landing under the protective cover of Stringham's shallowest vessels, the *Harriet Lane,* the *Monticello,* and the *Pawnee.* A freshening easterly wind stirred up considerable turbulence along the beach, capsizing two iron surf boats when they reached the breakers. Two wooden boats were crushed to matchsticks. The troops were thoroughly soaked as they floundered ashore through breakers. Some 315 men only were got on shore and two small howitzers, one with a carriage wheel crushed. Most of the ammunition had been saturated by the surf. No water, no provisions had been put on the beach.

By 12:25 P.M. the flags on both the forts had been shot away or lowered. Through the smoke, the garrison of smaller Fort Clark could be seen abandoning their works and running toward Fort Hatteras. What happened on shore could not be too clearly seen from the flagship, the forts being in a straight line from the flagship and obscured by smoke. But it was clear enough that the Federals on the beaches were racing toward the abandoned fort. At 12:30 P.M. the flag officer ordered cease fire. At 2:00 P.M. the American ensign was raised over Fort Clark to the cheers of the Union seamen and soldiers. The light-draft *Monticello* was ordered to enter the inlet and take possession of the larger Fort Hatteras. The latter, however, had not yet surrendered. The *Monticello,* coming within range, was fired upon. She drew twelve feet, and was caught in a narrow hole in the wall.

Stringham resumed his fire against Fort Hatteras to cover the *Monticello.* The little vessel absorbed several hits from the fort, but sustained no casualties, and in less than an hour wriggled back out of the channel. But Fort Clark, occupied by Federal troops, lay in a direct line with Stringham's target,

Fort Hatteras. Some Federal shot, falling short, frightened Butler's troops into abandoning Fort Clark and returning to their original landing place up the beach.

By evening, when Stringham ceased fire, the weather had thickened and the breakers were more formidable than ever. No water or provisions had been, or could be, sent to the troops on shore and the big ships had to gain an offing to avoid being beached. During the night shallow-draft steamers stood inshore to protect the troops.

On shore the stranded Federals scooped holes in the sand but found only brackish water. They seized a few sheep and geese, however, which they spitted on bayonets and roasted over campfires.

Happily the threatened storm blew over. Early the next morning Stringham was able to return and renew the bombardment. He now cut his fuses longer so as to overwhelm Fort Hatteras with a rain of ten-inch shells.

Reinforcements, meanwhile, arrived for the Southern forts, but, since their guns were outnumbered and outranged by the heavies of the fleet, these Confederate troops were not disembarked from the steamers that brought them across Pamlico Sound. Only Commodore Samuel Barron, formerly of the U. S. Navy and a snow-haired veteran of 1812, disembarked from the Rebel steamer and was persuaded by the fort's commander to take over the responsibility of command. With naval projectiles falling into Fort Hatteras at the rate of thirty a minute and the fort's magazines threatened, Barron at 11:10 A.M. on the twenty-ninth raised the white flag. Stringham's gunners mounted into the rigging to cheer the victory.

General Butler, in the canalboat *Fanny,* transported Commodore Barron and two other Confederate officers out to the flagship to deliver their swords and sign an unconditional surrender.

The next day, Federal troops were landed to garrison the Hatteras Inlet forts, and about seven hundred prisoners were embarked upon the *Minnesota.* Confederates too badly wounded to be moved were cared for at Fort Hatteras by Federal surgeons. Other wounded were placed on the *Adelaide* for transportation to the military hospital in Annapolis.

Since the Federal troops had brought rations and water for only ten days, it was now imperative that fresh supplies be sent them immediately. To persuade Washington to retain Hatteras as a naval base rather than destroy its forts and block its channel, General Butler left Hatteras on the *Adelaide* at 2:30 P.M. on the thirtieth. Half an hour later Stringham with a shipload of prisoners of war set sail for New York.

Butler stopped briefly at Hampton Roads to report the victory to General Wool and obtain his permission to go on to Washington. Stringham entrained for Washington as soon as he had disembarked the prisoners in New York.

To the uninitiated newspaper men, as well as to some captains on the blockade, the sudden return of the two commanders to Washington resembled a foot race between them to see who would be first to carry the good news, but in this instance interservice rivalry was more apparent than real. In Washington Butler put across his own and Stringham's idea about Hatteras. Stringham brought to the Navy Department the flag captured at Fort Hatteras. Fresh orders were obtained not to sink the block ships but to hold Hatteras and convert it into a base. Supplies were got off to the garrison troops left there.

National salutes were fired at all navy yards, and there was sincere rejoicing throughout the North as the first Federal victory of the war was hailed as an offset to Bull Run and an augury of greater victories to follow.

It was only in later weeks that the joke about the foot race between Stringham and "Old" Butler went sour, after Butler had detached himself from Fortress Monroe with a commission from Lincoln to raise troops in New England for further combined operations down the coast, and after Stringham had failed to follow up the success at Hatteras by scourging the inland waterways of North Carolina and Virginia as the newspapers demanded that he should, or even by sinking block-ships in other inlets, as Welles had directed. Then it was that the press began needling Mr. Lincoln's Navy by pointing out that the Hatteras expedition had suffered no casualties whatever and by hinting of bad blood between the Army and Navy.

Under censure from the press, Stringham resigned and Welles was pleased to accept the resignation.[10]

The time had come for the Navy Department to divide the Atlantic blockade coast into two sections, and Welles believed that even if Stringham had not resigned he would probably have had to be relieved because of his oversensitivity to the reduction of his command. Upon appointing two greatly junior officers, L. M. Goldsborough and S. F. Du Pont respectively, to the commands of the North and the South Atlantic Blockading Squadrons, Gideon Welles made clear his intention henceforth not to be bound by the consideration of rank in choosing flag officers, but to seek out the best talents in the service. He now had a retirement board at work weeding out the well-meaning but inefficient. His blockade, he warned the new commanders, must be made strict. Obstruction of the inlets on the coast "neglected since the capture of Hatteras . . . should be executed with as little delay as possible," and without specifically mentioning Port Royal, for security reasons, he made clear the government's determination to carry through the Port Royal plans with vigor.[11]

To smother the fire beneath the newspaper smoke, Lincoln, through his War and Navy Departments, specifically instructed Du Pont and T. W. Sherman that there must be complete cooperation between the services. "The President, Commander in Chief of the Army and Navy," wrote Scott to Sherman, "requires and expects the most effective and cordial cooperation between the commanders of the expedition." And Welles warned Du Pont: "The President expects and requires . . . the most cordial and effectual cooperation . . . and will hold any commander of either branch to a strict responsibility for any failure to procure harmony and secure the results proposed."[12]

Two weeks of excellent October weather came and went while the expedition was being assembled. The Port Royal venture was larger than any amphibian movement the United States had ever attempted and involved about 75 vessels. In addition to men-of-war, the Navy employed 20 colliers and 6 supply vessels, while the Army amassed 25 transports to carry Sherman's 16,927 soldiers, and miscellaneous specialized craft to carry live cattle for provisions and horses as mounts for generals and their staffs. The horses were loaded on the transport *Union* on October 14, and Sherman's troops were embarked at Annapolis on the twentieth. By October 22 the entire expedition was in Hampton Roads waiting for the weather to clear before sailing. During the delay General Sherman discovered that his supply vessels had been loaded upside down, and that it would take four days of unloading to dig out his small arms ammunition from the holds of the vessels. General Wool obligingly supplied him with 350,000 rounds of cartridges from the magazine at Fortress Monroe. But a week later, the expedition had still not been able to sail and Sherman wore thin his welcome when compelled to ask General Wool to replace the cooked rations that his men had consumed while waiting.

The weather finally clearing, Du Pont and Sherman sailed south from Hampton Roads on October 29. The flagship *Wabash,* out in front, led the parade like a drum major. Eight naval ships in two columns followed. Then came the transports in three columns, each headed by an ocean liner—the *Vanderbilt,* the *Baltic* and the *Atlantic.* Two naval craft guarded each flank of the transport group, and two served as whippers-in in the rear.

Off Cape Hatteras the symmetry of Du Pont's formation was shattered by a hurricane. The *Union,* loaded with horses, and the *Osceola,* an army supply vessel, were wrecked on the North Carolina coast and seventy-three members of their crews were taken as prisoners to Raleigh. The supply vessel *Peerless,* loaded with cattle, broke up in the trough of the waves. A small boat manned by some of the crew of the U.S.S.

Mohican at great peril brought the crew of the *Peerless* to safety on board their own ship. The converted naval steamer *Isaac Smith* sprang leaks at her water line and had to dump her guns overboard. The seventeen-year-old-side-wheeler *Governor,* chartered in Boston to carry a battalion of marines to Port Royal, rolling heavily, lost smokestack and rudder. Fortunately the stricken transport floundered into the vicinity of the sailing frigate *Sabine,* herself blown off from her blockade station. The *Sabine*'s commander, Cadwallader Ringgold, dropped anchor and by paying out his cable drifted his ship toward the wreck. About forty marines leaped to the rescuer's deck, six fell short and disappeared under the churning water, and the rest a few hours later jumped into the sea to be rescued by a small boat from the *Sabine.*

On Saturday morning, November 2, there was only one sail in sight from Du Pont's flagship. Sealed orders, however, had been distributed to the captains, notifying them of the rendezvous, to be opened in case they were separated. The gale moderated the next day and by Monday some twenty-five of the scattered vessels had appeared off Port Royal bar. As this bar lay ten miles to seaward of the harbor, with no prominent shoreline features from which to take bearings, Du Pont had brought Coast Surveyors to sound and buoy the channel, and while this was being done he sent in a reconnaissance group.

At 8:30 A.M. on Thursday, November 7, eight days after his departure from Hampton Roads, Du Pont headed into the sound to deal with the Confederate forts. Behind him at anchor about eight miles from shore were the transports. So many small boats had been destroyed by the hurricane that it was not feasible to take the troops ashore to cooperate as planned by assaulting the forts. The Navy was going it alone. Ahead of him loomed the two forts, for whose eighty heavy land-based guns Du Pont, a seaman of the old days of wood and sail, had great respect. Fort Walker to port, on Hilton Head Island, was the larger; Fort Beauregard lay to starboard on the southern tip of St. Helena Island. In the sound, looking as belligerent as possible, were Confederate Commodore

Tattnall's force of one river steamer and two tugs mounting one or two guns each. Unable really to make any reasonable retort to Du Pont's massive gunpower, turtle-jawed Josiah Tattnall waited for the first shot to be fired at himself, then dipped his blue flag in acknowledgment of the compliment and scurried for safety into nearby Skull Creek. Upstage in the distance were steamers with sightseers from Charleston and Savannah, filled with high hope that the Federal Navy, violating South Carolina's waters, would be sunk by the forts.

Du Pont's main strength lay in nine ships and gunboats proceeding slowly in line as follows: [13]

Wabash, flagship, steam frigate, 3,274 tons, 46 guns, Commander C. R. P. Rodgers

Susquehannah, side-wheel sloop, 2,450 tons, 12 guns, Captain J. L. Lardner

Mohican, screw steamer, 994 tons, 6 guns, Commander S. W. Godon

Seminole, screw steamer, 801 tons, 6 (?) guns, Commander J. P. Gillis

Pawnee, steam sloop, 1,289 tons, 10 guns, Lieutenant Commander R. H. Wyman

Unadilla, screw gunboat, 507 tons, 4 guns, Lieutenant N. Collins

Ottawa, screw gunboat, 507 tons, 4 guns, Lieutenant T. H. Stevens

Pembina, screw gunboat, 507 tons, 4 guns, Lieutenant J. P. Bankhead

Vandalia, sailing sloop, Commander E. S. Haggerty

The last vessel in line, without steam power, was being towed into action by the *Isaac Smith,* which, under Lieutenant Commander J. W. A. Nicholson, had steam power but had discarded her guns during the storm.

Alongside and moving in a parallel line to the right of the main column was a flanking squadron of five gunboats:

Bienville, side-wheel gunboat, 1,557 tons, 8 guns, Commander Charles Steedman

Seneca, screw gunboat, 507 tons, 4 guns, Lieutenant Daniel Ammen

Curlew, screw gunboat, 380 tons, 5 (?) guns, Lieutenant G. P. Watmough
Penguin, screw gunboat, 389 tons, 5 guns, Lieutenant T. A. Budd
Augusta, steamer, 1,310 tons, 9 guns, Commander E. G. Parrott

Du Pont's plan was to pass up the channel with his main battle line midway between Forts Walker and Beauregard to a point about two and one half miles beyond the forts, then, by turning repeatedly to port, to pass and repass Fort Walker at varying ranges. After its first run past the forts, the flanking squadron was to take a fixed position inside the sound from which to encounter Fort Walker on its weakest flank and at the same time to enfilade its two water faces, while Du Pont attacked them from the front.

The action took place on a stretch of the sound five miles long and two and one half miles wide, the latter being the distance between the forts.

The battleships filed slowly up the channel, with just enough speed to overcome the tide and preserve the order of battle without becoming a fixed mark for the enemy's fire. Everything moved according to plan, steadily, scientifically, inexorably.

Captain Steedman of the *Bienville* was a South Carolinian. After Du Pont's first turn Steedman dropped anchor with others of the flanking squadron and enfiladed Fort Walker. At noon, Commander Percival Drayton, another South Carolinian, arriving in the *Pocahontas,* joined Du Pont's group. Ironically Commander Drayton was entering battle against his own brother, Confederate General Thomas F. Drayton, who commanded the force on Hilton Head. Steedman, recognizing his friend Percival Drayton, swung his cap overhead and shouted, "Three cheers for South Carolina!" "Three cheers for South Carolina and the American flag!" called back Drayton in stentorious voice.[14]

On both sides the firing was too high. Upon entering the stage in the middle of the action, Drayton had seen shells from the fleet fall as much as a mile and a half behind the forts. These shells gouged furrows through near-by cotton fields. Some also landed in front of the fort, splashing geysers of sand into the air. Much damage was inflicted by the Confederates upon the rigging of the ships. One shell bored a clean hole through the mainmast of the *Wabash* about twelve feet above the deck rail.

At 1:15 P.M. the *Ottawa* signaled that Fort Walker had been abandoned. The flagship made a wide turn at the outer end of the channel. As soon as the *Wabash* and the *Susquehannah* had come about and brought their guns to bear upon Fort Walker for the third time, Du Pont lowered his gig and sent ashore his aide, Commander John Rodgers, under flag of truce. The Confederate garrison was decamping across the cotton fields. Rodgers at 2:00 P.M. hoisted the United States flag—the first to be raised on the soil of South Carolina since Fort Sumter was lost—and brass bands throughout the fleet struck up "The Star Spangled Banner."

Du Pont honored Commander C. R. P. Rodgers, the *Wabash*'s captain, by sending him ashore with a boatload of marines and sailors to take possession. General T. W. Sherman now landed and occupied Fort Walker.

Fort Beauregard, too, was vacated by its garrison and was occupied by Sherman the morning after the battle.

H. J. Winser, reporter for the *New York Times,* prowling through the deserted camp behind Fort Walker, noted evidences of hurried departure. "Most of the tents had been undisturbed. Officer's furniture, uniforms and other clothing, dress swords, small stores, with here and there an article which told that even in camp the warriors had not been wholly bereft of the society of their wives, mothers, and sisters. . . . Over the meadow . . . were scattered blankets, knapsacks, (some of which, singularly enough, were recognized as those which had been cast away by our panic-stricken troops at Bull Run,) muskets, bayonets, cartridge-boxes, and a few dead mules and broken vehicles, not camp wagons, but family carriages, which had been used to carry away the dead and wounded." [15]

Commander Steedman, a native of Charleston, saw to the

burial of the eight South Carolinians whose bodies were found in Fort Walker, the chaplain of the *Wabash* reading the Episcopal burial service.

To Washington Du Pont sent the captured flags of the forts and the United States ensign which John Rodgers had raised over Fort Walker.

Gideon Welles acknowledged Du Pont's great victory with "hearty congratulations," and national salutes at all navy yards. Lincoln recommended, and Congress passed, a joint resolution of thanks to Captain Samuel F. Du Pont "for the decisive and splendid victory achieved at Port Royal on the seventh day of November last." [16]

After slow and disheartening beginnings, Mr. Lincoln's Navy had at last won a substantial victory. But, even while Du Pont's victory was hanging in the balance, there occurred in an obscure channel off the east coast of Cuba an incident which threatened to embroil the struggling American republic in war with England.

7.

Wilkes and the Trent *Affair*

THEIR AGENTS, HAVING FAILED TO PERSUADE Europe to recognize Southern independence, the Confederate Government in the fall of 1861 appointed two former United States senators as ministers plenipotentiary to England and France. Perhaps through their skillful argument Europe might be induced to sign treaties of amity or to give military assistance in lifting the blockade. Ex-Senator James M. Mason of Virginia was chosen as minister to Great Britain and ex-Senator John Slidell of Louisiana as emissary to France. No secret was made of these appointments in Richmond, whose *Examiner* praised Mason as a well-mannered English type of gentleman who would promptly eclipse Charles Francis Adams, "the Puritan representative of freedom." [1] Slidell was a leader prominent in New Orleans, and a brother-in-law of the Creole General Beauregard.

The North feared the power of these "Rebel traitors" to move a Europe already leaning toward the South. The announcement that the Southern emissaries would run the blockade at Charleston and travel to England on board the Confederate commerce raider *Nashville* was met by angry cries to stop them at all costs. Mere mention of England aroused the Yankee temper. Was not England supplying arms to Southern Rebels? Had not English consuls connived at illegal transfers of Southern vessels to foreign registry? Were not British seaports in near-by New Brunswick, Bermuda, and the Bahamas entrepots for blockade-runners? Few Americans realized that British trade with the blockaded South was but a fraction of their commerce with the United States, or that in November of 1861 Yankee buyers in London had actually cornered the market for saltpetre.[2]

In October, when Mason and Slidell reached Charleston, the Washington government doubled the number of blockade ships off that port and dispatched the U.S.S. *James Adger* to the English Channel to intercept the *Nashville*.

The C.S.S. *Nashville* was a converted side-wheeler whose deep draft would compel her to use the main channel out of Charleston. Every afternoon the nimble coasting packet *Theodora* sprinted across the bar off Charleston to see whether the coast was clear for the *Nashville*. One evening Mr. Slidell and his two daughters made this trip on the *Theodora*. The swift little craft would tease the blockaders by advancing toward them, but always remained prudently beyond range of their exasperated guns. At length, however, this cat-and-mouse game began to pall. Rather than accept the greater risk of capture on the *Nashville,* the commissioners chartered the *Theodora* to take them to Cuba.

At 1:00 A.M. on Saturday, October 12, under cover of a rain squall, the *Theodora* scurried out of Charleston Harbor with Mason and Slidell and their secretaries, Messrs. Eustis and Macfarland. Mrs. Slidell, with the four Slidell children, and Mrs. Eustis completed the party. As they ran the blockade, they counted the lights of four Federal ships and passed within a mile and a half of the nearest. After skirting the coast a short distance, the speedy *Theodora* headed for the open sea, unnoticed by the blockade vessels.

Off Cardenas, Cuba, the blockade-runner's coal having given out, she was courteously escorted into the harbor by a Spanish gunboat. The Governor of the port dispensed with customhouse formalities in allowing the Confederates' baggage to land. At Havana, where they learned they would have to wait three weeks for an interisland steamer to carry them to St. Thomas and the English line, the Confederate agents were entertained like ambassadors of recognized powers. The

British Consul General, Joseph T. Crawford, extended them every courtesy and introduced them to the Captain General of Cuba. Although Crawford explained later to his superiors that his actions were unofficial and that he had been acquainted with Slidell for thirty-six years and was an intimate friend of Mr. Mason's brother, his hospitality was given a more ample notice in the press than if it had been official. For three weeks before the event, the world knew that on November 7 Mason and Slidell planned to embark at Havana on board the English mail packet *Trent* for passage to St. Thomas, and thence by an English liner to London. There was no reason to conceal their intention since the *Trent* flew the neutral flag of Britain and was proceeding from one neutral port to another. So reasoned the travelers.

The factor they did not consider was Charles Wilkes. While homeward bound from the West Africa Squadron, Captain Charles Wilkes of the U.S.S. *San Jacinto* heard about Mason and Slidell when he put in at Cienfuegos, Cuba, for coal. Wilkes hurried around to Havana hoping to intercept the *Theodora.* The latter had departed before Wilkes entered Havana on October 31, but Wilkes's executive officer, Lieutenant D. M. Fairfax, a Virginian, recognized Mr. Mason in the parlor of the Hotel Cubana and learned what was common knowledge—that the commissioners planned to sail on the *Trent* on November 7.

The big question that puzzled Captain Wilkes was whether he had a right to capture the persons of these commissioners. During a week of desultory cruising to the north of Cuba, Wilkes studied various authorities on international law whose works were in his ship's library. Clearly a neutral ship carrying contraband dispatches, whose captain knew they were on board, was subject to capture. But Mason and Slidell were not dispatches in any literal sense, and nowhere could Wilkes find a case to precisely cover that point. In the end Wilkes reached the quarter-deck decision that, since they could have no passports from a recognized government and were avowedly engaged in a mission "adverse and criminal to the

Union," their status was that of "conspirators, plotting and contriving to overthrow the Government of the United States." [3] Wilkes decided that these men were subject to capture and that, since the captain of the *Trent* had known in advance of their character and intentions, he had in effect embarked "live dispatches" essentially contraband, and rendered his ship liable to capture.

While Captain Wilkes was immersed in his study of Kent, Wheaton, and Vattel, the *San Jacinto,* in the course of a routine boarding operation, ran foul of a French brig and knocked out the Frenchman's bowsprit and foretopmast. Wilkes sent carpenters on board and escorted the craft to Havana. When he ran into Key West for coal, his executive officer, who disagreed with Wilkes's conclusion as to the Rebel commissioners' status, suggested that Wilkes consult with Judge Marvin of Key West, but he soon saw that Wilkes's decision had been made and did not press the matter.

Charles Wilkes had won fame in the prewar Navy as scholar and explorer. As a lieutenant he had commanded the expedition which discovered the Antarctic continent, and afterwards had spent twenty years on shore writing and editing the reports on his explorations. A man of science, at his own expense he had constructed the first naval observatory in Washington. Willful as his own shock of unruly hair, impatient when listening to others, impetuous, stubborn, he had been courtmartialed once, primarily because of his stubbornness, but had learned nothing from the experience. Such was the character of the Federal commander who on November 8 took station 230 miles east of Havana at a point where the Old Bahama Channel becomes so narrow that a single ship can effectively patrol it. Here Wilkes placed the *San Jacinto* to waylay the *Trent.*

The *San Jacinto*'s guns were run out, muzzle stoppers removed, crews readied at battle stations. At 1:00 P.M. on the eighth when the *Trent* appeared, Wilkes directed a shot across her bow, and, as the oncoming vessel merely slowed her engines, he fired a shell which exploded half a cable's length ahead. She then hove to. Captain Wilkes handed written orders to Lieutenant Fairfax to man and arm the cutters. On boarding the *Trent,* the lieutenant was directed to demand her passenger list. "Should Mr. Mason, Mr. Slidell, Mr. Eustis, and Mr. Macfarland be on board, you will make them prisoners and send them on board this ship immediately, and take possession of her as a prize." [4] Fairfax was to seize all their papers, trunks, cases, packages, and to convey Captain Wilkes's offer of accommodations on board the warship for their families.

Lieutenant Fairfax was determined to give the skipper of the *Trent* no unnecessary provocation, for he disagreed with Wilkes's earlier decision and hoped to avoid seizing the vessel. As executive officer, he well knew how difficult it would be for the *San Jacinto* to make up a prize crew to man the *Trent* in case of her seizure. Leaving the armed men in the cutter in charge of Second Assistant Engineer Houston and Boatswain Grace, Lieutenant Fairfax went on board the *Trent* alone and was shown up to the quarter-deck where he met Captain James Moir. The British merchant captain resented the procedure and refused to show his passenger list. Fairfax calmly and courteously told him that he had information that Messrs. Mason, Slidell, Eustis, and Macfarland had embarked on the vessel at Havana and that he must satisfy himself whether they were on board. Slidell, hearing his name mentioned, came up and asked Fairfax if he wished to see him. Mason, Eustis, and Macfarland also identified themselves, and vigorously protested when they learned that they were to be arrested and transferred to the United States warship.

The *Trent's* passengers closed in with such angry shouts and threats as to bring Engineer Houston and Boatswain Grace on board with six or eight marines.[5]

"Did you ever hear of such an outrage?"

"Marines on board! Why, this looks devilish like mutiny."

"These Yankees will have to pay for this."

"This is the best thing in the world for the South."

"England will open the blockade."

"Did you ever hear of such a piratical act?"

"Why, this is a perfect Bull Run."

"They would not have dared to have done it if an English man-of-war had been in sight."

Above the clatter arose the loud angry voice of Richard Williams, a retired commander of the Royal Navy, who, as agent of mails and the only English Government official on the *Trent,* denounced "this act of piracy, carried out by brute force." [6]

The *San Jacinto*'s marines cleared the passengers from around the cabins where the Confederates had gone to pack their baggage. Since Mason and Slidell refused to leave the ship unless force was applied, Fairfax summoned a second cutter. Two officers grasped Mr. Mason by the shoulder and with this gentle application of force walked him to the cutter. In their stateroom Slidell's distraught family became hysterical. When Lieutenant Fairfax urged Mr. Slidell to come, the latter's seventeen-year-old daughter flung herself across the doorway to bar his entrance. A slight lurch of the ship at this moment upset the girl's balance and she grasped Lieutenant Fairfax's arm to right herself—a trivial incident which the newspapers later rendered as "having slapped Mr. Fairfax's face," "she did strike him in the face three times," and "went so far as to bare her breast, defying death itself." [7]

To escape the hubbub Slidell stepped out of a window into a passageway, where, with Federal hands clapped on his shoulders, he was marched to the cutter. Mrs. Slidell and Mrs. Eustis rejected Captain Wilkes's permission to accompany their husbands.

Back on board the *San Jacinto,* Lieutenant Fairfax presented as reasons for not seizing the vessel the large number of enraged passengers who would be put to inconvenience and the shortage of officers and men on the warship. Captain Wilkes permitted the *Trent* to proceed on her voyage.

Wilkes's bold action, climaxing a period of popular suspense, took the American public by storm. Figuratively at least Gideon Welles tossed both his hat and his henna-gray wig into the air, for this sort of forthright initiative was precisely what he wished to inculcate in the captains down the blockade coast. Let there be no more pussyfooting of the sort that had lost the Pensacola and Norfolk Navy Yards! Henceforth, let there be more bold, forthright quarter-deck decisions.

"Sir: I congratulate you on your safe arrival," wrote the Secretary to Wilkes, "and especially do I congratulate you on the great public service you have rendered in the capture of the rebel emissaries. Messrs. Mason and Slidell have been conspicuous in the conspiracy to dissolve the Union, and it is well known that when seized by you they were on a mission hostile to the Government and the country. Your conduct in seizing these public enemies was marked by intelligence, ability, decision, and firmness, and has the emphatic approval of this Department. It is not necessary that I should in this communication, which is intended to be one of congratulation to yourself, officers, and crew, express an opinion on the course pursued in omitting to capture the vessel which had these public enemies on board, further than to say that the forbearance exercised in this instance must not be permitted to constitute a precedent hereafter for infraction of neutral obligations." [8]

The only member of the Cabinet who questioned the legality of Wilkes's act was Blair, a kinsman of whom had once suffered from a quarrel with Wilkes. Blair recommended that Wilkes be ordered to transport Mason and Slidell to England and deliver them to Lord Palmerston. Otherwise, he predicted, England would make war. Seward, the Cabinet member most concerned with foreign relations, "scouted the idea of letting the prisoners go." [9] Lincoln knew little about the fine points of admiralty law but was concerned for the personal safety of the prisoners themselves, in view of the tirades that were being made against them. He feared they would be "white elephants on our hands." [10] With Lincoln's approval,

Welles directed Wilkes to take the prisoners to Boston and lodge them for safekeeping in Fort Warren.

Boston banqueted and toasted the new naval hero. The mayor praised his "sagacity, judgment, decision, firmness." Governor John A. Andrew extolled his firing across the bows of "the ship that bore the English lion's head." New York gave Wilkes an ovation. Representatives in Washington proposed that he be tendered a vote of the thanks of Congress, and demanded that the President confine Mason and Slidell "in the cells of convicted felons." [11]

Newspapers of the North had a field day. "There is no drawing back to our jubilation," proclaimed one metropolitan paper. "The universal Yankee nation is getting decidedly awake. As for Captain Wilkes and his command, let the handsome thing be done. Consecrate another 4th of July to him, load him down with services of plate and swords of the cunningest and costliest art." [12] A cartoonist hit a popular note when he depicted a salty American sea dog in the act of lifting two "skunks" with the faces of Mason and Slidell out of John Bull's back pockets. Representative Clement L. Vallandigham called upon the President to approve Wilkes's act "in spite of any menace or demand of the British Government." [13]

Meanwhile, the attitude that England might take toward the *Trent* case was anyone's conjecture. Wall Street was the first to have qualms. On November 20 "war with England was the theme, and stocks were thrown out with the same eagerness that they were sought for only a day or two ago." The *New York Times,* deploring this "want of ballast" in the public mind, continued to exult over the capture of the two "distinguished malignants," than whom "it would be difficult to find two men more thoroughly imbued with the views of treason." [14]

Two weeks would be required for news of the *Trent* incident to reach London. Then two more weeks for Britain's first reactions to be returned to America. As a straw in the wind, the American press quoted the Toronto *Leader*'s "horror at Yankee audacity" and its characterization of Wilkes's action as "the most offensive outrage which Brother Jonathan has dared to perpetrate upon the British flag." [15] From Nassau, New Providence, the supercargo of a Confederate blockade-runner reported on December 10 to Judah P. Benjamin, then Confederate Secretary of War: "The affair of the *Trent* I find creates a universal feeling of indignation among the Britishers. I heard an officer say that if the Government did not resent it becomingly he would forever renounce his title as Englishman." [16]

England first learned of the incident with the publication of two highly emotional and fiction-spiced narratives furnished by the purser and the mail agent of the *Trent*. A popular "typhoon of fury" broke loose, so tremendous that in advance of diplomatic investigation the government at once ordered preparations for war. The English squadron in American waters was alerted. Queen Victoria on December 4 signed a proclamation forbidding the exportation from the United Kingdom of gunpowder, saltpetre, nitrate of soda, percussion caps, and lead.[17]

Onto the British ship *Melbourne* at Woolwich were loaded some thirty thousand Enfield rifles from the Tower, together with military clothing and other stores to be sent to Canada. There was a certain tongue-in-cheek character to this business, since the St. Lawrence River was frozen and the London press noted that it was "not unlikely that the *Melbourne* will go to Portland, and that the stores will be conveyed by railway to Quebec, across the State of Maine!" [18] The first of eight thousand picked troops to be dispatched to Canada embarked from London on the *Adriatic,* an American-built British steamer which only a few months ago had been operating with American registry under the United States flag.

Through diplomatic channels, despite the fanfare of the press and the quite genuine agitation on the part of the peoples of Britain and the United States, the *Trent* affair was speedily settled. Seward notified Charles Francis Adams that Wilkes's action had not been authorized by the government in Washington. Palmerston's demand for the release of the prisoners and a suitable apology was "toned down" by the Prince Consort before it left London and was tactfully conveyed in Washington by Lord Lyons. Secretary Seward found a way to release Mason and Slidell and at the same time save face, by arguing that Britain's present position with regard to neutral rights was identical with our own historical position. Seward's ingenious document of seven thousand words managed—to the private admiration of Welles and other members of the Cabinet—to reverse his own earlier views on the case, and to accede to British demands in a manner acceptable to the American public.

In secrecy, Mason, Slidell, Eustis, and Macfarland were released from Fort Warren on January 1, 1862, and conveyed by tugboat to Provincetown, to be put on board H.M.S. *Rinaldo.* This last act in the drama was so deftly and quietly managed that Boston and the country heard nothing about it until later.

With the surrender of Mason and Slidell disappeared the chance of any immediate military alliance between the Confederate States and Britain. "The American eagle," groaned the Richmond *Examiner,* "screeched his loudest screech of defiance—then 'Dropt like a craven cock his conquered wing' at the first growl of the lion." [19]

Within the month Anglo-American relations had become so pacific that Britain's expeditionary force was given permission to march across American soil to Canada, the St. Lawrence being solid ice; while in London, the Queen's withdrawal of her royal embargo on the export of munitions caused Anglo-American trade to spring back quickly to a wartime norm.

8.

The Merrimack *Threat*

LINCOLN'S EARLY HOPE THAT THE WAR WOULD be short, which was reflected in his calling for volunteers to serve only three months, appeared also in his ignoring the need to build ironclad warships. By the spring of 1861 the armored battleship was still in a primitive stage of development. Iron-sheathed floating batteries had been employed in the Crimean War, and since then France and England had riveted protective armor about the vitals of conventional steam warships. But the few existing armored ships had required many months to build and were designed for use against an overseas enemy. Lincoln's Navy was called upon chiefly for shallow-draft work in harbors, inlets, coastal sounds, and rivers.

During the first months of the war Lincoln's Navy Department was badgered by politicians urging the completion of the Robert L. Stevens ironclad battery, begun in Hoboken in 1843 and abondoned several years before the Civil War upon the death of its builder. Congressional appropriations totaling over half a million had been sunk in Stevens's experiment. Its basic design had been modified several times during construction, the inventor never having drafted a set of coherent plans. At length the unfinished ironclad had become a "lost cause" to its proponents and a "laughing stock" to the disillusioned. Secretary Welles stood among the latter group. Having no technical knowledge, he was nevertheless a tightfisted skeptic who considered armored ship experimentation too costly and the utility of the product too dubious; and he disliked pressure groups. He would appoint no board to examine the Stevens battery until August when Congress specifically required him to do so. For three months he refused to be sidetracked from building up the blockade navy, to which purpose he was driving every factory in the country that was capable of producing marine engines, even the six firms whose financial conditions were "doubtful," and during this time he brushed aside all critics who sought to divert him into building ironclads.[1]

In the end it required a major threat to his blockade fleet to enlist Gideon Welles's interest in this new type of ship. This threat was posed by the *Merrimack*.

The once proud steam frigate of the U. S. Navy, which had been scuttled and burned to the water's edge when Norfolk was lost, was raised and hauled into the undamaged dry dock, where the mud was sluiced from her engines. Early in June the Confederate naval secretary Stephen R. Mallory ordered the vessel to be rebuilt as an ironclad ram. Aware that the South must compensate for her want of industrial power by emphasizing novel weapons, Mallory planned to use the rebuilt *Merrimack* to break the Federal blockade at Hampton Roads—its most important single point—either by ramming and staving in the wooden sidewalls of the ships in the Roads or by destroying with hot shot the hulls that sought shelter under Fortress Monroe. After the work of conversion had been under way for more than a month, Mallory called on the Norfolk Navy Yard to devote every possible facility to the *Merrimack* "at the expense and delay of every other work on hand if necessary." [2]

Mallory's plans and the progress of the work on the *Merrimack* having forced themselves upon the attention of the Federal Navy Department, Welles, on July 4, 1861, presented the problem of ironclads to the special session of Congress. It was a poor time to be conducting experiments, he averred, and officers competent to form "correct conclusions" were occupied with other pressing and essential duties. England and

France "have made it a special object in connection with naval improvements; and the ingenuity and inventive faculties of our own countrymen have also been stimulated by recent occurrences toward the construction of this class of vessel." [3] Welles recommended the appointment of a board to investigate, and he left Congress to decide whether on a favorable report they would order "one or more iron-clad steamers or floating batteries." Congress, after some preliminary kicking around of the Stevens battery "football," on August 3 authorized the Secretary to appoint a board "of three skilful naval officers" to investigate ironclads, and appropriated $1,500,000 to build "one or more armored or iron or steel-clad steamships or floating steam batteries." [4]

Welles promptly advertised for offers to build "iron-clad steam vessels of war, either of iron or of wood and iron combined, for sea or river service, to be of not less than ten nor over sixteen feet draft of water. . . . The vessel to be rigged with two masts, with wire rope standing rigging, to navigate at sea." [5] The deadline for presenting bids was fixed at September 9, and on August 8 a board was appointed to study the whole problem of ironclads, and to winnow the incoming proposals and recommend which, if any, should be accepted. As members of the Ironclad Board Welles's choice fell upon two senior officers in the Department: Commodore Joseph Smith, an ever-watchful bureau head who, according to popular belief, slept with one eye open to guard his yards and docks, shrewd old Commodore Hiram Paulding of the Office of Detail, and, as the junior member, Commander John A. Dahlgren, the ordnance expert. Dahlgren, already filling the jobs of commandant of the Washington Navy Yard and superintendent of naval craft used in the defense of Washington in addition to supervision of naval gunnery, requested to be relieved of the added duty, and Commander Charles H. Davis, currently serving on Du Pont's strategy board, was substituted in place of Dahlgren. The shift was not altogether satisfactory. Davis was a fluent writer, useful as its secretary, but the board needed, if not an expert in ordnance, then an expert in naval construction. They asked that an experienced naval constructor be detailed to assist them, but Welles had literally no one not already overworked as inspector of vessels being built.

The Ironclad Board approached its researches with humility in the face of the unknown, "distrustful of our own ability . . . having no experience and but scanty knowledge in this branch of naval architecture." [6] Among naval and scientific men they found sharply conflicting opinions obscuring almost every aspect of the subject. Objections to ironclads seemed clear enough: enormous weight of iron, greatly increased breadth to insure stability, shortage of coal bunker space, necessity of greater propulsive power, increased construction cost.

With the impending crisis in Hampton Roads in mind, they admitted that "wooden ships may be said to be but coffins for their crews when brought in conflict with iron-clad vessels." [7] They conceded that armored ships or batteries could be employed advantageously "to pass fortifications on land for ulterior objects of attack, to run a blockade, or reduce temporary batteries on the shores of rivers and the approaches to our harbors."

As there was no way of foretelling what particular kind of armored craft would stand up best in fighting, the board decided to recommend that vessels of several types be built—as many as the appropriation would allow. Another decision was to award the contracts to American builders. English manufacturers, they believed, might produce better vessels, more quickly and cheaply, but international situations could complicate delivery of such ships, and they felt that the Yankee craftsmen "should be capable of constructing it themselves."

One proposal they accepted was for a ship built on conventional lines with belt armor around the vital midship sector (later the *New Ironsides*), and a second was a gunboat armored on the "rail and plate" principle, with closely fitted bars on edge, covered by thin plates (later the *Galena*).

John Ericsson, the great Swedish marine and military inventor, who might logically have been expected to submit a bid, failed to do so, and the members of the Ironclad Board, aware of Ericsson's ancient feud with the Navy Department, were evidently reluctant to stir him up. In the 1840's Ericsson, at the request of Captain R. F. Stockton, had drafted plans and served as professional consultant during the construction of the U.S.S. *Princeton,* the historic first American warship to use the screw propeller. Upon completion of the ship in 1844, Stockton had neglected to share honors with the sensitive inventor and following the explosion on board the *Princeton* of Stockton's gun, the *Peacemaker,* an inexact copy of a gun invented by Ericsson, a quarrel had developed between Ericsson and the Navy Department which had left the inventor feeling that he had been shabbily treated.

Actually during the current national emergency Ericsson had wished to be approached by the Navy. He had in his files the plans and model of an ironclad, turreted vessel which he had tried to sell to Napoleon III during the Crimean War, a shallow-draft affair that would be ideal for use in Southern harbors and rivers. But he could not bring himself to submit a proposal to the Navy's Ironclad Board. On August 29, 1861, he drafted a letter to President Lincoln:

> Sir: The writer, having introduced the present system of naval propulsion and constructed the first screw ship of war, now offers to construct a vessel for the destruction of the rebel fleet at Norfolk and for scouring the Southern rivers and inlets of all craft protected by rebel batteries.... Please look carefully at the enclosed plans and you will find that the means I propose to employ are very simple—so simple, indeed, that within ten weeks after commencing the structure I would engage to be ready to take up position under the rebel guns at Norfolk.... I have planned upward of one hundred marine engines and I furnish daily, working-plans made with my own hands of mechanical and naval structures of various kinds, and I have done so for thirty years.... I cannot conclude without respectfully calling your attention to the now well-established fact that steel-clad vessels cannot be arrested in their course by land batteries, and that hence our great city [New York] is quite at the mercy of such intruders....[8]

As he was placing the plans into an envelope, it occurred to Ericsson that it was unsafe to entrust them to the mails and he added a postscript, stating that he was withholding the plans, but that, if summoned, he would bring them to the White House within forty-eight hours. He now probably decided that without the plans there was no point in forwarding the letter. The original or a copy of it was later found among Ericsson's papers by his biographer, and there is no evidence of its having reached Lincoln.

Intelligence of Ericsson's invention did reach the Ironclad Board, however—after the time for submitting proposals had elapsed.

Cornelius S. Bushnell, one of the successful bidders, went to consult Ericsson professionally about the ironclad he had projected. Following the interview, Ericsson exhumed from a pile of refuse in a corner the dusty cardboard model of his turreted ironclad. Bushnell persuaded the inventor to allow him to show it to Mr. Welles. The latter promptly requested the Ironclad Board to consider it.

The junior member of the board told Bushnell that he might take the little model home and worship it "as it would not be idolatry, because it was made in the image of nothing in the heaven above or on the earth below or in the waters under the earth." But the two senior members, with encouragement from the Secretary, persuaded Ericsson to come to Washington to explain the properties of his proposed vessel and to demonstrate that it would have enough buoyancy to float. Ericsson's little model amused Lincoln, and he approved it with a wisecrack: "All I have to say is what the girl said when she put her foot into the stocking, 'It strikes me there's something in it.' "[9]

Without waiting to receive the Ironclad Board's formal report, Gideon Welles polled them individually and authorized Ericsson to go ahead at once. Thus, the keel plates for the new craft began rolling through the mill before the clerks of the Department had completed the drawing of the contract. Between the Secretary and Commodore Smith there was a private understanding, Welles recorded later, that the test which Ericsson's contract called for would be that his vessel should go to the Norfolk Navy Yard and destroy the *Merrimack* in dry dock.

To speed the construction of the naval vessel so as to complete it in one hundred working days—as the inventor rashly promised to do—Ericsson and his financial backers (C. S. Bushnell, J. G. Winslow, and J. A. Griswold) let out parts of the work to subcontractors. The hull was built by Thomas F. Rowland's Continental Iron Works at Greenpoint, Long Island, in whose ship house the essential parts were installed before the launching; the engines by Delameter & Co.; the turret by the Novelty Iron Works, with armor plates manufactured in Baltimore.

"Ericsson's Folly," as the vessel came to be called, had two hulls.[10] The lower one, to be entirely submerged, was about six feet deep, built of half-inch iron, flat-bottomed, with inclined sides. In this were located boilers, engines, turret-turning mechanism, staterooms, and magazines. The second, or upper hull, had straight sides, was longer and broader than the under one, was five feet deep, and fitted upside down over the lower hull. The vertical sides of the upper hull were heavily plated, the heavy wooden deck itself was covered with one-inch plates, and inlaid in the center of this deck was a wide brass ring upon which the circumference of the turret rested. The turret was a cylinder nine feet high and twenty across, pierced for two heavy-caliber Dahlgren guns mounted side by side. The turret's weight was borne by a twelve-inch iron spindle which extended from the top center of the turret to the keel of the lower hull and was turned by a donkey engine and a system of gears. The craft's two guns were designed to be fired "on the fly" as the turret was slowly revolved.

Ericsson divided his time between his office in lower Manhattan and the shipyard at Greenpoint. The designs for each of the three thousand parts of the mechanism went directly from Ericsson's drafting board to the craftsmen in factory or blacksmith shop who fashioned them. If for any reason a part failed to fit, Ericsson might indicate in chalk on the piece itself where it was to be cut off or hammered in so that it would fit. Necessarily the inventor, working at white heat, freely modified his original plans as he went along, and—to the consternation of Commodore Smith, whose obligation was to see the contract fulfilled—forgot what the terms of that out-of-date instrument were. As an example, because of the vessel's restricted space for coal bunkers the contract specified that she should be provided with "masts, spars, sails, and rigging of sufficient dimensions to drive the vessel at the rate of six knots per hour in a fair breeze." Ericsson ignored this clause entirely. As "Ericsson's Folly" neared completion, bets were made in Manhattan as to whether she would sink at her launching. Since the Mason and Slidell incident was bruited in the press at this time, Ericsson suggested that his ironclad battery be named the *Monitor* to admonish not only Southern leaders but the English as well. " 'Downing Street' will hardly view with indifference this last 'Yankee notion,' this monitor." [11]

"You cannot imagine the intense and almost agonizing anxiety of all the heads, from the President down," wrote Griswold to Ericsson on January 10, 1862, "to have one boat *to use.*" [12] An old Negress from Norfolk had brought Mr. Welles a note from a Unionist workman on the *Merrimack.* The Confederate threat to the blockaders in Hampton Roads was nearing completion. She had been cut down to her berth deck and an armored citadel with sloping walls had been built over the central portion of the ship. The walls of this gun fortress, canted at an angle of thirty-five degrees above the horizontal to cause shot to glance from them, consisted of four inches of iron plates backed by twenty-one inches of oak and pine. At either end of the vessel, beyond the casemate, the prow and stern were to be nearly awash, just high enough to add buoyancy but too low to interfere with the firing of her guns. Below the water line a fifteen-hundred-pound castiron "shoe" had been fitted across her bow for ramming.

Ericsson's little two-gun *Monitor,* the smallest of the three ironclads ordered by the Ironclad Board, was the only one that might possibly be finished in time to meet the *Merrimack.* The *Monitor's* keel had been laid on October 25. Steam was first applied to her engines on December 30, and on January 30 she was launched.

A large crowd gathered on the cold, drizzly day of her launching, curious to see whether the weird craft would float under her weight of armor. A few minutes before 10:00 A.M. the braces were knocked away and the vessel began to skid toward the water. United States flags at each end of the *Monitor* fluttered as she started. John Ericsson demonstrated his own confidence by riding his craft down the ways, although he and the little knot of people who stood with him on the deck about twenty feet from the vessel's stern had a small boat by them as a precaution. "Amidst the greatest anxiety on shore and on board, the vessel moved easily into the water, not immersing more than six feet of her forward deck, and sailing gracefully out into the stream for some distance." [13] The crowd on shore, including some who had lost bets on her buoyancy, cheered and waved rain-soaked hats and handkerchiefs and, immediately upon her being moored to the dock, rushed on board to be shown over the ship by the proud inventor and workmen.

The Federal flag officer whose segment of the blockade was threatened by the *Merrimack* was Louis M. Goldsborough of the North Atlantic Blockading Squadron. Goldsborough seems to have obtained his flag appointment by knowing the right people. Born in the Navy, the son of a chief clerk in the Department, he had at age eleven received his midshipman's warrant predated to 1812, for reasons patriotic but also practical since the maneuver gave him five extra years on the seniority list. His talk was often blustery, but well meant. Midshipmen, while he was superintendent of the Naval Academy, took advantage of his deceptive geniality when they set fire to his backyard privy and provoked his classic outburst:

"I'll hang them! Yes, I'll hang them! So help me God, I will!" [14]

A "rough sailor" by reputation, he had harried pirates in the Greek Archipelago and led a landing party in hand-to-hand fighting at Tuspan. He played backgammon with skill, was highly sensitive about rank, and did not always see eye to eye with the Secretary. His first disagreement with the latter probably occurred in a strategy conference just after Welles had placed the initial orders for the three ironclads. Goldsborough contended, and he could never advocate anything quietly, that only *three* such ships would be of no practical use.[15] He wanted the department to build thirty, and allow the Army to mark time until the iron ships were ready to advance!

Although Goldsborough in February of 1862 had fifty vessels with which to maintain the blockade from Washington, D. C., down the coast to the northern boundary of South Carolina, he still did not have all the ships he needed. There were three distinct areas within his command, each with its own special problems: the Potomac and lower Chesapeake Bay, the North Carolina sounds, and the ports of Wilmington and Beaufort, North Carolina.

Only off the latter harbors did the blockaders perform the simple routine chores of boarding merchantmen, keeping Rebels in port and outsiders out, with an occasional capture of a willful violator to break the monotony. As young blockade officer Alfred T. Mahan wrote, "Day after day, day after day, we lay inactive, roll, roll." [16] It was a welcome relief to Commander O. S. Glisson of the *Mount Vernon* when General B. F. Butler's transport went aground off Wilmington. Glisson and his men buoyed a channel for the embarrassed troopship and took on board for the night Mrs. Butler and her maid when the general feared his vessel would break up.

The operation that chiefly engaged Goldsborough during the winter of 1861-62 was carrying the war into the North Carolina sounds in cooperation with General Ambrose Burnside. A logical outgrowth of Stringham's capture of Hatteras

Inlet, the Burnside-Goldsborough amphibian venture won General-in-Chief McClellan's approval and an allotment of thirteen thousand troops. As at first conceived, it had a threefold aim: the capture of Roanoke Island on the gut between Pamlico and Albemarle Sounds, operations against the towns on Albemarle Sound with the blocking up of the Chesapeake and Albemarle Canal, and a strike inland toward Raleigh to cut the railroad from Richmond to Charleston. Only the first two of these objectives were accomplished, for McClellan ruled out the strike against Raleigh by recalling Burnside's troops for use in the Peninsula campaign.

Goldsborough and Burnside sailed from Hampton Roads on January 12 and spent three weeks getting army transports and supply ships across the bar into Hatteras Inlet and then lightening the vessels further in order to drag them across the inner bar into Pamlico Sound.

At Roanoke Island, forty miles to the north, Goldsborough's eighteen light-draft warships knocked out a Confederate mosquito fleet of armed tugboats and pounded three land batteries. Burnside disembarked his troops unopposed. In a quick march the length of the island, Burnside flanked and captured the smaller Confederate army that attempted to check him. The capture of Roanoke Island on February 8 gave the Federals the key to all the rear defenses of Norfolk—Albemarle and Currituck Sounds, eight rivers, four canals, and two local railroads. Effectively it cut off Norfolk from four-fifths of its supply of corn, pork, and forage, and deprived Richmond of convenient blockade-runner bases north of Beaufort.

After seizing Roanoke Island, the Federal forces might well have concentrated upon an inland strike against the Confederates' north-south railroad, instead of frittering away their strength in petty excursions against coastal towns. The Federals, however, never lost hope that Union men in the area would rise up and throw off the Confederate yoke as soon as the Yankee troops arrived. True, some nine out of thirty-five Confederates captured by the Navy at one point did prefer to remain with their captors rather than return home on parole; but for the most part the Unionist sentiment that flourished in the sound country was among Negroes. The Burnside-Goldsborough expedition has gone down in history as notable for the large number of blacks who flocked to the Federal camps. So many came that Roanoke Island itself had shortly to be converted into a colony for these fugitives.

Hampton Roads continued to be the North Atlantic Blockading Squadron's primary supply base, but its role was complicated by later developments. Confederate river craft darting out of the James or Elizabeth Rivers sometimes captured unwary supply boats of the army at Fortress Monroe and Hampton Roads. When checked by Federal naval police they would simply retire to the cover of Confederate land batteries at Sewell's Point or Pig Point. On the Potomac below Alexandria, the Confederates continued to menace Federal river traffic to and from the capital. Nor could the Navy's repeated shelling permanently rid the river of these dangers, for McClellan refused to risk small army garrisons which might be captured by the Confederates.

After the sinking of the stone fleet in Charleston Harbor, British and French warships put into Hampton Roads to convey consular mail to Norfolk. Their presence called for an exchange of civilities which took time from the flag officer's blockade duties and raised the ever-present danger of violations of trust, when not only messages but persons were illegally smuggled through the blockade. Confederate floating mines necessitated nightly boat patrols around the large blockade ships. Some of these infernal devices were lifted out and taken to the Washington Navy Yard for Captain Dahlgren to analyze. Another activity in Hampton Roads was the staging here of the expedition of Farragut and Butler whose as yet secret destination was New Orleans. Vessels from the Gulf squadrons having engine trouble would put in for repair. Occasionally the blockaders would have to serve as coast guards, as when the *R. B. Forbes* of Commander D. D. Porter's bomb fleet was wrecked off the Virginia capes.

Early in March, everyone in the Hampton Roads area was keyed up to expect the long-awaited visit from the C.S.S. *Virginia* as the Confederates had newly christened the *Merrimack,* when General McClellan received final approval to shift his offensive army from Washington to Fortress Monroe to proceed against Richmond via the Yorktown peninsula. It was this projected shift of military forces that caused Secretary Welles on March 6 to order the *Monitor* under Lieutenant John L. Worden to "come direct to Washington, anchoring below Alexandria." [17]

The first Federal ironclad, fresh from her trials, cleared Sandy Hook at 4:00 P.M. the same day, towed by the steam tug *Seth Low.* At first in fair weather and on a smooth sea the *Monitor* made good progress, but next day in a moderate breeze her eccentricities as a seagoing ship were revealed. Small waves flowed across her deck, as Ericsson had intended they should, but larger ones dashed against the turret with sufficient violence to force out the oakum around the turret's base. Her executive officer later wrote: "The berth-deck hatch leaked in spite of all we could do, and the water came down under the turret like a waterfall. It would strike the pilot-house and go over the turret in beautiful curves, and it came through the narrow eyeholes in the pilot house with such force as to knock the helmsman completely round from the wheel. The waves also broke over the blower-pipes, and the water came down through them in such quantities that the belts of the blower-engines slipped, and the engines consequently stopped for lack of artificial draught, without which, in such a confined place, the fires could not get air for combustion." [18] Two engineers trying to repair the blowers were asphyxiated and had to be carried to the top of the turret to be revived. The steam pumps could not be operated because the fires were low, and hand pumps lacked the force to throw the water out through the top of the turret, which was the only usable opening to the outside. Toward evening, wind and sea subsiding, the engines once more were started. Yet after midnight, in passing over a shoal, they again hit rough water. They spent the greater part of the night plugging leaks, but found smooth water again just before daylight.

The *Monitor* passed Cape Henry at 4:00 P.M. on Saturday, March 8, and as she headed westward into the entrance of Chesapeake Bay she heard the booming of heavy guns in Hampton Roads thirty miles off.

At 12:45 P.M. on the same day the blockade vessels in Hampton Roads had discovered what appeared to be three small Confederate steamers coming out past Sewell's Point. A few minutes later, when the new arrivals shifted course and steered across the roads toward Newport News, it had become apparent that one of them, which resembled a barracks roof submerged to the eaves and surmounted by a large smoking funnel, was the *Merrimack* (*Virginia*).

Although Flag Officer Goldsborough himself was in the North Carolina sounds, the trap he had devised now closed in on the Confederate ironclad.

Two heavy ships, the *Minnesota* and the *Roanoke,* decks cleared for action and steam up continuously during the past month, left their stations under Fortress Monroe and followed the *Merrimack* to cut off her escape and to bring her between their own guns and those of the sailing ships *Cumberland* and *Congress* that were stationed in the mouth of the James River off Newport News. As the *Roanoke*'s main shaft was broken, she blew off steam through her exhaust valves to deceive the enemy, while being hauled toward the scene of impending action by tugs.[19]

The Confederate ironclad under Flag Officer Franklin Buchanan had been hurried into action. Workmen had been busy on board her as far down as Craney Island. Her crews were still new to the ship, undrilled at the guns. Her engines had scarcely been turned over. She was so short of ammunition that Secretary Mallory had advised Buchanan to use his ram as much as possible. Buchanan headed straight for the *Cumberland* and the *Congress.*

About two o'clock when the *Merrimack* came within range, the *Cumberland,* the *Congress,* and the Army's shore batteries at Newport News opened fire. The ironclad, without veering from her chosen track toward the *Cumberland,* acknowledged the fire with her bow gun and the action became general. For fifteen minutes, while the *Merrimack* covered the last mile and a half, shot of the heaviest caliber struck her slanted, tallow-greased casemate and glanced off. Futile Federal projectiles ricochetted in every direction across the entrance to the James. At 2:30 P.M. the *Merrimack's* cast-iron beak, driven at four to five knots, plunged into the *Cumberland's* starboard bow. Captain Buchanan heard the underwater crash above the roaring cannonade. Her metal prow was wrenched off when the *Merrimack* backed free and went down with her victim, which sank—as Captain Buchanan admiringly phrased it—"gallantly fighting her guns as long as they were above water." [20]

Leaving the *Cumberland* on the bottom, with masts jutting above the surface and flag still flying, the *Merrimack* next opened fire on the *Congress.* She was joined now by C.S.S. *Yorktown* and *Jamestown,* which, coming out from the James River, also fired on the *Congress* and the *Minnesota,* which by now had run on the Middle Ground shoal. Toward three o'clock the *Congress* hoisted her jib and sheeted home her topsails, but progressed only a ship's length when she too grounded on the sandbanks south of the entrance to the James. In this situation, with no relief in sight, the surviving officers of the *Congress* at 4:00 P.M. struck her colors and hoisted a white flag at the gaff.

The *Merrimack* by now having executed a wide-radius turn, Buchanan ordered Lieutenant Commander Parker of the C.S.S. *Beaufort* to take possession of the *Congress,* secure her officers as prisoners, allow the crew to land, and burn the ship. Parker ran alongside the *Congress* and received on board Commander William Smith and Lieutenant Pendergrast, who handed over the ship's ensign in token of surrender, along with their own side arms. While the Federal officers, now prisoners, returned on board the *Congress* to get off the wounded, the Confederate vessels were fired upon both by

Federal soldiers on shore and by gun crews on the *Congress* who were yet ignorant of the vessel's surrender. Buchanan himself became so enraged at this "treachery" that he leaped up on top of the *Merrimack's* casemate to protest and was himself drilled through the thigh by a Minie ball. He fell back into his impregnable iron fortress and ordered the *Congress* to be burned with heated shot and incendiary shell. The Federal batteries at Newport News, having exhausted their powder supply, were "silenced," a large Federal transport alongside the wharf was blown up, a schooner was sunk, and another was captured by the Confederate mosquito craft and taken to Norfolk.

With the *Congress* in flames, the wounded Buchanan turned over command of the *Merrimack* to his executive officer, Lieutenant Catesby Jones, and the victorious ironclad at 7:00 P.M. set her course for Norfolk.

Panic now swept the surviving Federal blockade ships. The sailing frigate *Roanoke,* with three tugs dragging her up North Channel toward the battle scene, ran aground, as did the *Minnesota* and the *St. Lawrence.* What saved all three of these vessels was the fact that the *Merrimack* elected to return home via the deeper passage to the south of Middle Ground. The victorious Confederates looked upon these wooden Yankee pachyderms as fat prizes to be seized on the morrow.

The flames of the *Congress,* dying relic of a departed era, gave an awesome light to Hampton Roads until 1:00 A.M., when her magazines blew. Then dark came quickly.

9.

The Monitor *and the* Merrimack

FOR TEN MONTHS, STRATEGIC HAMPTON ROADS had communicated with Washington by dispatch boat up the Potomac, or by bay line steamer from Old Point Comfort to Baltimore and thence by wire to Washington. In February of 1862, with the *Merrimack's* emergence imminent and McClellan's shift to Fortress Monroe in the offing, wires were strung from Delaware to Cape Charles, from which point a submarine cable was being laid to Old Point Comfort. The laying of the cable was not completed until 4:00 P.M. on Sunday, March 9. Until that hour, then, Lincoln and his Cabinet of necessity must sweat it out with only the frightening news of the day before to plague them.

For so kinetic and vividly imaginative an individual as Stanton, the suspense of this day became well-nigh unbearable. In his alarm, he foresaw the *Merrimack* compelling the surrender of Fortress Monroe and the naval craft in its vicinity, and possibly before nightfall ascending the Potomac to threaten Washington.[1] Only recently had Stanton succeeded to the office of Secretary of War, and already he was fighting McClellan as well as the Confederate foe, his nerves were on edge, his disposition was sour. Gideon Welles, on the contrary, prided himself on being cool while under stress and on this day was as silent as Stanton was vocal. En route to the White House on this black Sunday, Welles had stopped at St. John's Church to inform Commodore Smith, whose son had commanded the *Congress,* of yesterday's disasters, and the rest of the day Welles was haunted by Smith's instinctive premonition (later proved correct) that his son Joe was dead. Seward, who feared difficulty with foreign nations if the *Merrimack* had raised the blockade, was without his usual bounce, "rendered more timid," Welles surmised, "by the opinion and alarm of Stanton." [2]

Lincoln, like Stanton, paced the floor and went frequently to the window to gaze down the Potomac, as though expecting the *Merrimack* to arrive and shell the White House. At length the restless President drove to the navy yard to enquire of Dahlgren whether the *Merrimack* could ascend the Potomac. Dahlgren thought she might have difficulty getting across Kettle Bottom Shoals. Lincoln then asked a pilot who said that she could come over them, so the President was left in as great uncertainty as before.

The Secretary of War, disregarding proprieties in dealing with a sister service, ordered Dahlgren to load canalboats with stone and tow them to the Kettle Bottoms ready to block the channel if the *Merrimack* should appear. Lest the dread ironclad proceed to New York and other cities and "lay them under contribution," Stanton telegraphed a warning to the governors of New York, Massachusetts, and Maine: "The opinion of the naval officers here is that the *Merrimack* will not venture to sea, but they advise that immediate preparations be made to guard against the danger to our ports." [3]

Stanton questioned Welles about the Ericsson battery, and when he learned that the *Monitor* carried only two guns "his look of incredulity and contempt" went beyond Welles's power to describe. In the belief that the Hampton Roads disaster would have to be retrieved by the country's best brains outside of the Navy Department, the distraught Secretary of War dispatched an emergency plea for a number of prominent citizens of New York to consult together secretly as a committee "to devise the best plan of speedily accomplishing the capture or destruction of the *Merrimack.*" [4]

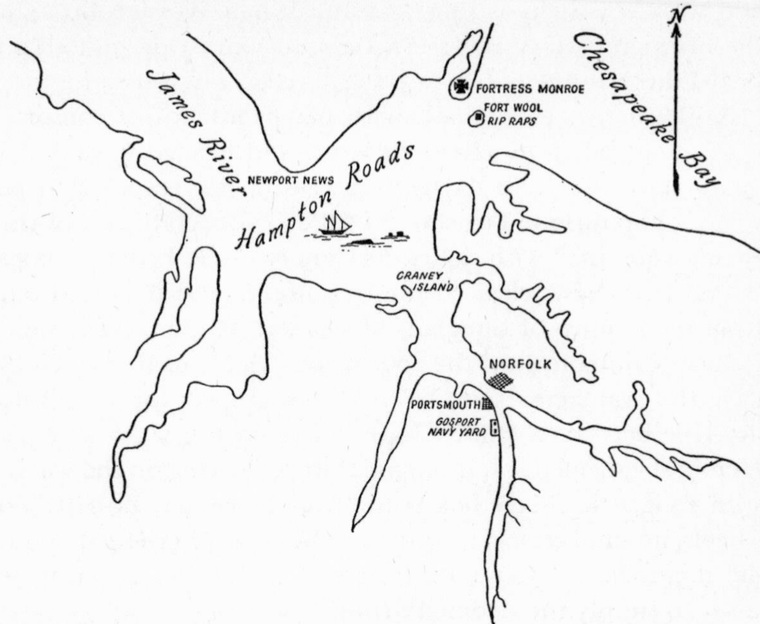

HAMPTON ROADS, first battleground of ironclad warships.

Meanwhile, just after the *Merrimack's* destructive raid on the previous afternoon, the *Monitor* entered Chesapeake Bay and proceeded slowly across the thirty-mile stretch toward Hampton Roads. While she was still under tow, her canvas shelter was removed from over the turret; blower pipes and funnels were unshipped and stowed below. At 9:00 P.M., stripped for action, she hove to alongside the *Roanoke* to report to the senior officer. Captain John Marston directed Worden to go to the aid of the battered and wounded *Minnesota,* which was now fast aground off Newport News.

Obtaining a pilot, Worden cast off the tow and proceeded under his own power toward the *Minnesota,* which was soon visible in the light from the burning *Congress*. Several tugs were trying to pull the *Minnesota* free at 2:00 A.M. when the *Monitor* arrived, but the big frigate's hull, having recoiled under her broadsides, had worked itself into a cradle of mud, and was there held as in a vacuum. When Worden brought the Ericsson battery alongside, Captain Van Brunt and all on board the *Minnesota* felt vastly relieved.

At dawn the *Merrimack,* with her paddle-wheel consorts, again emerged from Elizabeth River and headed toward the *Minnesota,* which, as daylight increased, was revealed to be in her old position. The shores of the Confederate side of the Roads were lined with sightseers from Norfolk. Federal troops at Newport News cheered the tiny *Monitor* as it moved out from the shadow of the giant blockader. As the raftlike newcomer steamed toward the roof-shaped victor of the previous day, the watchers from both shores groped for words to describe her. To a Confederate officer on the C.S.S. *Patrick Henry,* she seemed "an immense shingle floating on the water, with a gigantic cheese box rising from its center; no sails, no wheels, no smokestack, no guns." [5] Other Southerners thought she might be a water tank on a raft or a floating magazine come to supply the doomed *Minnesota.*

But these surmises were eliminated when shortly after eight o'clock the *Monitor* advanced to meet the *Merrimack.* To Captain Van Brunt of the *Minnesota,* the contrast between the two ironclads was that of "a pigmy and a giant." "Gun after gun was fired by the *Monitor,* which was returned with whole broadsides from the rebels with no more effect, apparently, than so many pebblestones thrown by a child. After a while they commenced maneuvering, and we could see the little battery point her bow for the rebels, with the intention, as I thought, of sending a shot through her bow porthole; then she would shoot by her and rake her through her stern. In the meantime the rebel was pouring broadside after broadside, but almost all her shot flew over the little submerged propeller, and when they struck the bombproof tower the shot glanced off without producing any effect." [6]

Her pilothouse, the *Monitor's* most difficult and the most vulnerable part, was a square box rising five feet above the deck about fifty feet forward of the turret, and connected with the latter by voice tube. This brain center of the ship—barely large enough to hold captain, pilot, and helmsman—was a crib of nine- by twelve-inch iron logs neatly mortised at the corners and covered by a heavy lid. Eyeslits a quarter-inch deep permitted conning and steering. As the voice tube to the turret broke early in the action, Captain Worden had to transmit orders to the gunners through two volunteer landsmen unaccustomed to naval idiom.

Lieutenant S. D. Greene, who was in charge of the turret, had to be careful not to fire on the vessel's own pilothouse. He had to sight the *Merrimack* target through the narrow margin of clearance between gunbarrel and edges of the port, and to pull the lanyard while the turret was in motion, firing the guns "on the fly." Once the heavy turret had been started on its "revolving journey" it could not be readily halted or reversed. Thus it was scarcely possible to take deliberate aim, to try, for instance, to place every shot at the same point on the *Merrimack* so as to crush through her shield. The engagement began with the ironclad duelists a mile apart. By mutual consent the Union David and the Confederate Goliath closed in and fought most of the time at ranges of less than a hundred yards. Sometimes they grated ponderously against each other. At these short distances the *Monitor*'s problem in sighting her guns was minimized, and this was well, for the bearing marks that had been chalked on the deck were obliterated shortly after the turret began revolving. For a while Lieutenant Greene was perplexed not to have these marks indicating starboard, port, bow, and stern. "I would continually ask the captain, 'How does the *Merrimack* bear?' He replied, 'On the starboard beam,' or 'On the port-quarter' as the case might be. Then the difficulty was to determine the direction of the starboard-beam, or port-quarter, or any other bearing." [7]

Sixteen gunners served the *Monitor*'s two eleven-inch Dahlgren guns. These famous naval cannon, because of their shape called "soda-water bottles," operated on special platforms that Ericsson had devised to absorb their recoil. When the guns were withdrawn into the turret for recharging, metal port stoppers like pendulums swung down to close the ports.

The men in the *Monitor*'s turret were deafened by the thunder of their own guns and by the clang of the *Merrimack*'s projectiles against their revolving citadel, but soon they breathed easily when they found Ericsson's armor to be shotproof. The laminated walls of the turret were built up of eight thicknesses of one-inch wrought-iron plates, standing vertically with overlapping joints and firmly riveted together. Glancing blows from the *Merrimack* scarcely scratched this armor, while the heaviest straight-on shots punched indentations up to two-and-one-half inches deep, but did not crack the plates. The only casualties in the turret were three men who leaned against the armor when it was struck. These were temporarily stunned and had to be carried below.

In a battle lasting four hours, the *Monitor* fired forty-three projectiles. As storage space inside the turret for ready ammunition was limited, the vessel had to haul off across a stretch of shallow water where the deep-draft *Merrimack* could not follow. A hole in the turret floor had to be brought to rest over a scuttle so that a fresh supply of powder and shot could be handed up from the magazine below.

During such a recess the *Merrimack* turned her attention once more to the *Minnesota* which was still aground. "Earlier in the morning she had put a 11-inch shot under my counter near the water line," reported Captain Van Brunt, "and now, on her second approach, I opened upon her with all my broadside guns and 10-inch pivot a broadside which would have blown out of the water any timber-built ship in the world. She returned my fire with her rifled bow gun with a shell which passed through the chief engineer's stateroom, through the engineers' mess room, amidships, and burst in the boatswain's room, tearing four rooms all into one in its passage, exploding two charges of powder, which set the ship on fire, but it was promptly extinguished by a party headed by my first lieutenant." [8]

The *Minnesota*'s marine officer stationed on the poop reported that at least fifty of his vessel's solid shot struck the *Merrimack's* slanting sides without effect.

When the *Monitor* returned, the *Merrimack* attempted to ram, although her cast-iron prow had gone down in the wreck of the *Cumberland*. The Goliath was ponderous in contrast to the David (263 feet long against 172 and in draft 23 against 10½), so that Worden was able by putting his helm hard over to avoid a direct blow. The *Merrimack* succeeded only in slicing her wooden stern across the sharp edge of the *Monitor's* side armor and starting a leak in her own hull. In attempting to ram the *Merrimack* in return, Worden found that the *Monitor* was only relatively nimble. He aimed toward his opponent's after quarter, hoping to crash her rudder and disable her steering gear, but he missed and slid past the target only three feet away.

The *Merrimack* now grounded in shoal water and, during the fifteen minutes when she was struggling to free herself, a 180-pound solid shot was planted by the *Monitor* in the stern of the Confederate's casemate. This shot ripped off some plating and splintered some of the wooden backing, but did not break through. Had the *Monitor* been able to land other shots in the same area, she would doubtless have pierced the *Merrimack's* shield. Or this shot alone might have broken through had it been propelled by a heavier powder charge. The standard powder charge used on board the *Monitor* on this momentous day was only fifteen pounds. Ironically enough, it was discovered later that the same guns could fire up to forty-five pounds with safety!

The *Merrimack*, after jerking herself off the mudbank, from close range concentrated her attention upon the *Monitor's* pilothouse. About 11:30 A.M. a shell fired from a gun not ten yards away struck the pilothouse, jolting askew the iron slab that formed the top and cracking one of the nine- by twelve-inch beams.

Lieutenant Worden was conning the ship immediately opposite the point of impact. Minute grains of dust were blown through the quarter-inch eyeslit into his eyes. "The flood of light rushing through the top of the pilothouse, now partly open, caused Worden, blind as he was, to believe that the pilothouse was seriously injured, if not destroyed; he therefore gave orders to put the helm to starboard and 'sheer off.' "[9] Lieutenant Greene, called from the turret, found the injured captain at the foot of the ladder leading to the pilothouse, and helped him to his cabin before himself taking control of the ship. After twenty minutes Greene steered the *Monitor* out of the shallows but toward an enemy who thought the fight was over and had set course for vital docking at Norfolk.

If, during this interval, the *Merrimack* had once again fired upon the *Minnesota,* Captain Van Brunt had planned to abandon his ship. Or if the *Merrimack* had been able to accept the *Monitor*'s belated offer to renew the engagement, she might have found the altered situation very much in her favor. In charge of the turret, after Greene had succeeded Worden, was Alban C. Stimers, who was not a naval officer but a civil engineer serving on board as a technician operating the turret-turning mechanism.

The battle ended with neither side scoring an appreciable advantage. "We had run into the *Monitor,* causing us to leak, and had received a shot from her which came near disabling the machinery, but continued to fight her until she was driven into shoal water," explained the *Merrimack*'s acting captain, Lieutenant Catesby Jones; "The *Minnesota* appeared so badly damaged that we did not believe that she would ever move again. The pilots refused to place us any nearer to her (they had once run us aground). About 12 [o'clock] the pilots declared that if we did not go up to Norfolk then, that we could not do so until the next day."[10]

Thus, the historic first contest between ironclad battleships, after four hours of thunderous but relatively harmless clatter of iron on iron, ended without decision. Each side claimed the victory, and each in a different sense was justified.

Assistant Secretary of the Navy Fox had come down from Washington to witness the epochal event, and was one of the first to go on board the *Monitor,* as cheer on cheer resounded from the Federal ships and forts. Fox sent the injured Worden to Washington on a tug and after the new telegraph cable had been connected, he sent over it the historic dispatch to the Secretary of the Navy: [11]

Headquarters, Fortress Monroe—6:45 P.M.

The *Monitor* arrived at 10 P.M. last night and went immediately to the protection of the *Minnesota,* lying aground just below Newport News.

At 7 A.M. today the *Merrimack,* accompanied by two wooden steamers and several tugs, stood out toward the *Minnesota* and opened fire.

The *Monitor* met them at once and opened her fire, when all the enemy's vessels retired, excepting the *Merrimack.* These two ironclad vessels fought part of the time touching each other, from 8 A.M. to noon, when the *Merrimack* retired. Whether she is injured or not it is impossible to say. Lieutenant J. L. Worden, who commanded the *Monitor,* handled her with great skill, assisted by Chief Engineer Stimers. Lieutenant Worden was injured by the cement from the pilot house being driven into his eyes, but I trust not seriously. The *Minnesota* kept up a continuous fire and is herself somewhat injured.

She was moved considerably today, and will probably be off tonight. The *Monitor* is uninjured, and ready at any moment to repel another attack.

G. V. Fox
Assistant Secretary

G. Welles
Secretary Navy

Two months of uneasy stalemate followed the battle. The *Merrimack* was put in dry dock to receive a new ram, a skin of metal across her bow, and new plates at the water line. The state of her preparations was so closely guarded that the Federals kept outside Hampton Roads with steam up and men at battle stations momentarily expecting her to return. A sloping metal shield with solid wood backing was built around the *Monitor's* pilothouse to cause shot to glance from it. Several of the heavy frigates upon their release from grounding were sent to Northern shipyards and replaced by lighter gunboats with powerful rifled ordnance. For the few army supply ships that were allowed to enter the strategic area between Fortress Monroe and Newport News, an unusual number of tugs was held in readiness to pull them out of danger should the *Merrimack* reappear. During this period of watchful waiting, the *Monitor* took station between Fortress Monroe and the Rip Raps to prevent the *Merrimack* from getting out into the lower Chesapeake Bay where McClellan's transports and supply vessels were anchored. Bushnell's ironclad battery, named the *Galena,* was finished in the New York yard and rushed to the *Monitor*'s side, as was also the lightly armored battery of E. A. Stevens known as the *Naugatuck.*

Both Federals and Confederates improvised novel methods for crippling each other's ironclad. Ladders to enable boarders to scale the *Merrimack*'s tallow greased sides, hoses of scalding steam, hand grenades to be tossed inside her casemate or down her stack were matched on the Confederate side by wet sailcloth to stuff down the *Monitor*'s smokestacks, wedges to scotch her turret, and sheets to throw over the low pilothouse to blind her helmsman.

General McClellan, although he feared the power of the *Merrimack* to disrupt his communications on the Yorktown peninsula, nevertheless followed through with his plans. Perhaps overprudently, he accepted the continued threat of the *Merrimack* and landed at Old Point Comfort, anchoring his ships outside of Hampton Roads where they could be protected by Fortress Monroe, the *Monitor,* and the battery on the Rip Raps known as Fort Wool. When he had difficulty turning the Confederate defenses at Yorktown, he called for the *Monitor* to bombard the shore batteries at Yorktown, but Flag Officer Goldsborough was under strict orders from Lincoln himself that he was not to risk the *Monitor* against any Confederate shore positions until after the *Merrimack* had been destroyed.

On April 11 the *Merrimack* showed herself off Sewell's Point, accompanied by the *Jamestown*, the *Yorktown*, and four smaller vessels. There was instantaneous activity in the upper roads. "Steam tugs ran whistling and screaming about, towing strings of vessels behind them, whilst sloops, schooners, and brigs, taking advantage of what air there was got up sail and moved out of harm's way." [12] The *Monitor* with steam up and in fighting trim lay quietly near her usual anchorage and was joined by the armored *Naugatuck*. Had the *Merrimack* proceeded across the Roads toward Newport News, the *Monitor* would have interposed to cut off her retreat to Norfolk, or had she tried to get at the shipping in the lower bay there would have been a fight. But the Confederates merely staged a show, remaining close by the Confederate land batteries at Sewell's Point. And while the ironclads assiduously tried to outface each other, the *Yorktown* with bold impudence side-wheeled across the Roads and captured three of McClellan's small transports that were caught in a bight without wind or tugs.

Time, however, was on the side of the *Monitor*, which in this particular game had only to prolong the stalemate in order to win. The *Vanderbilt* and several other fast passenger liners were strengthened as rams and sent to operate in conjunction with the *Monitor*. The ironclad *Galena*, built by Cornelius Bushnell who had introduced Ericsson's model, joined the *Monitor* on April 24. In vain, the Confederates, deficient in resources, tried to scrape together enough iron to plate a second vessel at Norfolk. But, with McClellan finally advancing toward Richmond, Norfolk's days as a Confederate stronghold were numbered.

As early as March 24, only a week after the first of McClellan's troops had arrived at Fortress Monroe, the commandant of the Norfolk Navy Yard was ordered by the authorities in Richmond to push work on the second ironclad at night even if they had to use girls to hold candles for the workmen, since the loss of Norfolk within twenty days was expected. Two days later he was instructed: "Begin at once, without attracting special notice to the subject, to carefully pack and get ready for transportation all the fine machinery and tools not required for your operations in your workshops." [13] The last of McClellan's hundred thousand troops reached the peninsula by April 2. On May 4 the Confederates abandoned Yorktown. McClellan trailed the retreating garrison along the York River, with light gunboats scouting ahead as far as White House, Virginia. Almost immediately Confederate troops began evacuating Norfolk. In the disordered state of affairs, Commodore Tattnall, in command of the *Merrimack,* received conflicting orders to defend Norfolk and to prevent the Federal Navy from ascending the James. And while he was debating where to take his cumbersome vessel, the Federal forces advanced upon Norfolk and backed him up inside the Elizabeth River.

President Lincoln came to Fortress Monroe a few days after the fall of Yorktown, imbued with the desire to push General McClellan and possibly Flag Officer Goldsborough also. When McClellan requested a naval reconnaissance up the James, Lincoln on May 7 directed Goldsborough: "If you have tolerable confidence that you can successfully contend with the *Merrimack* without the help of the *Galena* and two gunboats, send the *Galena* and two gunboats up the James River at once. Please report your action on this to me at once. I shall be found at General Wool's headquarters." [14]

Accordingly, the *Galena,* the *Aroostook,* and the *Port Royal* were promptly dispatched up the James River. There they flushed and drove upstream the Confederate steamers *Jamestown* and *Yorktown.* Then after they had passed two land batteries without casualties, the *Galena* ran aground and stuck for thirty-six hours, before finally freeing herself and proceeding on up to Jamestown.

Meanwhile, the President directed Goldsborough to send the *Monitor* toward Norfolk to bombard the Sewell's Point batteries and smoke out the *Merrimack* so that the ram vessels could get at her. The *Monitor,* with three other vessels, approached the Elizabeth River and engaged Sewell's Point, while the fort at the Rip Raps also bombarded it from long range. On the tenth the Presidential steamer *Baltimore* came alongside the *Monitor* and Lincoln asked the latter's commander whether there would be any military impropriety in the *Monitor's* returning to Sewell's Point without prior orders from the flag officer. Commander Jeffers replied that it was necessary and proper for the flag officer to know that he had not acted without authority. Lincoln then assured Jeffers that he would notify Commodore Goldsborough and directed him to proceed on a reconnaissance of Sewell's Point to learn whether it had been reinforced or abandoned. When the works were found to have been abandoned, Lincoln caused General Wool's troops to be marched to Norfolk.

Early on the eleventh, Craney Island having been evacuated, Commodore Tattnall set fire to the *Merrimack* and she blew up at 4:58 A.M. It was "one of the grandest sights ever seen," officers on President Lincoln's boat reported.[15] X

Lincoln, with Chase and Stanton, could not resist the urge to visit Norfolk. Picking up Commodore Goldsborough and accompanied by the *Monitor* and three gunboats, Mr. Lincoln proceeded up the Elizabeth River on the steamer *Baltimore.* As though fearful that the Confederates might return to recover the guns in the Norfolk batteries and Navy Yard, Lincoln ordered Goldsborough to collect all of these and have them removed to Fortress Monroe. As they proceeded through water littered with debris from the exploded *Merrimack,* the flag officer fished up a length of yellow pine thought to have been a portion of her keel. This was eagerly split up and a section suitable for a walking stick was presented to the President, along with two Confederate flags picked up at Craney Island. The party arrived at Norfolk shortly before noon.

Lincoln did not go ashore, but surveyed the city from the vessel. "The President is a man of practical pluck, like Farragut, Du Pont, Porter, McClellan and Halleck," announced the New York *Herald,* "and has more genuine fight in him than all the members of his cabinet put together." His visit, reported the same source, "is understood to have been for the purpose of directing in person, as Commander-in-Chief, the cooperation of the navy with the execution of the plans of Gen. McClellan. . . . The sailors all unite in saying he is 'a trump,' and that he has at some time served an apprenticeship on board ship, so much at home did he seem." Possibly taking his cue from the Commander-in-Chief himself, the *Herald* reporter concluded, "We have this rebellion upon the hip. That fact is patent to all the world. With that one little vessel-of-war, the *Monitor,* we have broken up all the navies of Europe. . . ." [16]

Certainly Lincoln was in high spirits on his return to Washington. In passing Kettle Bottom Shoals he jested about the canalboats that Stanton had prepared for sinking two months ago. "Oh, that is Stanton's navy," said he. "That is the fleet concerning which he and Mr. Welles became so excited in my room. Welles was incensed and opposed the whole scheme, and it has proved that Neptune was right. Stanton's navy is as useless as the paps of a man to a suckling child. There may be some show to amuse the child, but they are good for nothing for service." [17]

With the removal of the *Merrimack* as a threat to McClellan's operations on the peninsula, the *Monitor* joined the *Galena,* the *Naugatuck,* and other ironclad gunboats for a quick thrust up the James River. The plan was to ascend to Richmond and by threatening bombardment to compel its surrender. McClellan, meanwhile, was moving up along the York River on the other side of the peninsula. At Drury's Bluff, eight miles short of Richmond, the *Monitor* and her consorts on May 15 found their passage blocked by sunken hulks and carefully built cribs of stone. Rifle pits along each shore forced all hands on the vessels to keep under cover, while heavy batteries on a cliff two hundred feet high rained conical, armor-piercing projectiles upon the gunboats. The ironclad *Galena* was riddled, with eighteen out of the twenty-eight shot that hit her penetrating, and she lost thirteen killed and eleven wounded. The *Monitor,* advancing to shield the *Galena,* found that she could not sufficiently elevate her guns at close range and was compelled to retreat downstream. The *Monitor,* hit three times, suffered no injury. The bursting of her one-hundred-pounder Parrott rifle rendered the little *Naugatuck* useless. Had McClellan been able to attack the Confederate land batteries in conjunction with the naval assault some progress might have been made, but that had not been possible.

The final chapter in the history of Ericsson's *Monitor* lacked the brilliance of the first. She remained in the James River throughout McClellan's campaign there, as part of the James River Flotilla under Commodore Charles Wilkes, keeping open the army's communications below the Confederate defense line. At the end of the year, while en route to the concentration of ironclads to attack Charleston, she foundered off Cape Hatteras. In her less than a year of active service, she had won a place in the history of navies and had rescued Lincoln's wooden Navy from the brink of disaster. Ericsson's magnificent pioneering, moreover, had done more than anything else to break the shackles of the past. Already in busy Yankee shipyards, several new classes of ironclad monitors were coming off the ways to change the character of the later naval fighting.

10.

Launching the New Orleans Campaign

TO MR. LINCOLN'S NAVY, NEW ORLEANS WAS A city of fabulous interest as keystone of the blockade in the Gulf, gate to the interior waterways of a continent, and the South's largest, richest, most cosmopolitan city. As the trading outlet in peacetime for over three thousand miles of navigable waters, she required wharves along the entire seven-mile crescent of her levee to accommodate the hundreds of river steamboats and ocean-going craft that handled her freight—lumber, grain, cattle, and hogs of the Middle West; turpentine, sugar, cotton of the Southern states.

In the summer of 1861 Welles's strategy board, compiling useful blockade data on New Orleans' outlets to the sea, were awed by her manifold and devious entrances and exits. "It will be apparent to a careful reader of this memoir that New Orleans has so many outlets and channels of trade, less direct and convenient indeed than the river, but not less certain and practicable, that the blockade of the river does not close the trade of the port." [1] A hundred miles below New Orleans the river branches off in three directions, forming, from east to west, Pass a L'Outre, South Pass, and South West Pass, the first and last of which were practicable for heavy seagoing ships. But, aside from these river channels through the deltas, New Orleans had lateral outlets through Lake Pontchartrain on the east and Barataria Bay on the west, and through in-

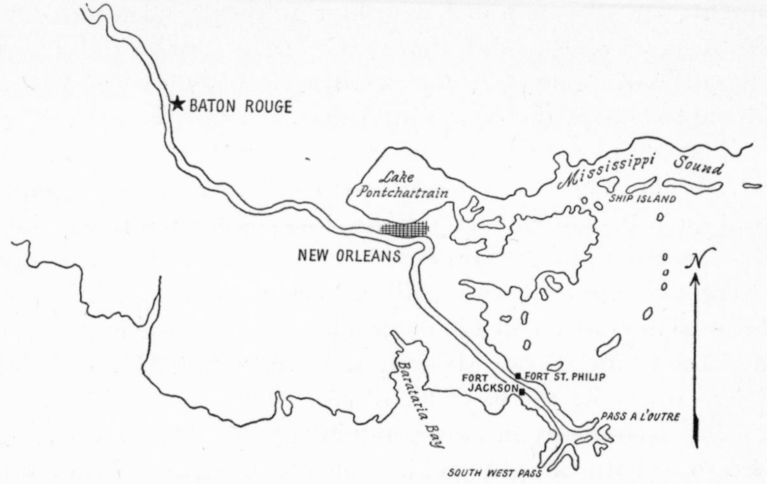

THE LOWER MISSISSIPPI RIVER, showing New Orleans' lateral outlets to the sea through Lake Pontchartrain and Barataria Bay, as well as the Delta passes. The best way to seal the port of New Orleans to blockade runners was to capture it.

numerable secondary inlets sprinkled all around the coast from the Lake Pontchartrain channel to Atchafalaya Bayou, a distance on the arc joining these eastern and western extremities of 170 miles.

Ultimately New Orleans itself had to be captured, but this, in the board's opinion, would require a large number of smaller, more powerfully armed gunboats than the Navy possessed in the summer of 1861, "a great many troops, and the conduct of sieges, and it will be accomplished with slow advances." [2] After capturing the two masonry forts, a slow and bloody advance by the Army might be expected against any secondary positions between the forts and New Orleans, in which operations the naval ships would enfilade the Confederate positions ahead of the troops. Two considerations deterred the board from recommending that a seagoing expedition be undertaken in the near future. There was a chance that the War Department's campaign in the West might, with the help of fresh-water gunboats, take New Orleans from above; and there were the "nearer and more urgent" salt-water operations against Hatteras Inlet and Port Royal to occupy the Navy's attention.

The political situation in the Middle West, however, as Mr. Welles knew, was urgent, with the harvest approaching and the usual commercial outlets closed. Some positive action was essential. So the strategy board recommended, and the Secretary approved, two palliative measures: the seizing of Ship Island outside of Lake Pontchartrain and the capture of a point inside of the Mississippi River at the Head of the Passes to render the blockade of New Orleans more effective.

Ship Island was an easy conquest for the blockaders as it was but halfheartedly held. The Confederates themselves early in the war had burned its fort and barracks and, when they later reconsidered their hasty action and began to rebuild their defenses, a few broadsides from the blockader *Massachusetts* so discouraged them that they abandoned the island permanently.[3] From the middle of September the Navy used the fine anchorage in the lee of Ship Island as a refuge from storms, but not for several months did they make use of the island as a naval base. On November 2, when the first contingent of General B. F. Butler's troops was ready to advance down the coast for another "Hatteras" expedition, those troops were sent to Ship Island as an advanced staging area for operations in the Gulf.

The seizure of a position inside the Mississippi River at the Head of the Passes was also easy enough, since there were no Confederate shore defenses below Forts Jackson and St. Philip. But thus to apply a tourniquet to the great artery of the river would be to invite the most determined opposition from New Orleans. The ships necessary to maintain such a position, thought Du Pont's strategy board, ought actually to be powerful enough to run the gantlet of the forts above and attack New Orleans; "here, if anywhere," the board advised, "is the place for ironclad ships." [4] But such vessels not existing in October of 1861, the Gulf blockaders sent into the river two inefficient sailing sloops that had to be towed and one steamer to set up the interior base.

The steamer *Richmond,* shepherding the sailing sloops *Vincennes* and *Preble,* early in October entered the river and began unloading lumber and other gear inside the river at the Head of the Passes. While so employed they were kept under surveillance by a Confederate river boat which lobbed occasional shells at them from a range outside that of the Federals' guns. The *Richmond* hurriedly sent to Tortugas for long-range rifles, but before these guns could be received the Confederates launched a fierce night attack. The *Richmond* was caught by surprise while coaling. As she was struggling to unleash herself from the collier, the *Richmond* was butted by the Confederate iron-sheathed ram *Manassas* and had three of her planks stove in under water. Several Confederate fire rafts joined together by chains and, stretching across the river blazing fearsomely, were now pushed downstream toward the Federal intruders. In the contrary currents the infernos ran afoul of snags and driftwood along the bank and harmlessly burnt themselves out. The shallower *Preble* escaped, but the *Richmond* and the *Vincennes,* in their haste to clear out of the river, grounded on the bar at South West Pass, where for two hours they were kept under fire by the long-range guns of the Confederates. They were saved from destruction only by the excessive range and the almost juvenile marksmanship of their assailants.

During the confusion while grounded and unable to reply to the Confederates' fire, the commander of the *Vincennes* heaved his thirty-two-pounder guns overboard and, misinterpreting a signal from the *Richmond,* abandoned his ship. Fortunately the slow match which he had lighted to explode his magazines fluttered out and he was able later to reboard his vessel, but not until after he had become a laughingstock and made the Gulf Blockading Squadron appear ridiculous.

Reports on the affair reached Washington, along with the excitingly good news of Du Pont's victory at Port Royal, and Lincoln's Navy Department was convinced that the time was right to launch an attack on New Orleans. Du Pont's success afforded grounds for believing that the navy's wooden ships were capable of executing a quick thrust up the river past the forts. Assistant Secretary Fox declared it feasible, as did Commander David D. Porter, newly arrived from the Gulf.

Porter was an old cruiser in the lower Mississippi. During a slack season after the Mexican War, he had obtained leave of absence and commanded a mail steamer making regular trips to New Oleans, and he claimed to know "every inch of the river." [5] The energetic Porter, surprised and pleased to find that Welles would listen to him after he had absconded with the *Powhatan* to Fort Pickens, gave a graphic description of conditions of the blockade off the deltas, and, when Welles mentioned to him the department's secret plan to organize an expedition to take New Orleans, Porter entered into the project with zest and relish. To further insure the success of the navy's thrust past the forts, Porter suggested a preliminary bombardment by regular army mortars mounted on schooners.

Lincoln, Welles, Fox, Porter, and General McClellan met in a secret conference at the latter's home on November 15, 1861, to debate the reasons for and against a joint army-navy expedition to New Orleans. McClellan, newly installed as general-in-chief and in command of all the armies, was at this time concentrating upon building up the Army of the Potomac. He stated that fifty thousand troops would be required to lay siege to Forts Jackson and St. Philip and that so many could not be spared. Porter contended that only sufficient troops to occupy New Orleans were required, and explained his plan for bombarding beforehand with thirteen-inch mortars. Once the fleet had run the gantlet and cut off the forts from New Orleans, the forts must shrivel like fruits on a severed vine. The bombardment idea appealed so strongly to McClellan that he "came readily into the arrangement" and agreed to furnish ten thousand troops to accompany the Navy in addition to the two thousand belonging to General Butler that had already been sent to Ship Island.[6]

Whether even General Butler was informed at this early time that the destination of the expedition was New Orleans is not clear. Welles in his diary noted that this top-secret information was "withheld from the War Department [now under Simon Cameron] and all others . . . because secrets could not then be kept but inevitably leaked out, contractors became importunate, and the Rebels often were forewarned." [7] The dynamic Butler, moreover, was now in New England raising troops in competition with the state officials, and managing through a personal feud to stir up a mare's nest over states rights. McClellan was doubtless happy to find a place for him so far from the national capital, where, as Welles phrased it, Butler's "energy, activity, and impulsive force might be employed in desultory aquatic and shore duty in concert with the navy." [8]

Gideon Welles, having scrapped the practice of awarding important billets to the hoaryheaded according to rank, appointed young Porter as commander of the Mortar Flotilla, and combed the roster to pick the right officer to head the naval contingent. Welles had studied the list, but each time he had passed over the names of Southern officers as "particularly suspect." Now he felt he might trust a Southern-bred officer whose loyalty had remained unshaken through eight months of war. The Secretary was especially attracted to Captain David Glasgow Farragut, foster son of the famous Commodore David Porter. Since his boyhood battle experiences in the War of 1812, Farragut had earned a modest reputation as a gunnery officer and had established the West Coast navy yard at Mare Island. Upon the secession of Virginia he had promptly abandoned his home in Norfolk and moved to New York City, where, after six months, he had been given responsible duty on the retiring board. Impressed by Farragut's decisiveness in breaking off his Southern connections, Welles inquired among naval officers as to Farragut's ability to head "a great and active campaign against Mobile or some other point." [9] Most officers, while speaking well of Farragut as a person, questioned his power as an administrator. Du

Pont thought him "a fair fighting officer, of ordinary standing" but "doubted if he was equal to the position." Smith of Yards and Docks considered him "a bold, impetuous man, of a great deal of courage and energy," but felt that "his capabilities and power to command a squadron was a subject to be determined only by trial." [10] Porter, whose family connections with Farragut were closer than those of anyone else consulted, expressed confidence in him, and, since Porter himself was to have a conspicuous part in the expedition, his word carried weight. After Porter and Fox had sounded Farragut unofficially, Gideon Welles invited him to his home for a delightful and heartwarming chat, after which, sure of his man, the Secretary secretly revealed to Farragut that his real destination was New Orleans, and announced to the press the selection of Farragut as flag officer of the newly formed Western Gulf Blockading Squadron.

Farragut at sixty, with a boyish vivacity that belied his forty-nine years in the Navy, on December 21, 1861, wrote a note to his wife: "Keep your lips closed, and burn my letters; for perfect silence is to be observed—the first injunction of the Secretary. I am to have a flag in the Gulf, and the rest depends upon myself. Keep calm and silent. I shall sail in three weeks." [11]

Farragut departed from Hampton Roads in the flagship *Hartford* on February 2. He had been briefly delayed by ice in the Delaware River but had not wasted the time. Since he expected to pass so close to the Confederate forts that the men in his tops would be able to fire down upon the enemy and in turn be exposed to the musketry of the latter, he had mounted extra guns in the tops, along with a shield of quarter-inch boiler iron to protect his men. "This is a little kink of mine," he explained to Dahlgren, "but if it saves one man only, I will consider myself well repaid for the trouble; should a ball occasionally pierce the iron, they must take their chances." [12] His arrival at Ship Island on the twentieth was without fanfare. He busied himself with organizing the Western Gulf Blockading Squadron and did not advance immediately toward the deltas, since he wished to prolong the doubt in Confederate minds as to the precise point of his attack.

Commander Porter sailed from Washington in the *Harriet Lane* on February 11. For three hectic months he had shuttled between New York and Washington organizing the Mortar Flotilla: purchasing twenty schooners, ordering thirteen-inch mortars from Pittsburgh, mounting the mortars as they arrived at the navy yard in New York, assembling seven steamers to tow the floating mortar platforms into the Mississippi, recruiting officers and men from the merchant service. "Black Dave" Porter moved in the vortex of administrative hubbub that delighted his soul, and had already brought order out of chaos when he reached Key West on February 28.

Here, while waiting for his steamers, he divided the mortar schoolers into three groups under Lieutenants Watson Smith, W. W. Queen, and K. R. Breese, and set them to practice firing at barrel targets. Several of the mortar captains, who chafed under naval discipline, Porter clapped in irons and gave their places to other men. After a week of shaking down, he was convinced that he had the finest organization in the world, and, although but four of his steamers had now arrived, he pushed on to Ship Island. As he would learn later, two of his flotilla's steamers, *Clifton* and *R. B. Forbes,* had collided in fog off the Virginia capes. The latter, having to be beached, was wrecked, while the ex-Manhattan ferryboat *Clifton* was delayed by a trip to Baltimore for repairs.

General Butler was the last of the three chief leaders of the New Orleans expedition to get away and his near failure to do so jeopardized the success of the undertaking. The embarkation of the second contingent of Butler's troops in January was the moment chosen by Governor Andrew of Massachusetts for a final showdown with General Butler. Through the Massachusetts Senators, Governor Andrew hurled loose charges of corruption and malpractice on the part of Butler during his three months of recruiting. Governor Andrew sent his state adjutant general, and finally went himself, to

Washington to belabor the President and the War Department. The chief difficulty concerned the appointment of officers for the regiments Butler had raised in Massachusetts. Butler insisted on rewarding with officer billets his Democratic political friends who had helped him with recruiting; while Governor Andrew, an abolitionist-Republican, declined to sign their commissions in the belief that they were not "proper" representatives of the state. From Secretary Cameron the redoubtable Butler had obtained an appointment to command the so-called "Department of New England"—a Federal post which, as Butler contended, made him coordinate with, rather than subordinate to, the Governor, and this maneuver by the sharp lawyer general had antagonized the governor all the more. Lincoln made a personal appeal to Andrew to sign the commissions so as not to hold up Butler's army, and, when the governor refused, he had the adjutant general of the United States quietly issue Federal commissions as though that were a regular procedure.

Unfortunately, General McClellan, in mid-January when the Butler-Andrew storm broke, was all too willing to oblige the Governor by nullifying "Butler's expedition" and diverting his recruits to the Army of the Potomac.

Fox appealed to Stanton who was new in office, having but recently relieved the ineffectual Cameron. This was the first that Stanton had heard of an expedition for New Orleans. In principle he heartily approved of such a move, but he went through the formality of requiring a report on the project from McClellan. The latter, once more thinking in terms of fifty thousand troops to besiege the forts, on January 25 recommended that "what is known as 'General Butler's expedition' ought to be suspended." [13]

To counteract this adverse decision of the general-in-chief, Fox and Butler, with considerable aid from General J. G. Barnard, who had been a member of the naval strategy board which had originally considered the New Orleans problem, worked directly with Secretary Stanton, marshaling figures explaining the navy's plan of operations. Stanton at length rendered the decision that Butler should go on to the Gulf as originally planned. Stanton's bold move saved the carefully wrought project of Lincoln's Navy for one of the war's most important expeditions, although, as the canny Secretary of the Navy surmised, it marked the beginning of the personal rift between Stanton and McClellan. Butler received his orders on February 23 and at once put to sea. Mrs. Butler, no less hardy than the redoubtable general, accompanied him.

On the way south Butler's transport, the S.S. *Mississippi,* ran aground off Wilmington, North Carolina, on Frying Pan Shoals.[14] When her captain dropped an anchor overboard in the shallow water, the wind drove the ship against it and punched a hole in her bow. A navy blockader buoyed a channel and stood by until she floated the next day. Continuing on down the coast to Du Pont's naval base at Port Royal, she lost twelve days there getting her hull repaired. That finished, she backed into a shell bank, broke tiller ropes, ran crazily on shore a mile away, and stuck until released by navy tugs at high tide the next morning. To appease his now frightened troops, Butler put the transport captain under arrest and made the final lap to Ship Island under a young officer loaned to him by the Navy.

Ship Island lay midway between Mobile Bay and the mouths of the Mississippi. It was about sixty-five miles east of New Orleans as the crow flies and ninety-five north of the deltas. Above the flat white sands of the western end of the island arose the silhouettes of a lighthouse, a rude fort, and the breeze-whipped tents of the soldiers.

By the U.S.S. *Pensacola* which reached Ship Island on March 2, Flag Officer Farragut received from the Navy Department sketches and a detailed description of the New Orleans forts for his own and General Butler's use. "The most important operation of the war is confided to yourself and your brave associates," read Welles's covering letter, "and every light possible to obtain should be carefully considered before putting into operation the plan which your judgment dictates." Although there were only fifteen feet of water at the deepest entrance into the river, Farragut was urged to lighten the huge frigate *Colorado,* which had a 22-foot draft, so as to have the use of its enormous fire power when passing the forts. "The Department relies upon your skill to give direction to the powerful force placed at your disposal, and upon your personal character to infuse a hearty cooperation amongst your officers, free from unworthy jealousies. If successful, you open the way to the sea for the great West, never again to be closed. The rebellion will be riven in the center, and the flag to which you have been so faithful will recover its supremacy in every State." [15]

Farragut's squadron was a heterogeneous group of vessels that included sailing sloops, converted merchant steamers of assorted sizes, old steam frigates, and a class of brand-new gunboats whose shakedown cruise was their voyage to Ship Island. The U.S.S. *Mississippi* was a lumbering side-wheel battleship, veteran of Perry's opening of Japan. The *Varuna* was a light merchantman purchased only a month before Farragut left for the Gulf. The Mortar Flotilla was made up of whaling schooners and a miscellany of side-wheel ferryboats and new navy-built "double-enders" like the *Miami.*

For weeks after he reached Ship Island, it looked as though Farragut would not be able to move for lack of coal. The small supply the Navy had ordered was requisitioned by ships of the Atlantic squadrons, or the sail-driven colliers were blown off course, or they thoughtlessly unloaded at Key West, which had been the base of the Gulf Squadron before its reorganization into eastern and western units. Farragut borrowed seventeen hundred tons from General Butler, and afterward towed Butler's steam transport into the river to conserve coal. The flag officer was short, too, of such essentials as fuses, lint for bandages, and medical supplies, and wrote worried letters to the department about these matters during the first few weeks while he was distributing his sailing ships along the thousand miles of Gulf coast that had been allotted to his Western Gulf Blockading Squadron and drawing in his steamers for the push upriver to New Orleans.

Farragut's well-intentioned friends had persuaded the department that the frigate *Colorado* could be got into the river, and their unfortunate advice cost the flag officer several weeks of anxious delay. The *Colorado's* coal and movable gear were transferred from the deep-bellied vessel to a chartered merchantman, but, since the removal of twenty tons lightened her only an inch, the business was tedious. After a conscientious struggle to carry through the department's wish, Farragut gave up the effort, appointed the *Colorado's* elderly skipper, Captain Theodorus Bailey, as leader of a gunboat division, and shifted the ship's best guns and gun crews to other ships that could enter the river.

On the bar at Pass a l'Outre, the trim *Brooklyn,* drawing only fifteen feet, had remained stuck for seventeen hours. Farragut took her around to South West Pass, where, in a deeper channel that had previously been sounded and marked by the Coast Survey, she grounded for only an hour before sliding over the bar into the deep water inside the river. It had now been twelve months since normal peacetime traffic through the mouths of Big Muddy had ceased. The tons of silt brought down daily by the two-and-a-half- to four-mile current were piled up in tough, gummy clods on the bars, constantly filling the ship channels or causing them to shift about.

Farragut's trim sloops, the *Hartford,* the *Brooklyn,* and the *Richmond,* had little trouble negotiating Southwest Pass, but the *Pensacola* and the *Mississippi,* even after a trip to Ship Island to lighten them, proved difficult. The plan was to heel over the *Pensacola* and to pull her through on her side. Porter's mortar steamers thus dragged her part of the way across the bar when the vessel's pilots waved Porter's towing vessels aside. The *Pensacola* now barged ahead under full steam and, running aground on a sunken wreck a hundred yards off the main channel, nosed over so far that her spinning screws were exposed. "The fool of a first Lt. and a very ignorant and gassy Pilot, who never cast a lead," Porter reported to Fox, "overshadow the old Captain and if they don't get in they will have no one to blame but themselves. Neither skill nor energy has been displayed in the management of that vessel; there are too many 'can't do this' and 'can't do that' to expect much from her." [16] Porter, pocketing his disgust, once more hitched three or four of his steamers in tandem and tugged at the distressed ship. But neither the *Pensacola* nor the side-wheeler *Mississippi,* which could not be careened without smashing a wheel, was brought through until a strong southerly breeze the second week in April raised the water on the bar almost enough to float them.

After his ships had crossed over the bar, Farragut's coal arrived, so that he was able to begin the attack.

Fleet Captain H. H. Bell he sent to examine the Confederate defenses, eighteen miles north of the Head of the Passes. The first barrier Bell found to be a chain of hulks across the river below the forts. A few months earlier the defenders had blocked the river with a raft of logs joined by underslung chains, but the raft had been carried away by the tremendous weight of driftwood that had piled against it during recent floods. In its place was a barrier composed of seven anchored hulks chained together at the bow. Of these the masts and rigging had been chopped away and allowed to trail astern to foul an enemy's propellers. Captain Bell noted that trees along the bank had been felled to give Fort Jackson's heavy casemated guns a clear sweep down the river.

From General Butler, who had sent a landing party ashore at Biloxi, Mississippi, Farragut received a batch of New Orleans newspapers which attested the Confederate belief that New Orleans was unassailable from below. "The Mississippi is fortified so as to be impassable for any hostile fleet or flotilla." "Forts Jackson and St. Philip are armed with one hundred and seventy heavy guns." The *Merrimack*'s phenomenal success of March 8 had given the people of New Orleans confidence in the iron-sheathed vessels they were themselves building. "In a day or two we shall have ready two iron-cased floating batteries. . . . Each iron-cased battery will mount twenty sixty-eight pounders, placed so as to skim the water, and striking the enemy's hull between wind and water. We have an abundance of incendiary shells, cupola furnaces for molten iron, congreve rockets and fire-ships. Between New Orleans and the forts there is a constant succession of earthworks." [17]

At Pilot Town, a muddy village on South West Pass whose houses were perched precariously on posts to keep them above floodwater, Farragut placed all the inhabitants on parole and requisitioned several buildings as storage sheds for masts, spars, and other gear not wanted up the river, and he prepared other dwellings for possible use as hospitals.

To his captains he now issued detailed instructions for preparing the ships for action. "I wish you to understand," he concluded, "that the day is at hand when you will be called upon to meet the enemy in the worst form for our profession. . . . I expect every vessel's crew to be well exercised at their guns. . . . Hot and cold shot will no doubt be freely dealt to us, and there must be stout hearts, and quick hands. . . . I shall expect the most prompt attention to signals and verbal orders. . . ." [18]

11.

The Seizure of New Orleans

FORT JACKSON, THE LARGER OF THE CONFEDERATE strongholds, was a star-shaped pentagon of brick 110 yards on a side with bastions at the corners. The U. S. Army engineers who built it, being sticklers for blueprints, surrounded it with a wet ditch, although the fort was mired down in swamp. Within its two curtains which bore on the river, Fort Jackson had twenty-four smoothbores and howitzers in casemate.[1] When perfectly horizontal, these guns, owing to the fort's foundations having settled into the ooze, were just about on a level with the top of the levee. They could fire horizontally and strike Farragut's ships somewhere above the water line, but could not be depressed enough to hull them "between wind and water." These guns were encased beneath vaulted roofs and could not be put out of action by Porter's mortar shells. Up on the parapets, however, and in her adjacent water battery, Fort Jackson had forty-two guns which were open to the sky. To smother these guns the mortars would be useful.

Fort St. Philip on the opposite side of the river was an antiquated, Spanish-built fortification, to which had been added modern bombproof magazines and shelters. Fort St. Philip had only forty-nine guns bearing on the river, all in barbette and exposed to mortar fire. But St. Philip was favorably placed on the kneecap of the bend in the river so that its guns commanded a longer sweep of the river than Jackson's. Farragut would have to head directly toward St. Philip's guns

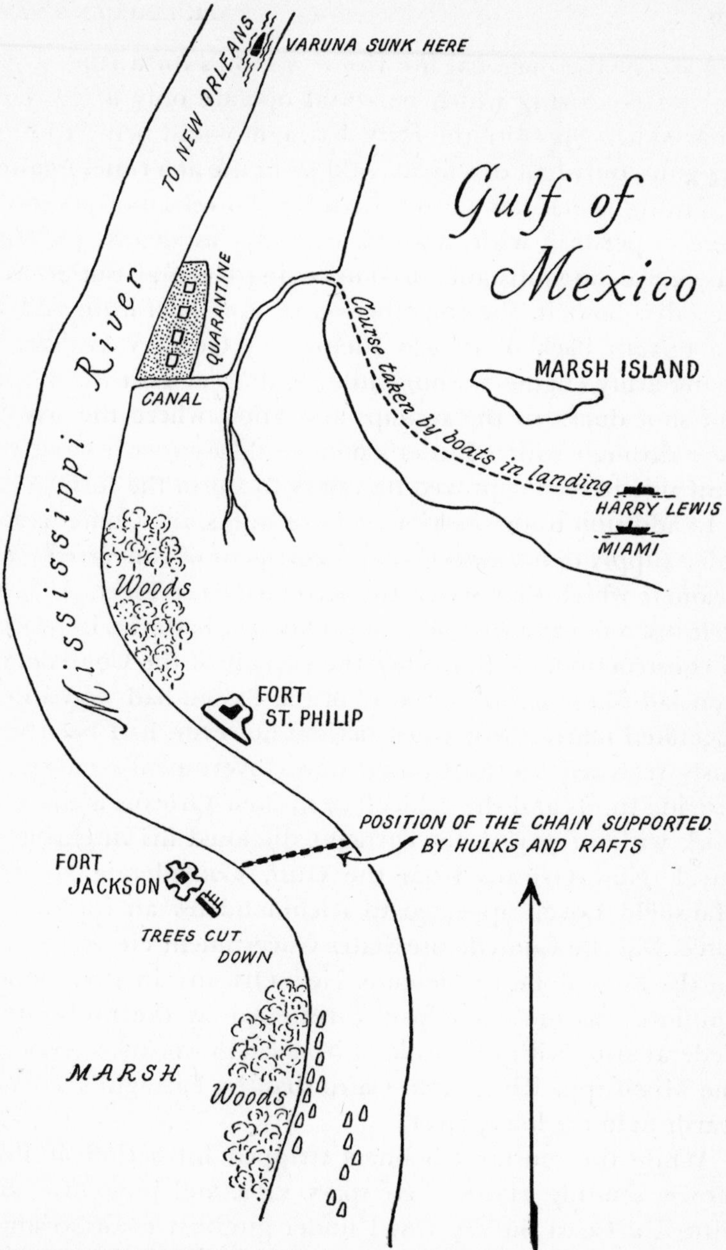

THE NEW ORLEANS FORTS. After Farragut ran the gantlet, Butler's troops landed from the Gulf side at Quarantine, to isolate Forts Jackson and St. Philip.

and accept the diagonal fire from Jackson's for a run of several miles, during which he could operate only a few bow guns. When opposite the forts, Farragut could bring to bear 154 guns, only half of which could be in use at a time. Against St. Philip, which was 3,680 yards away, Porter's mortars could scarcely perform with the same efficiency as against Jackson, only 2,850 yards distant. Accompanying General Butler, as a specialist both in the construction of Fort St. Philip and in the terrain back of it, was Lieutenant Godfrey Weitzel, a young army engineer who, while on duty at Fort St. Philip, had shot ducks in the swamps and knew where the bayous were through which Butler's men could approach from the Gulf side in case it proved necessary to storm the fort.

In addition to the barrier chain of hulks, the Confederates had a supply of fire rafts and an assortment of converted river steamers which they styled the River Defense Fleet. At New Orleans, too, were several ironclad floating batteries in process of construction.[2] These, since the exploit of the Confederate ironclad *Manassas* at the Head of the Passes, had won an exaggerated fame. Their construction, however, had been seriously retarded by the Confederate Government's failure to provide funds and the reluctance of New Orleans artisans to work without pay. After Farragut disclosed his intention to attack New Orleans from the Gulf, Confederate General Mansfield Lovell appealed to Richmond for an increase of force. But the Confederate States Government elected to rely on the forts alone for defense. New Orleans, in Richmond's opinion, was more seriously threatened by the midwestern Federal army with its flotilla of ironclad gunboats descending the Mississippi River from Cairo than by Farragut's wooden warships in the lower river.

While the mortar schooners stripped for action at Pilot Town, sending ashore their spars, sails, and inessential furniture, a Coast Survey vessel under gunboat escort triangulated the river below the forts to mark positions and ranges for the mortar schooners. There was bitter fighting between boats' crews protecting the surveyors and Confederate sharpshooters in the flooded forest who sniped at the Federals by day and removed their surveyors' markers by night.

A *New York Times* reporter, impressed by the energy displayed in mosquito-infested Pilot Town, wrote: "The mortar captains, a jolly set of fellows, may become ill . . . if something is not done soon. They begin to fret at the lack of opportunity for ridding themselves of the large amount of superfluous energy with which they are imbued." [3] Regular sea dogs in Farragut's squadron shook their heads and predicted that the bottoms of the mortar schooners would drop out at the tenth fire. But these oldsters approved of the smart dress parade which Porter staged when he towed his schooners up the river to battle positions. "They looked very pretty," confessed a seaman on the *Hartford,* "as they ranged along the shore in line of battle, with their flagship, the *Harriet Lane,* at their head." [4]

The three divisions of the flotilla were anchored in marked positions. The First and Third Divisions under Lieutenants Watson Smith and K. R. Breese were placed along the western bank below the lower limit of Fort Jackson's casemate fire and were sheltered behind cottonwood trees laden with vines. The Second Division under Lieutenant W. W. Queen was moored on the east bank in a position exposed but favorably located for attacking Fort St. Philip. The crippling of two vessels in this group shortly after the bombardment began caused Porter to place it below the other divisions against the western bank.

The bombardment, continuing past the anticipated forty-eight hours, lasted for six days and nights. The schooners dressed their tops with bushes, both to hide masts and to shield spotters who perched aloft to check accuracy of firing. Trees on shore shortly became black with powder dust, as did the gunners themselves. "The enemy's fire was excellent," wrote General J. K. Duncan, commander of the forts, "a large proportion of his shells falling within Fort Jackson. The . . . parapets and platforms were very much cut up, as well as much damage done to the casemates. The magazines were considerably threatened, and one shell passed into the casemate containing fixed ammunition." [5]

After rowing up the river the first night to check on damages, Porter was convinced that the mortars alone might compel a surrender. Farragut permitted him to prolong his firing, especially since the high wind now blowing from the north would retard vessels in passing the forts. Shot from Fort Jackson tore through the point of forest which shielded the "bombards," splintering and uprooting trees. As rapidly as the brush was stripped from the schooners' masts, it was replaced by the powder-streaked gunners. Here and there a vessel's crew would take time out to sleep on a quivering deck not twenty feet from their next neighbor's thundering mortar.

Porter found that too many shells exploded in midflight. After fruitlessly struggling to adjust the length of the unreliable fuses, he finally put in full-length fuses to burst the shells after they had entered the ground. The swamp had encroached upon the fort as a result of bomb damage and recent rains, and the bombshells, after embedding themselves twenty feet in the ground, blew geysers of mud into the air, "not doing a great deal of harm, but demoralizing the men." [6]

To obtain relief from the concentrated rain of thirteen-inch mortar shells, General Duncan sent fire barges down the river and made repeated calls upon Commander J. K. Mitchell of the Confederate ironclad battery *Louisiana* to bring down from New Orleans his uncompleted vessel to draw some of the fire away from the forts. Commander Mitchell shifted his ironclad with workmen and tenders to a mooring half a mile above Fort St. Philip, where work on her was continued.[7] Although 150 men were now detailed from the forts to man the ironclad's guns, the vessel's engines were not functioning, so that she could not be employed against Farragut. Fire rafts at first caused confusion among Farragut's closely packed vessels. Several ships collided or lost anchors in working clear of these menaces. But the Federals developed a system for grappling and dowsing or towing the barge torches clear of the fleet. One night the crews of fifty small boats quenched an inferno by pouring on buckets of water and salvaged a barge load of fat pine logs. Another night a fire raft that had been guided through the fleet ignited the trees for half a mile along the bank where it was brought to rest.

On the night of April 20 Farragut sent Captain Bell, his fleet captain, up the river to break the chain barrier. In the swift current and under fire of the forts, Bell's vessels fouled the obstructions, ran aground, and broke electric wires leading to petards placed on the hulks, but one of his gunboats, after slipping the chain over the bow of a hulk, rammed into the chain and broke it, opening a gap in the barrier wide enough for the fleet to enter in single file.

In preparation for running past Forts Jackson and St. Philip, all of Farragut's ships hung sheet cables up and down on the sides as a sort of loosely woven chain mail to protect their engines. And, since they would be exposed to raking fire from the forts before they could bring their own broadsides into action, each commander tried to stop fore and aft shot from penetrating boilers or machinery by packing in exposed areas clothes bags and hammocks, sacks of ashes, sand, and coal. Some lined their bulwarks with hammocks, others with splinter nettings of woven rope. Some rubbed their vessels with mud to make them less visible, and whitewashed their gundecks to make tackle, marline spikes, and ammunition visible without use of lanterns.

Farragut organized his attack squadron into three divisions: Bailey's flying the red pennant, Farragut's the blue, and Bell's the red and blue. These groups were constituted as follows: [8]

RED DIVISION—Captain Theodorus Bailey

Cayuga, screw gunboat, 507 tons, 2 guns, Lieutenant N. B. Harrison

Pensacola, screw sloop, 2,158 tons, 23 guns, Captain H. W. Morris

Mississippi, side-wheeler, 1,692 tons, 17 guns, Captain M. Smith

Oneida, screw corvette, 1,032 tons, 9 guns, Commander S. P. Lee

Varuna, screw corvette, 1,300 tons, 10 guns, Commander C. S. Boggs

Katahdin, screw gunboat, 507 tons, 2 guns, Lieutenant G. H. Preble

Kineo, screw gunboat, 507 tons, 2 guns, Lieutenant G. M. Ransom

Wissahickon, screw gunboat, 507 tons, 2 guns, Lieutenant A. N. Smith

Blue Division—Flag Officer David G. Farragut

Hartford, screw sloop, 1,990 tons, 24 guns, Commander R. Wainwright

Brooklyn, screw sloop, 2,070 tons, 22 guns, Captain T. T. Craven

Richmond, screw sloop, 1,929 tons, 24 guns, Commander J. Alden

Red and Blue Division—Captain Henry H. Bell

Sciota, screw gunboat, 507 tons, 2 guns, Lieutenant E. Donaldson

Iroquois, screw corvette, 1,016 tons, 7 guns, Commander J. DeCamp

Pinola, screw gunboat, 507 tons, 2 guns, Lieutenant P. Crosby

Kennebec, screw gunboat, 507 tons, 2 guns, Lieutenant J. H. Russell

Itasca, screw gunboat, 507 tons, 2 guns, Lieutenant C. H. B. Caldwell

Winona, screw gunboat, 507 tons, 2 guns, Lieutenant E. T. Nichols

Bailey's division, with the stout *Pensacola* and the *Mississippi,* was expected to pass close by and devote its chief attention to Fort St. Philip. Farragut, with the three heaviest broadsides of the fleet, planned to concentrate upon Fort Jackson; while Bell with the light gunboats, primarily useful for maneuvering in the upper river, would simply sprint upstream while covered by the first two divisions.

During Farragut's attempt to run the gantlet, the mortars behind Point of Woods were to increase their rate of fire; and Porter, with six of the light steamers of the Mortar Flotilla, was to move up into an exposed position close to the barrier and enfilade Fort Jackson's water battery. The attacking steamers under Commander David D. Porter were: [9]

Harriet Lane, side-wheeler, 619 tons, 3 guns, Lieutenant J. M. Wainwright
Westfield, ex-ferryboat, 891 tons, 6 guns, Commander W. B. Renshaw
Owasco, screw gunboat, 507 tons, 2 guns, Lieutenant J. Guest
Clifton, ex-ferryboat, 892 tons, 7 guns, Lieutenant C. H. Baldwin
Miami, double-ender, 730 tons, 5 guns, Lieutenant A. D. Harrell
Jackson, ex-ferryboat, 777 tons, 7 guns, Lieutenant S. E. Woodworth

At 2:00 A.M. on April 24, two dull red lanterns hung from the mizzen peak of the flagship *Hartford* signaled to the fleet to get under way, but, because of difficulty in purchasing their anchors, the line did not begin moving until after three. Captain Bailey, in his little "pilot fish" *Cayuga,* led the procession through the gap in the barrier at 3:30. A quarter of an hour later the forts opened fire. The *Cayuga* sped through the area of danger between the forts in fifteen minutes and was struck forty-two times. Her masts were mangled, smokestack riddled, but, with her crews prone on deck when not serving her two guns, she came through with only six wounded.

In the blackness the slower *Pensacola* lost sight of the leading gunboat, and, after cruising close alongside of her appointed target, Fort St. Philip, lost her bearings and sheered to the opposite side of the river where she came under the cross fire of both forts. Lieutenant Roe, who conned the ship, saw gun crews decimated with horrible groans, shrieks, and wails. "My signal quartermaster and my boy aid (Flood) were both swept away from my side. The quartermaster lost his leg by a cannon ball . . . shell burst all about me. At daylight I found the right leg of my pantaloons and drawers cut away by the knee, and the skirt of my coat cut in a strip; yet my body was untouched." [10] The muzzles of the *Pensacola*'s guns almost scraped the plated sides of the dreaded Confederate *Manassas,* but this turtle-backed ironclad ran on downstream squaring off for a bout with the side-wheeler *Mississippi.*

The Confederate ram attempted to butt the port paddle wheel of the *Mississippi* and was balked in her effort by Lieutenant George Dewey who maneuvered the big ship so skillfully that she received only a glancing blow on her quarter. The future hero of Manila Bay, leaning far out over the rail, saw in the lurid light from shellburst and fire raft, where planks had been ripped off his vessel, about fifty gleaming ends of copper bolts "cut as clean as if they were hair under a razor's edge." [11] A few minutes after the *Manassas* had made a feint toward the flagship, Farragut hailed the *Mississippi* to run down the ram. The *Mississippi,* quickly backing one wheel and driving forward the other, turned on her axis and dashed after the *Manassas* only to see her plough into the river bank. The *Mississippi* poured two broadsides into the stalled Confederate and left her breathing out smoke through a row of fresh punctures that resembled portholes.

The Confederate tug *Mosher* pushed a fire barge toward the flagship, in attempting to avoid which Farragut's ship ran aground. The inferno continued to be shoved against the grounded ship. Flames blowing through the ports and running up the rigging endangered the *Hartford* as much as the gunfire of the forts which was now concentrated against her. But she extinguished her flames, backed herself free of the bank, and proceeded upstream, her gunners the while never slacking in the broadsides they delivered to the forts.

In the darkness and blinding smoke the captain of the *Brooklyn,* next in line after the *Hartford,* lost sight of the latter, missed the gap in the barricade, and crashed over one of the anchored hulks. "For a few moments I was entangled and fell athwart the stream, our bow grazing the shore on the left bank of the river," wrote Captain T. T. Craven. "Whilst in this situation I received a pretty severe fire from Fort St. Philip. Immediately after extricating my ship from the rafts her head was turned upstream and a few minutes thereafter she was feebly butted by the celebrated ram *Manassas.* She came butting into our starboard gangway, first firing from her trapdoor when within about 10 feet of the ship, directly toward our smokestack, her shot entering about 5 feet above the water line and lodging in the sandbags which protected our steam drum. I had discovered this queer-looking gentleman while forcing my way over the barricade, lying close in to the bank, and when he made his appearance the second time I was so close to him that he had not an opportunity to get up his full speed, and his efforts to damage me were completely frustrated, our chain armor proving a perfect protection to our sides. He soon slid off and disappeared in the darkness." [12]

Above the forts there was a brief melee between Farragut's van ships and the Confederate River Defense Fleet. These latter river craft and steam tugs, some of them fitted with rams and light metal plating across the bow, made a heroic struggle. The *Governor Moore,* under Confederate Lieutenant Beverly Kennon, twice rammed the Federal *Varuna,* and, being unable otherwise to aim his pivot gun at his target, fired downward through his own vessel's bow. The *Varuna,* the only converted merchantman to attempt to run past the forts, was the only vessel sunk by the Confederates. Her skipper, Commander C. S. Boggs, ran her into the bank, let go her anchors, tied her to the trees, and, while she was slowly sinking, continued to operate her guns until the muddy water swirled around her gun trucks. Then he abandoned ship. Only three small gunboats at the rear of Farragut's line failed to get through. One was crippled by a boiler injury, and the others, daylight having arrived, found the wrath of the forts concentrated against them. By simply dropping their crews on deck, the *Kennebec,* the *Itasca,* and the *Winona* drifted downstream out of action.

At the quarantine station four miles above the forts, Farragut stopped long enough to bury his dead and temporarily plug the leaks in his vessels. His losses had been 36 killed and 135 wounded. To Porter he sent a cheerful note—"You supported us most nobly." [13] Leaving two gunboats to protect General Butler's landing of troops, Farragut pushed on toward the city of New Orleans. All the morning of the twenty-fifth his ships dodged the evidences of panic in New Orleans. "Cotton-loaded ships on fire came floating down, and working implements of every kind, such as are used in shipyards." [14] At the English Turn, the site of Andrew Jackson's victory over the British in 1815, Farragut discovered new earthwork forts on both shores. About 10:30 A.M., with his fleet in two lines, Farragut passed between these defenses. The river here was too narrow actually for two vessels to operate in tandem; his crews were so excited that the flag officer's greatest fear was that they would fire into each other. "Captain Wainwright and myself were hallooing ourselves hoarse at the men not to fire into our ships," Farragut wrote to Fox. But this engagement, "one of the little elegancies of the profession; a dash and a victory," was quickly decided and Farragut moved on up to the city and dropped anchor.[15]

Meanwhile, when Confederate General Mansfield Lovell at New Orleans learned of Farragut's passing the forts, he evacuated his troops from New Orleans, taking with them as much food and military stores as the retreating trains could carry. Then he ran a torch along the length of the levee. Patriotic citizens participated in the frenzy of destruction by emptying warehouses, tossing cotton on the fires, or staving in barrels of molasses and sugar and pouring them in the gutters. When Farragut arrived he found the levee "one scene of destruction; ships, steamers, cotton, coal, etc., were all in one common blaze, and our ingenuity much taxed to avoid the floating conflagration." [16]

"The river was filled with ships on fire," wrote the New York *Herald* reporter billeted on board the *Hartford,* "and all along the levee were burning vessels, no less than eighteen vessels being on fire at one time and the enemy firing others as fast as they could apply the torch. . . . The atmosphere was thick with smoke and the air hot with flames. It was a grand but sad sight. . . . At the levee just by the Custom House lay a burning ram (the *Anglo-Norman).* The unfinished frames of two or three more were on the stocks at Algiers [across the river]. . . . While men were hastening up the levee firing ships and river craft as fast as possible, the people were rushing to and fro. Some of them cheered for the Union, when they were fired upon by the crowd. Men, women and children were armed with pistols, knives and all manner of weapons. Some cheered for Jeff. Davis, Beauregard, etc., and used the most vile and obscene language toward us and the good old flag. Pandemonium was here a living picture." [17]

Farragut seized all steamboats that had not been destroyed and sent them down to quarantine to bring General Butler's troops to New Orleans. He ordered Lee of the *Oneida* to seek out the unfinished Confederate ironclad *Mississippi,* but that vessel, having already been set afire and cut from her moorings, presently drifted through the fleet in flames.

Captain Theodorus Bailey was sent ashore to demand surrender of the city. He could find no civil official willing to undertake that responsibility. Mayor John T. Monroe claimed that the city was ruled by General Lovell under martial law. Lovell, when summoned, returned the city to the mayor, as his troops had now departed. Monroe replied that he would not haul down the Louisiana State flag. Any citizen who did so, he avowed, would be mobbed. Lowering the Confederate flag "would have to be performed by the invading forces themselves." [18]

The Stars and Stripes emblem which Captain Morris of *Pensacola* raised over the United States Mint building was torn down by a group of hot Secessionists and desecrated. Farragut sent a battalion of marines to lower Secession flags and raise the Stars and Stripes over public buildings. To Mayor Monroe, Farragut wrote on the twenty-sixth: "I shall speedily and severely punish any person or persons who shall commit such outrages as were witnessed yesterday by armed men firing upon helpless women and children for giving expression to their pleasure at witnessing the 'old flag.' " To this Monroe answered that the people of New Orleans "do not allow themselves to be insulted" by deserters in their midst who "might remind them too forcibly that they are the conquered and you the conquerors. . . . Your occupying of the city does not transfer allegiance from the government of their choice to one which they have deliberately repudiated, and they yield the obedience which the conqueror is entitled to extort from the conquered." [19]

Meanwhile, for three days the situation below the forts was one of uncertainty. Farragut's fleet had gone to New Orleans leaving the forts unreduced and, in the absence of accurate information, the ram *Louisiana* was believed to be "as lively as ever." Under flag of truce Porter demanded surrender of the forts, and, the demand refused, he expended the remainder of his available ammunition in renewed bombardment. Then he sent the defenseless mortar schooners to Pilot Town twenty-five miles away and with his light steamers mounted guard behind the Point of Woods.

General Butler, with naval assistance, transferred the Twenty-sixth Massachusetts from inside the river below the forts, out through Pass a L'Outre, and around to a landing from the Gulf side behind Fort St. Philip. The troops made their way up a bayou known as Maunels Canal which empties into the Gulf and, after their galleys touched bottom, they waded the last mile and a half in water and mud that was sometimes hip deep. After they reached quarantine, some were ferried by Farragut's gunboats, the *Wissahickon* and the *Kineo,* across to the Fort Jackson side of the river. Both forts were thus cut off from their escape routes to New Orleans, since the flooded condition of the countryside left only these narrow trails of dry land along the levees which were now occupied by Federal troops.

At midnight on the twenty-seventh the troops in Fort Jackson seized the guards and posterns and turned their guns on the officers who sought to check their mutiny, and the next day General Duncan came off to the *Harriet Lane* and surrendered the forts. Because of disunity between the Confederate forces ashore and afloat, the Confederate ships were not included in the capitulation. While the surrender negotiations were in process between General Duncan and Commander Porter of the Mortar Flotilla, word was brought to the

Harriet Lane that the ironclad *Louisiana* had been set on fire and cast adrift. "This is sharp practice," Porter remarked to the Confederate officers, "but if you can stand the explosion when it comes we can. We will go on and finish the capitulation." [20] Several minutes after the signing was completed the boom of the explosion was heard. Everything in the cabin was jolted from side to side, but not an officer left his seat.

"New Orleans falling seems to have made a stampede in 'Secessia,' " Porter jubilantly wrote to Fox. "You may put the rebellion down as 'spavined,' 'broken-backed,' and 'wind-galled'. . . . You good people at home can go to work now cut down the Navy's pay, and disrate us to your heart's content. You will soon have no use for us in this contest." [21]

Butler's transports arrived in New Orleans on May 1, and Farragut turned over to the political general the arduous chore of governing New Orleans. Fortunately, Butler proved to be unusually gifted in what to the United States Army was then the novel science of military administration. Quasi-rebellious citizens were held in check. The destitute were fed. Law and order were made to prevail. The sanitary situation was corrected as it had never been before. And these matters were of no small import in view of the use to be made of New Orleans as a naval base for future operations both within the river and on the Gulf coast.

If Lincoln's Navy in seizing New Orleans had not yet suc ceeded in opening the Mississippi River and splitting the Confederacy in two, it had made a long stride in that direction.

12.

Early Operations on the "Inland Sea"

✓ ✓ ✓ ✓ ✓ ✓ ✓ ✓ ✓ ✓ ✓ ✓ ✓ ✓ ✓ ✓

At the outset of the war in the middle West, the Confederate States, adopting a strategy of perimeter defense, set up several small batteries overlooking the Mississippi River at Columbus, Kentucky, and built Forts Henry and Donelson on the Tennessee and Cumberland Rivers. Although single-track railroads had begun to stretch across the fields and forests of the Middle West, the rivers were still the natural arteries of this region. From the Southern strategists' point of view, the Mississippi, which bisected the Confederacy, and the Tennessee and Cumberland Rivers, which gave easy access into the heart of Tennessee, were the most dreaded paths of invasion.

Once the Confederate batteries had been erected at Columbus, Kentucky, the Federals, whether they wished to invade or not, were forced to take military action to open the Mississippi. Like an ax across the trunk of a tree, the Columbus batteries cut across the middle of the Mississippi's main stem, converting its upper reaches, the Ohio, the Missouri, and their many tributaries into an "inland sea" of navigable water many hundred miles in length. As early as January, 1861, when war became inevitable, the governors of Midwestern states had already forecast a bloody struggle among the canebrakes and wood yards of the lower Mississippi.[1] And after Fort Sumter, although the cotton states continued to "import" grain, cattle, and hogs from the North, it was manifest that the Confederate Government might at will dam up all outbound traffic from the inland sea by a simple order to commanders of the river forts. The Northern states had been long accustomed to cheap transportation by flatboat and river steamer. They considered rail freight rates prohibitive for shipping their bulky produce and in any case the railroads, now largely pre-empted by the military, were not equipped to take over the immense hauling job from the river craft.

To open the Mississippi, then, constituted for Lincoln's government vital economic and political objectives, as well as a prime military necessity.

Late in April, after Lincoln had proclaimed the blockade of the Southern coast line from Virginia through Texas, there appeared in Washington a spokesman from the Midwest who proposed a military blockade on the Western waters. He was James B. Eads, a prominent engineer of St. Louis who, as president of a wrecking company, was familiar with navigation on the river. Eads suggested that shore batteries be set up (1) at Cairo, where the southern arrow tip of Illinois thrusts into the confluence of the Mississippi and the Ohio, and (2) on the Illinois shore of the Ohio River opposite the mouths of the Tennessee and the Cumberland Rivers. Stop the southward flow of food and the cotton states would be starved out, Eads believed, in six months. Eads also offered to the government a large snag boat operated by his wrecking company to be converted into a floating battery or gunboat to enforce this blockade.[2]

Eads's ideas, originally submitted to the Navy, were relayed to the War Department. The latter, borrowing naval experts, undertook not only a blockade from fixed positions but a regular advance along the lines of the rivers into the heart of the South. The Eads snag boat was eventually converted into the largest ironclad on the rivers, and Eads himself built for the government four novel ironclad river gunboats that shortly made history in their battles against the Confederate perimeter forts.

Commander John Rodgers II, son of Commodore Rodgers of 1812, and a kinetic and efficient officer in his own right, was assigned to assist the Army at Cincinnati and was authorized to call upon the Navy for ordnance and crews. Unhappily for himself, Rodgers assumed that the gunboats were the navy's business. He stretched his slender measure of authority to include requisitions upon the Navy Department for money to buy boats and everything necessary to convert them. His charging the purchase price of three river steamers to the Navy Department brought him a prompt rebuke from Gideon Welles. Rodgers had been sent out "to aid, advise and cooperate" with the Army, Uncle Gideon snapped, to be under their direction *and at their expense*. Welles would supply navy guns and crews "but nothing further." [3]

The military commander of the Army of the West in these early days was Major General John C. Frémont, the famed "Pathfinder," presidential candidate, and political controversialist. As Frémont remained in his headquarters in St. Louis, Commander Rodgers saw little of him. Nevertheless, Rodgers managed to obtain War Department sanction for his purchases and personally scoured the countryside from Buffalo to Chicago for equipment and men. His three Ohio River steamers, the *Lexington,* the *Tyler,* and the *Conestoga,* splendid three-tiered wedding cakes of thin white pine topped with the usual carved woodwork, were cut down to one deck, and engines and boilers were lowered in the hull and shielded by bulwarks of five-inch oak, which made them musket-proof. These became useful patrol craft around the army's floating naval base at Cairo and plowed up and down the river to succor Union citizens from bands of Confederate marauders.

To obtain vessels for ascending the Tennessee and Cumberland Rivers against Fort Henry and Donelson, Rodgers, assisted by Naval Constructor Samuel M. Pook, worked out a simple plan of armor-clad gunboat: a rectangular paddle-wheeler, armored with two and one half inches of iron across the bow and half way back on either side. Later, for fighting downstream descending the Mississippi, it was planned to use mortar boats. Gustavus V. Fox, Assistant Secetary of the Navy, had suggested the mortar boats. Siege mortars, their operation already familiar to army men, were to be mounted on flatboats with reinforced hulls. Without engines of their own, they were to be hauled into firing position by tugs. General Frémont contracted for thirty-eight of these scows to be constructed in St. Louis, and their heavy guns and mortar platforms were scheduled to be cast in Pittsburgh.

In August, after four months of exhausting labor, Commander Rodgers had built the nucleus of the army's Western Flotilla, a mosquito fleet of three shallow-draft, musket-proof scout vessels. The exigencies of the situation in the West, however, had left him no time to observe amenities toward his punctilious superior, General Frémont. On August 9 the latter, through Postmaster General Blair, sent word to the President that he wished Rodgers removed. Lincoln, not yet ready to recall Frémont himself and sensing a certain amount of friction between the services, gave Mr. Welles the nod and the Secretary recalled Rodgers and sent in his place a salt-encrusted seaman, Captain Andrew H. Foote.

The latter, a Connecticut schoolmate and friend of Secretary Welles, was shifted from the Brooklyn Navy Yard to the ambivalent "command of the naval operations upon the Western waters, now organizing under the direction of the War Department." Foote was ordered to "place himself in communication with Major General John C. Frémont, U. S. Army, who commands the Army of the West" and to cooperate fully and freely with him as to his movements. Although Foote's requisitions were to be made upon the War Department, Welles promised to provide "whatever the Army can not furnish," if this could be done after supplying the squadrons on the coast.[4] Thus was Captain Foote tossed like his predecessor into the uncertainties of a new fresh-water command in which ships of novel type had yet to be built with army money and manned by field and forest hands who had yet to be recruited and trained.

When Foote assumed command on September 6, 1861, nine

ironclads, colloquially known as "Pook turtles" after Naval Constructor Pook, were in various stages of construction at river ports from St. Louis to Cincinnati. It disturbed Captain Foote that these river gunboats were armored only across their square bows and along the sides abreast of their engines. These partially iron-plated vessels were built for fighting headon and upstream, as when operating against Forts Henry and Donelson. But in moving downstream past hostile batteries, as at Columbus, Kentucky, they must perform the almost impossible ballet-step maneuver of keeping their protected bows always turned toward the enemy. Chances were that in the swirling currents these unwieldy craft would be swung around willy-nilly to present as targets their unarmored hindquarters.

For four months Captain Foote's chief business was to get the vessels built and obtain guns, powder, and crews. Secretary Welles did not have them to send during these early months. Establishing the salt-water blockade and mounting the expeditions to Hatteras, Port Royal, and New Orleans made it impossible for Lincoln's naval establishment on the seacoast to supply also the Western Flotilla. Failing to get naval ammunition for the *Lexington,* the *Tyler,* and the *Conestoga,* Foote was compelled to accept army powder, which was unsatisfactory. He even appealed to Governor Morton of Indiana to furnish the flotilla with suitable powder.

With Eads and the four other builders of the Pook ironclads Foote had little difficulty. Worries he had in plenty. Could the armored riverboats be floated over the several bars in the Ohio below Cincinnati, for instance? But he had no such troubles with the gunboats as he had with the mortar boats.

The day General Halleck relieved General Frémont, Captain Foote called on him at St. Louis. Halleck put him off till next day. Foote then requested categorical replies to three questions: "May I fit out the Mortar boats?" "Will you give me Captain Constable [to be in charge of them]?" "May I send Capt. Pike to Pittsburgh for the Mortars?" "No," answered Halleck to every question. "I have no authority and it cannot be done and I cannot give you an officer or a man." Foote urged further: "General Meigs says you have instructions and refers me to you about the Mortar and tug Boats." "General Meigs is mistaken," declared Halleck.[5]

Recruiting for the flotilla was retarded by lack of money. The crews of the *Lexington,* the *Tyler,* and the *Conestoga,* unpaid for two months, clamored for money for their destitute families. The War Department authorized the transfer to the flotilla of soldiers with naval experience, but army officers refused to permit such men to leave their companies. One group whom Foote had recruited and sent to St. Louis to take charge of the mortar boats was seized by General Halleck and impressed into a company of artillery in Sedalia, Missouri.

Foote was caught in an anomalous situation. He was in the War Department but not of it. Many army officers with whom he had to deal were ignorant of, and hostile toward, the work of his flotilla. To improve his bargaining position in dealing with army officers, Foote urged Fox to get for him the rank of flag officer. Since the Army of the West rated him with lieutenant colonels, every officer of higher grade could interfere with his movements. At Cairo, where he was without a base on shore but possessed only an establishment afloat, consisting of a wharf boat, a blacksmith boat, and a barge to house supplies for his flotilla, he had to fight to prevent a brigadier general from taking away his supply barge for other purposes! To Fox, Foote complained: "No imagination can fancy what it is to collect materials and fit out Western Gun Boats with Western men without a Navy Yard—in the West, where no stores are to be had." [6]

By January of 1862, when the army's campaign on the Western rivers was scheduled to begin, the mortar scows were lined up off the levee at Cairo, but their mortars and mortar beds or platforms were not yet ready. Through lack of funds, through dilatoriness of Halleck and others, the Western Flotilla was without one of its major weapons.

Fox brought the matter to the attention of the President.

Lincoln was quick to grasp the nature of the interservice friction which had handicapped Captain Foote. By telegraph Lincoln lighted a bonfire under the contractor at Pittsburgh.

"The President is very much exercised in the matter, and I do not blame him," Fox reported to Foote on January 27. "He telegraphed to Pittsburgh and they replied that *two* [mortar] beds were ready. I doubt if the history of any war ever furnished such an exposure." [7] To keep immediately in touch with the situation in the flotilla, Lincoln directed Captain Foote to send him a daily report by telegraph, "stating the progress or lack of progress in the mortar business." [8] The daily message was sent through H. A. Wise, an assistant in the Naval Ordnance Bureau, who either carried the telegram to the White House or showed it to John Hay, one of Lincoln's secretaries, with whom Wise frequently lunched.

Wise assured Foote that his almost superhuman efforts were now appreciated by his friends in Washington "from the President down," and that, with regard to the mortar rafts, "Uncle Abe, as you already know, has gone into that business with a will, making his first demonstration *entre nous,* by pitching General Ripley out of his [War Department] Ordnance Bureau. . . . Yesterday a.m. came your second telegram, which I immediately sent to the White House. . . ." [9]

Henceforth, telegrams to the White House became a regular feature of Captain Foote's day, by means of which Foote obtained prompt action not only upon mortars but upon steamboat purchases, transfer of seamen from the Army, carpentry and machine work on the gunboats, procurement of supplies, and every other aspect of flotilla business as well. Even Secretary Welles fell into the new quickstep and found it possible to divert a contingent of regular salt-water officers and seamen to man the river gunboats. And, through the diplomatic efforts of the ever-cooperative Assistant Secretary, Captain Foote's title was inflated to "Flag Officer of the Western Flotilla."

The first week in February, winter's ice having cleared away and early rains swelling the streams, Flag Officer Foote set out from Cairo to test four of his new ironclad gunboats. These were the *Cincinnati,* flagship, under Commander R. N. Stembel; the *Essex,* under Commander W. D. Porter; the *Carondelet,* under Commander H. A. Walke; and the *St. Louis,* under Lieutenant Commander Leonard Paulding. With these went also the veterans of the mosquito fleet: the *Conestoga,* under Lieutenant Commander S. L. Phelps; the *Lexington,* under Lieutenant Commander J. W. Shirk; and the *Tyler,* under Lieutenant Commander William Gwin.

It was to be the first time that American-built ironclads had been tested in battle and the first time that any American naval officer had fought in such craft. Moreover, this first hot experimental battle against Fort Henry was to be the opening move in the Western Army's first campaign. On passenger steamers Brigadier General U. S. Grant's army of seventeen thousand followed the gunboat convoy as it moved up the Ohio and turned right into the Tennessee.

With Foote's aid, Grant had persuaded the reluctant General Halleck to adopt the following strategy: Grant, with gunboat support, was to attack the Confederate center at Fort Henry, isolating the strong Confederate wing positions at Columbus and Bowling Green. After Foote's ironclads had punched through Fort Henry, his light craft were to ascend the Tennessee River as far as Muscle Shoals, capturing and destroying enemy boats and stores, and knocking out the bridge of the Memphis and Clarksville Railroad. Grant's troops, meanwhile, were immediately to move eleven miles east of Fort Henry to invest Fort Donelson, while Foote's ironclads ascended the Cumberland to assist with their heavy ordnance. Fort Donelson subdued, the capital of Tennessee, Nashville, would be uncovered.

Ascending the mud-yellow Tennessee River, the black iron gunboats, each measuring 175 by 51½, with draft of 6 feet, picked their way around snags, inundated trees, and other navigational hazards. On February 6, as they rounded Panther Island, just before reaching the Tennessee state line, they discovered two miles in the distance the low lines of Fort

Henry on the east bank. Grant disembarked his troops below the gunboats with the intent of circling to attack the fort from the rear while Foote's guns hammered it from the water. The soldiers marched to the beat of drums and brass bands and sang national airs, but, as the forest was drowned by back-waters, their progress was slow and they arrived too late for the combined assault.

Foote's four ironclads moved abreast toward the fort, with shutters open and eleven heavy cannon protruding through their forward gunports.[10] At 12:36 P.M. these bow guns began a duel with the fort that lasted an hour and a quarter, in which the ships moved slowly upstream firing at ranges diminishing from seventeen hundred to six hundred yards. The din of cannon from fort and gunboats reverberated through the forest, muffling the labored puffing of the steamers and the swish of paddle wheels that pushed the heavy craft upstream.

Shot after Confederate shot clanged against slanted black Federal armor. Midway in the fight, a ball entering one of the ports of the *Essex* clipped off the skull of the captain's aide and coursing aft exploded a boiler. Escaping steam painfully scalded Commander William D. Porter, two pilots, and thirty others, and the vessel drifted downstream out of action. Commander Porter, a brother of Commander D. D. Porter of the Mortar Flotilla below New Orleans, was a tough and ingenious sea dog. Returning from the Pacific to find his wife gone South and his sons in the Confederate Army, William Porter had obtained a divorce and an appointment to command the *Essex*. The distinctive feature of the *Essex,* which rendered her so vulnerable in river fighting, was that Porter had rigged every mechanical device on board to be powered by steam. With boilers shot, she could not even operate her bilge pumps. Small wonder that in fright several of her scalded seamen jumped overboard and were drowned. The *Cincinnati,* flying Foote's pennant, received seventeen hits, suffered scratches on casemate and armored pilothouse, and minor perforations in chimneys and unarmored upper works.

The *Cincinnati* lost one killed, nine wounded; the *Essex* one killed and thirty-eight casualties from steam and drowning. The *St. Louis* and the *Carondelet,* though receiving seven and six hits respectively, sustained no casualties.

Inside Fort Henry, whose guns were no match for Foote's, Confederate General Lloyd Tilghman fought a delaying action to permit the main portion of the garrison to retire upon Fort Donelson. Wooden cabins within and back of Fort Henry were turned into torches, walls were breached, guns dismounted. At 1:55 P.M., an hour before Grant's men had slogged through the muddy woods, Tilghman raised a white flag.

The Confederate Commander, wringing his hands, came on board the *Cincinnati* to surrender. Foote assured Tilghman that he had defended his post like a brave man and quietly led him by the arm into his cabin for dinner.

"Another fort knocked over by the Navy is my reward," jubilated Fox, forgetting that the Western Flotilla belonged to the Army.[11] Foote's telegram announcing the victory was sent immediately to Congress, where it was read in both houses and "gave intense satisfaction." Secretary Welles sent the Navy Department's "profound thanks." Wise, the ordnance inspector who had carried Foote's daily messages to the President, reported to Foote: "Uncle Abe was joyful, and said everything of the navy boys and spoke of you—in his plain, sensible appreciation of merit and skill. You will be . . . made a flag-officer for life." [12]

The Sunday following the victory at Fort Henry, Flag Officer Foote, who was back in Cairo to repair his vessels, attended services in a little Presbyterian church. The minister being absent, the newly famous first American flag officer to fight in an ironclad vessel ascended into the pulpit and preached a sermon on: "Let not your hearts be troubled; ye believe in God, believe also in me," a text which Foote's little niece living in Cleveland is said to have changed to: "Ye believe in God, believe also in gunboats." [13]

When General Grant pushed on immediately to invest

Fort Donelson on the Cumberland, he realized that this position was much more powerful than that of Fort Henry. The latter had been improperly located on low ground with two miles of marsh behind it. By contrast Donelson was built on a series of rolling hills with batteries strategically mounted on their crests, the whole surrounded by flooded creeks, abatis of felled trees, and extensive entrenchments. Reinforced by the garrison from Fort Henry, it was stronger now than ever. Grant's first concern was to isolate Donelson to prevent its receiving further reinforcements from either of the Confederate wing positions at Columbus and Bowling Green.

In isolating Fort Donelson, Grant employed Foote's flotilla like cavalry. While Foote returned to Cairo to repair the injuries on the *Cincinnati* and the *Essex,* his three mosquito boats under Lieutenant Commander S. L. Phelps ranged up the Tennessee River, destroying Confederate military supplies, capturing the *Eastport,* a partially built Confederate ironclad, and other river boats. Since Phelps failed to destroy the railroad bridges (the Memphis to Bowling Green at Danville and the Memphis to Chattanooga at Florence, Alabama), Grant dispatched Commander Walke in the ironclad *Carondelet* to destroy the first of these bridges and cut off Donelson from support coming from Columbus on the west. He then ordered the *Carondelet* around to the Cumberland River in the hope that she might be able to pass up above Fort Donelson and isolate it while Grant's troops invested the fort on its land faces. The *Carondelet* was checked, however, by Donelson's stair-stepped batteries along the river.

On the theory that his fifteen thousand men today were worth more than fifty thousand next month, Grant hemmed in Fort Donelson's garrison of twenty-one thousand and called for immediate help from the gunboats. Grant's men were without tents in sleeting weather and many had foolishly discarded their blankets on the march from Fort Henry. To support Grant, Foote found it necessary to shift crewmen from his disabled vessels to two new ironclads just completed, the *Louisville* and the *Pittsburg*—an unpopular necessity which prompted three dozen of his men to desert the flotilla. Against his own better judgment, the flag officer hastened up the Cumberland, convoying Grant's reinforcements as he went.

Foote's problem at Fort Donelson was to silence the three tiers of batteries on the river bluffs, and, thrusting upstream past the fort, to enfilade Confederate rifle pits on their left wing in conjunction with Grant's assault.[14] The Cumberland was narrower than the Tennessee and in its swifter currents the unwieldy gunboats lurched about. One gunboat lobbed a shell into another because of an unexpected swirl in the current. Foote attacked at 3:00 P.M. on February 14 with four ironclads: the *St. Louis,* flagship, the *Carondelet,* the *Louisville* and the *Pittsburg;* and two wooden gunboats: the *Tyler* and the *Conestoga.* As at Fort Henry, the ironclads fought in line abreast with bows toward the enemy batteries. The wooden vessels remained behind them, firing at extreme range. In a contest lasting an hour and a half, Foote's gunboats repeatedly drove the Confederate gunners back from their batteries, but they always returned as soon as the flotilla slackened its fire. Moreover, Confederate cannon on a fifty-two-foot elevation had a distinct advantage when Foote moved up within four hundred yards, for, at this distance, the line of fire against the ironclads' shields becoming almost a right angle, they were able to penetrate the iron targets. One of the *Carondelet*'s rifled guns burst during the engagement, and her steering gear was disabled by a shot in her wheelhouse. The *Pittsburg* received several shots in her hull, forward of her casemate, and a 128-pound shot in her pilothouse which sent her out of action. Shipping water, she had to shift guns aft to raise her injured bow out of water. One of the fifty-nine shots that found its way into the flagship *St. Louis* carried away her steering wheel and injured the flag officer by a painful splinter wound on the left foot. Both the *St. Louis* and the *Louisville,* whose tiller ropes were cut, drifted helplessly downstream. The remaining boats, nursing injuries, fell out of action a few minutes later.

On the sixteenth, while Foote at Cairo was preparing to tow up mortar rafts, Grant launched a general attack and took Fort Donelson. General Simon B. Buckner was captured with 15,000 men. An estimated two thousand had fallen in battle.

Grant's "unconditional surrender" victories at Forts Henry and Donelson tore open the center of the Confederate defense line. Up the Cumberland River, Clarksville surrendered to Foote's gunboats on February 20. Nashville was abandoned in favor of a new point of defense at Murfreesboro, back from the gunboat-harried river. The first-line Confederate wing positions, Bowling Green and Columbus, were evacuated, and a new defense system, anchored on the Mississippi at Island No. 10, was formed, extending through Shiloh and Murfreesboro to Chattanooga.

The suddenness of victory at Fort Donelson alleviated somewhat Northern disappointment in the mechanical failures of the flotilla. Henceforth, every Union military commander in the West wanted gunboat support. But the vulnerability of these craft to shot descending from an elevation upon steam drums, paddle wheels, and steering ropes, and the penetrability even of their thinly armored casemates and pilothouses were lessons not lost on the Confederates. For several hundred miles along the Mississippi, the Confederates possessed hilltop positions that were ideal for planting cannon to control the river. And while Farragut hammered away at the forts below New Orleans and Foote, with his newfangled ironclads and mortar rafts, threatened their position at Island No. 10, the Southerners busied themselves erecting batteries overlooking the river's horseshoe turn at Vicksburg.

For a variety of reasons Flag Officer Foote resolved not to let every brigadier general interfere with him at Island No. 10. He now had assimilated rank with major generals in the Army. Although technically "on loan" to the Army, he had never ceased to report his acts to the Navy Department. Both Welles and Fox hailed his successes as "victories for the Navy." The flag officer's badly bruised foot kept him on crutches, and he was unable to get around freely for personal inspections. He suffered chronically from headaches, and the death of his thirteen-year-old son William early in March depressed him. Furthermore, the situation at Island No. 10 presented greater hazards to his gunboats than the up-river fighting, and Army men were too impatient when Foote insisted on making necessary repairs. On March 4, Foote, accordingly, stated his new policy to Secretary Welles: "I shall decline moving, as I informed Generals Sherman and Cullum, unless I am ordered to do so by the Secretary of the Navy, as I must be the judge of the condition of the fleet, and when it is prepared for battle." [15] Uncle Gideon backed him in his declaration of independence from army control: "Friend, how gratified I have been and am with what you have done." [16]

Island No. 10, fifty-nine miles below Cairo, lay in a loop of the Mississippi River a few miles above the village of Madrid, Missouri, and immediately opposite the sloughs and swamps along the northwest corner of the state of Tennessee. The Confederate land batteries on the island were supplemented by cannon on the so-called "pelican" dry dock brought up from New Orleans and moored off the lower end of the island, and along the Tennessee shore opposite was a series of water-level batteries, about a mile apart and mutually supporting one another. The entire system of defense, comprised of about seventy-five guns and six thousand men, was unapproachable by Federal land forces from the upper river because of the moat formed by river and swamp.

While Foote was repairing his disabled gunboats and finishing construction on his largest ironclad, the *Benton,* Major General John Pope cut a six-mile canal through drowned forest and seized New Madrid on the Missouri shore below Island No. 10. It was possible now for Pope, could he but ferry his men across the river, to cut off the garrisons of the batteries on the Tennessee shore. The Confederate troops had no exit from their batteries except along the river. But the river was too wide for Pope's own artillery to support his troops in this passage. Pope, therefore, peremptorily demanded that Foote send down an ironclad to guard his troop landing on the Tennessee shore. Foote doggedly refused.

To pass downstream an ironclad would have to present its unarmored stern to a succession of enemy batteries along a ten-mile stretch. Once below, it could not return upstream under its own power but would have to be towed by tugs or other unprotected craft. Furthermore, Foote's new ironclads lacked maneuverability, and the Confederates were known to have river vessels that were prepared to use ramming tactics. Foote insisted on delaying until he could be joined by his largest ironclad, the *Benton*. The powerful *Benton* would be able from a safe distance to protect the mortar rafts while they in turn pounded the Confederate batteries.

President Lincoln took a heightened interest in the affairs of the flotilla at this time. "Immediately upon the receipt of your telegram of yesterday," wrote Wise to Foote on February 25, "I read it to the President, who instructs me to say in reply that the reasons for the delay of the *Benton* are satisfactory, and that he appreciates your services, which meet his entire approbation." [17] Three days later Lincoln approved Foote's request for a large wharfboat, directed Halleck to send Foote's gunboats out of the Cumberland as rapidly as possible to be repaired, and ordered Quartermaster General Meigs to send extra funds to the flotilla. No favor was too trivial to enlist the President's attention and aid. He wished Foote to be fully prepared "to rain the rebels out" with "a refreshing shower of sulphur and brimstone." [18]

Throughout the latter half of March Foote tried a cautious, long-range bombardment of the island and the Tennessee shore. Lest any of his gunboats be disabled and drift helplessly through the gun-toothed jaws of Island No. 10, the flag officer lashed them together in pairs and trios. Thus, the flagship *Benton* was lashed between the *Cincinnati* and the *St. Louis*. In a battle on March 17 an eight-inch shot penetrated the *Benton's* plating and, after bounding around the lower deck, came to rest on the flag officer's writing desk. About the same time a rifled gun burst on board the *St. Louis,* killing and wounding fifteen, and the *Cincinnati's* engines were crippled so badly as to necessitate towing her to Cairo for repairs. Mortars on scows tied to trees on the western bank of the river rained thirteen-inch shells weighing 215 pounds each upon the Confederate positions. At night the mortar shells described fiery arcs across the sky like shooting stars, but their defective fuses—said to have been manufactured before the Mexican War—often caused them to burst prematurely. They dealt but little damage to their widely spaced targets.

On the night of April 1-2, Foote sent a boat party from the gunboats to surprise and spike the guns of the first fort on the Tennessee shore. The cutters from five of the gunboats, hugging shadows along the bank, were not discovered until within a few yards of the fort. Confederate sentinels fired two volleys and decamped into the woods while, in the swashbuckling style of Stephen Decatur at Tripoli, the men from the cutters boarded the enemy, spiked his cannon, and were off up the river in tow of the tug *Spitfire* before the startled defenders realized what was happening.

The success of this boat party was a prelude for the attempt three nights later to run the *Carondelet* past the Confederate batteries. Commander Henry Walke, scrounging timbers from an old barge, improvised a shield to protect his boilers and engines, and piled hay, lumber, and chain cables along the unarmored portions of his vessel's sides. A loaded coal barge was lashed to her port quarter to shield magazine and shell rooms. Her upper deck was piled with cordwood, bags of coal, surplus chains, and hawsers. Cables were wound about the pilothouse as high up as the windows. The *Carondelet,* it was reported, "looked like a farmer's team, preparing for market." [19]

The run was made on a black night under cover of a thunder storm. To minimize noise Commander Walke had made arrangements for the engineers to blow off steam in the covered wheelhouse rather than vent it as usual through the flues. The consequences of this piece of foresight was that soot dried in her chimneys and when she came abreast of the first Confederate battery a chimney blaze leaped out, illuminating the upper deck and everything around.

During the next half hour seventy-three Rebel guns opened upon the presumptuous Yankee, while from their distant moorings upstream Foote's gunboats and mortars fired at the flashing Confederate batteries. Through the blackness, riven by gunflash, chimney fire, shellburst, and lightning, the *Carondelet* raced to safety dragging her coal barge. She braved the danger as quietly, reported the New York *Herald,* as "a stray washtub being pelted with pebbles by a party of schoolboys." [20] Pelted she was, but not hit. Confederate missiles, aimed too high, whizzed over her.

Signal guns notified Flag Officer Foote when the *Carondelet* reached New Madrid. Soldiers here cheered Commodore Foote and Captain Walke. With impartiality they cheered even the Negro cabin boy who went ashore in the gig with the sailors. Soldiers caught up the sailors in their arms and passed them from one to another.

The *Carondelet*'s passage proved decisive. In company with the *Pittsburg,* which ran the batteries a few nights later, the Union ironclad fended off the Confederate River Defense Fleet and guarded the beachhead while General Pope's troops disembarked from transports on the Tennessee shore. Union General Pope now captured six thousand Confederate troops from the swamp-surrounded batteries whose sole route of escape had been along the river road to Tiptonville.

Foote had made a wonderful start toward opening the Father of Waters. After building a novel river flotilla of considerable striking power, he had been the first American naval commander to fight with the new ironclads. He had demonstrated that, though mechanically vulnerable, they could stand up to, and win against, land fortifications. He had shown that they could successfully bypass land batteries. Quartermaster General Meigs suggested that Foote ignore all the Confederate batteries on the Mississippi and run down to New Orleans with his gunboats, thus relieving the possible danger to Farragut's wooden fleet from the Confederate metal-plated vessels there. But Flag Officer Foote at fifty-six had aged under the strain of war on the rivers. His swollen foot required rest. Increasingly he fretted over long hours at his desk. Like the prophet Moses with the Promised Land in view, he felt compelled to turn over the leadership of the squadron to a more active leader.

The man he recommended, and whom Mr. Welles appointed, was Captain Charles H. Davis, whose affable manner would enable him to get on well with the Army and whose scientific caution would discourage unnecessary risks of the flotilla.

Davis had not long to wait for his first excitement.

At daybreak the morning after Davis took over the flotilla, a sharp action occurred near Fort Pillow.[21] For several weeks the mortars of the flotilla had been bombarding Fort Pillow, both from above and below the fort, and each group of mortar scows had one or two gunboats close by to protect it. At 6:00 A.M. on May 10, Confederate Commodore J. E. Montgomery, with eight vessels of the Confederate River Defense Fleet, appeared suddenly from around a curve in the river, bent upon cutting out the Federal ironclad *Cincinnati,* at the moment moored four miles below the *Benton.* Several nimble Confederate vessels, their bows lightly plated with iron for ramming, drove into her first from one side then another. The *Cincinnati* fired into her attackers and temporarily disabled them, but was compelled to beach herself in shoal water to keep from sinking. The ironclad *Mound City* was also damaged by ramming and had to be beached before the arrival of other gunboats forced the Confederate craft to retire.

Had the Union ironclads now possessed steam power in proportion to their dead weight, they might have collected several disabled Rebel vessels as prizes, but under the circumstances these damaged boats simply floated downstream and lived to fight again in the skirmish at Memphis on June 6.

Since Memphis was an "open" town, evacuated by the

military, the river fight here was not preceded by the pyrotechnics of mortar bombardment. But for the host of citizens who crowded its water front the melee was not without spectacle. At Memphis the Federal flotilla first used vessels fitted for ramming. The initiative in creating the so-called Ellet Ram Fleet had been taken by one Charles Ellet, a river man who had all sorts of zeal for the Union cause and absolutely no sense of danger. Lincoln, who admired daredevils with ingenuity, commissioned Ellet to purchase and convert river steamers suitable for his purpose, and to recruit and drill his own crews to man them. Without guns and relying solely upon speed, Ellet planned "to drive [his] rams against the enemy's armed vessels and transports wherever they can be found." [22]

Flag Officer Davis surprised eight craft of the Confederate River Defense Fleet at their Memphis moorings early on June 6. While his ironclads engaged them at long range, Colonel Ellet's swift rams, darting out from among the pachyderms, converted the affair into a running melee, lasting an hour and carrying the flotilla ten miles below the city. Of the eight Confederate steamers all but one were sunk or driven ashore and captured. The C.S.S. *Van Dorn* alone escaped down the river.

With the upper reaches of the Mississippi cleared of enemy forts and naval craft, Flag Officer Davis descended to the mouth of the Yazoo River, a few miles north of Vicksburg where, on July 1, he joined Flag Officer Farragut's seagoing warships that had just come up from New Orleans.

13.

Farragut on the River

AFTER THE OCCUPATION OF NEW ORLEANS IN early May, Farragut faced the difficult question of where to turn next. Should he ascend the Mississippi, join forces with the Western Flotilla, and clear the Rebels from the great river? Or should he attack Mobile? The river was now at flood stage. If his cumbersome salt-water ships went aground on the hundreds of shifting bars up the river and the water level should fall off, he could expect no presently incoming tide to float him, but must sit there, perhaps all summer, waiting for it to rain in Kansas. In the upper river, the armor-clad gunboats under Flag Officer Davis were infinitely better suited for inland work than the *Hartford* or the *Brooklyn,* and Farragut personally preferred to leave the opening of the interior waterways to Davis. Several of Farragut's best vessels were too heavy to go higher than New Orleans. In fact only his smaller gunboats were sufficiently light in draft for river work and their fire power was limited. If his wooden-hulled ocean ships encountered the Confederate ironclad rams, which were reported as being built at Memphis, they could hardly cope with them.

The dog-eared orders of January 20, framed by Welles and Lincoln before the New Orleans campaign, which Farragut consulted anew, did not resolve his dilemma. In fact, these ancient instructions squinted in both directions. "If the Mississippi expedition from Cairo shall not have descended the river, you will take advantage of the panic to push a strong force up the river to take all their defenses in the rear. You will also reduce the fortifications which defend Mobile Bay and turn them over to the army to hold." [1]

Farragut, splitting his forces, sent Porter's Mortar Flotilla to Mobile and Commander S. P. Lee with the *Oneida,* bearing nine guns, and several smaller gunboats up the river to Vicksburg. "My vessels are wanted everywhere," he wrote on May 3. "I have sent a force up the Mississippi to Vicksburg, and shall soon follow. I must protect this city [New Orleans], and I must send a large force to Mobile, where I must be present." [2]

Off Mobile the energetic Porter fumed and fretted at the flag officer's delay in coming to attack the forts, while in the river Captain T. T. Craven, the more senior skipper of the *Brooklyn,* envied young Lee his chance for personal distinction. As the weeks wore on, Captain Craven, an ambitious old man with a large family, began to resent his friend Farragut's penchant for giving more important commands to his juniors; but the flag officer did not sense this discontent until the climax of operations against Vicksburg, when Craven's failure to understand correctly his orders was construed by the half-sick and hot-tempered Farragut to have been deliberate.

On the way upstream, Farragut's gunboat captains demanded surrender of the river towns. Baton Rouge and Natchez, being undefended, allowed the Federals to raise the Union flag over their public buildings, but proud Vicksburg, having already mounted several batteries on her Chickasaw Hills, insultingly retorted "that Mississippians don't know and refuse to learn how to surrender to an enemy. If Commodore Farragut or Brigadier-General Butler can teach them, let them come and try." [3] Commander Lee gave the city twenty-four hours' notice in which to remove women and children to safety and instituted a strict blockade pending further orders from New Orleans.

Farragut, meanwhile, learned that the descent of the army's Western Flotilla was blocked by eighteen enemy gunboats at Memphis, where the Confederates had constructed an iron-cased ram. He dispatched a plea to Welles to send him all available steamers drawing less than sixteen feet, and, in company with a hastily improvised army attack force of fifteen hundred men under Brigadier General Thomas Williams, set out up the river.

There was now opened to the Federals a chance for a grand convergence upon Vicksburg which, if successful, might have won control of the Mississippi River. In mid-May of 1862, while the amphibian expedition of Farragut and Williams was proceeding northward from New Orleans and Davis with the Cairo ironclads was working downstream toward Memphis, Generals Halleck and Grant, with an army of 110,000, were waging their campaign against Corinth, Mississippi, a few hundred miles north and east of Vicksburg. It was necessary for the three Federal forces to close in quickly upon Vicksburg before the Confederates could entrench and mount new batteries, and before the seasonal drop in the water level should drive Farragut's great ships back toward the Gulf.

As he proceeded north, Farragut was not hopeful. Navigation difficulties worried him. The levees stood six feet above the surrounding plains, and inside the river the water swirled within a foot of the tops of the levees. From the deck of the flagship Farragut could see the heads of Negroes walking along the river road, and the lower halves of the slave cabins that lined the river were shut off from view by the embankment. "All the mansion grounds are densely shaded by live oaks, magnolias of rather a small growth, pecans and orange trees," Captain Bell noted in his diary, "nurseries for mosquitoes and chills and fevers. Dwellings generally low, with high-pitched roofs, galleries in front and rear. Live oaks are grand and gloomy by their thick foliage of deep green and long moss pendant from their boughs. . . . Not a token of friendship shown today except at one county seat, where they hoisted the Danish flag about 8 A.M." A gunboat captain who had preceded Farragut returned to report that the advanced gunboats were short of coal, and that the *Sciota* was having to repair an engine at Natchez. The enemy were sinking all their own coal or burning it in advance of the fleet. Beyond Baton Rouge the river became hourly more difficult, "every gunboat," Bell noted, "having grounded repeatedly, some of them three times a day." [4]

Licensed river pilots were not to be found. Farragut had to coerce into service as pilots ordinary rivermen from steamers or flatboats, "but they know little or nothing of the river's depth or channel for vessels of our draft." [5] The salt-water sailors who cast the leads were ignorant of "the feel" of the lead against the soft bottom of Old Muddy. The *Hartford* grounded at night at Tunica Bend, two hundred miles north of New Orleans, her green pilots having mistaken some flooded bushes on the mud bar for shadows of the more distant forest. With a draft of sixteen feet, Farragut's distressed flagship was now hard aground with but twelve feet of water under her bows and thirteen aft. Efforts to roll the ship by running her crew back and forth from port to starboard had no effect. Her guns and coal had to be shifted to other vessels. "I got her off in two days," Farragut reported to Welles, "but my health suffered from anxiety and loss of sleep." [6]

Coal became more difficult to obtain as the heavy ships made distance upstream, and wood as fuel would barely enable the warships to stem the current. To the complexities of procuring coal from transportation-short New Orleans were now added the seasonal river epidemics. Plagues of malaria and dysentery descended upon war craft and troopship. To cap his difficulties, the accompanying military force was ludicrously inadequate. General Williams had a mere handful of troops—fourteen hundred infantry and seventy-five artillerymen, with four field pieces—all that General Butler could find steamers for, all, in fact, that were not pinned down by necessary chores of the occupation in New Orleans or garrison duty in the captured forts. And this handful were packed on board the transports "more like livestock than men" in filth and dirt, as their commander testified, "to a disgusting and of course most unwholesome degree." [7]

Farragut reached Vicksburg on the twenty-third. Against the advice of several of his captains who considered navigation without pilots too hazardous for the heavy ships, he had brought up the *Hartford,* the *Brooklyn,* and the *Richmond,* along with eight gunboats. He believed, according to Captain Bell, that the Vicksburg defenses would be abandoned if he showed a sufficiently imposing force there. He proceeded at once to make a reconnaissance in company with General Williams and the naval commanders. Riding the nimble *Kennebec,* the commanders ascended to within two miles of Vicksburg's wharves.

The city of Vicksburg lies on the east bank at the bend of a horseshoe in the river. A series of terraces, commencing at wharf level, rises to a height of 250 feet at the crest of the Chickasaw Hills behind the town. Since Farragut's seizure of New Orleans, ten guns had been erected on the heights below the town, overlooking the lower shank of the horseshoe, and two above. Near the wharves were moored two Confederate gunboats. The sight of these enemy craft under the frowning land batteries, together with the insulting answer the Vicksburgers had given to Commander Lee, aroused in Farragut the fighting spirit of the old wood-and-sail Navy in which he had grown up. He called upon the gunboat captains to make a surprise attack after nightfall and capture these enemy vessels. His captains, however, led by Commander Lee, indicated that they considered such an exploit as sheer madness. "Lee," wrote Bell, "carried his objection so far as to say anyone who would undertake it might have his vessel." [8] Farragut removed Lee as commander of the division of gunboats, replacing him with Commander James S. Palmer. The reluctance of his officers to undertake a daring exploit so exasperated Farragut that he fell ill. He had, in fact, not recovered from the nervous strain of the grounding at Tunica Bend.

Across the river from Vicksburg and between the shanks

of the horseshoe lay a tongue-shaped peninsula of water-puddled lowland three miles long and a mile wide. On an embankment running lengthwise down the center of this peninsula was a railroad which in normal times brought cattle and grain from Louisiana and Texas to Vicksburg but which, because of washouts during the current floods, was not usable. It had been one of Williams' aims to destroy this road, but it was needless to land his men to achieve what nature herself had already done and what Commander Palmer's blockading gunboats could accomplish with a few shells whenever the enemy should repair the washouts. The only other military objective was to storm and occupy Vicksburg itself.

On the final day of the reconnaissance, Farragut was confined to his ship with illness, but he dragged himself to the conference of commanders which met in the *Hartford's* wardroom in the evening. General Williams said that he could not bring his frail transports to the wharves until after the fleet had silenced the heaviest hilltop batteries, and that then he could only attempt to scale the bluffs, spike the guns, and bring his men back to the ships. He could not occupy and hold the city with only fourteen hundred troops. His spies had informed him that there were eight thousand of the enemy within the city and that there were thouands of Confederate reserves at Jackson, only forty miles distant by railroad. Captains Craven, Bell, Wainwright, Lee, Russell, Nichols, and Donaldson all agreed that the broadsides of the fleet, with their horizontal fire, could not reach the highest batteries. Captains Palmer, Caldwell, and DeCamp wanted to "go into it and smash them up" because of their insult to Commander Lee. Captain Alden wavered, hiding his face in his hands, and then sided with the majority. Farragut, wrote Bell in his diary, "clearly wanted to chastise the enemy by destroying the town, but was reluctantly restrained by his better judgment, as the troops could not co-operate by land attack and spiking his guns." [9]

Leaving Palmer's gunboats to blockade Vicksburg from

below and to harass the enemy by occasional bombardments in order to draw off from Corinth as many Confederate troops as possible, Farragut the next day returned down the river, General Williams accompanying him.

The Confederates, still smarting over the loss of New Orleans, now claimed that Farragut had been repulsed, and Confederate partisan rangers or guerrillas attacked the withdrawing Federals. Williams disembarked two companies at Grand Gulf to pursue a band of guerrillas, and Farragut, who had been compelled to supply the Army with navy salt pork and hard tack, restocked his own larder by levying a "pretty considerable haul" of Confederate cattle and poultry. At Baton Rouge Farragut's gunfire followed a group of mounted guerrillas on their retreat through the center of town, and General Williams, whose men on the crowded transports had been unable to clean up for several weeks, landed his entire force and took possession of this bright little capital of Louisiana.

Meanwhile, two weeks before Farragut's return to New Orleans, Mr. Lincoln was perplexed by misleading Confederate reports from the lower river. For several months he had been receiving daily reports from the Cairo flotilla. He was within reasonably speedy telegraphic communication with Halleck at Corinth. But with Farragut, who was operating on the far side of enemy-held territory, Lincoln had to resort to fast courier steamers from Hampton Roads to New Orleans. After the seizure of New Orleans, the only quick news about Mr. Lincoln's Navy in the lower Mississippi River reached Washington via the Confederate press. On May 11, the Memphis *Appeal* carried a dispatch from Natchez that the Federal fleet had returned to New Orleans.[10] This incorrect news, relayed through Chicago and New York, reached Lincoln on May 16, along with the bona fide notice of the appearance of Union gunboats off Mobile. Fox questioned Captain Bailey on how many vessels Farragut had sent up the river, and the bearer of the New Orleans victory dispatches, who had departed from New Orleans on April 29, answered, "None." "Impossible," exploded Fox, "the instructions were positive." [11] Bailey volunteered that he thought Farragut had forgotten those orders. Lincoln was "so distressed" over the possibility that Farragut had gone to Mobile instead of Vicksburg that he had Welles and Fox send Farragut a dispatch in triplicate via fast steamers:

> Carry out your instructions of January 20 about ascending the Mississippi River, as it is of the utmost importance.[12]

And Fox in a private letter warned Farragut:

> This retreat may be a fatal step as regards our western movements, since our advance to Memphis would have been the means of forcing Beauregard to fight or retreat. . . . We hear of their fortifying the river with the utmost expedition to prevent your ascent, and you may now find formidable obstacles which you would not have done after the panic created by your magnificent dash; but still it is of paramount importance that you go up and clear the river with the utmost expedition. Mobile, Pensacola, and in fact, the whole coast sinks into insignificance compared with this.[13]

Lincoln's imperative orders found the flag officer in New Orleans licking his wounds. "The elements of destruction in this river," Farragut reported to Welles, "are beyond anything I ever encountered, and if the same destruction continues the whole Navy will be destroyed in twelve months. More anchors have been lost and vessels ruined than I have seen in a lifetime, and those vessels which do not run into others are themselves run into and crushed in such a manner as to render them unseaworthy. I have not at this moment one-third of the vessels fit for duty outside, and if struck by the ram, which they say is near Vicksburg, the *Arkansas,* there is not one that will resist her; their sides are smashed in, their cutwaters entirely broomed up and removed. . . . They all require docking—ribs broken, plank-sheer gone, stems torn off to the wood ends, etc." [14]

Lincoln's peremptory orders once more turned Farragut's battered fleet upstream to clear the river. This time he was determined to pass above Vicksburg to join forces with Flag Officer Davis regardless of navigational hazards five hundred miles inland from his ships' native element. To reach the hilltop hornet nests of Vicksburg, Farragut called Porter back into the river. With the high-angle fire of the mortars, he would now attempt to smother Vicksburg while the fleet ran the gantlet. General Butler managed to double the number of soldiers under General Williams and ordered him "to take the town or have it burned." [15] The ever-active brain of the Massachusetts politician general also conceived the idea of trenching across the peninsula opposite Vicksburg in such a way as to induce the river to scour for itself a new channel several miles to the west of the city, so as to bypass the magnificent natural defense amphitheater at Vicksburg.

On the return trip upstream every gunboat able to tow a coal barge or mortar schooner did so. The number of transports, supply vessels, mortar fleet, and naval craft on this second expedition was three times that of the first. They traveled slower. To minimize damage from grounding, running afoul of snags, and colliding with one another, Farragut ordered them to anchor at night. Even so, the heavy ships scraped bottom repeatedly. Off Union Point a brace of transports tugged seven hours to free the *Hartford,* with hawsers parting every few minutes. Finally, a sixteen-inch manila stream cable was located in the *Hartford*'s hold, and, with three towing vessels attached to this, the flagship was jerked free. "Hurrah! stream cable! All hands in high glee," recorded Captain Bell. "I felt sure the ship was here till next winter." [16] Guerrillas were active in sniping, and the ships were fired on from freshly emplaced Confederate batteries along the bluffs that formed the eastern "coast" of the river. At Ellis Cliffs these were particularly troublesome. In retaliation, the town of Grand Gulf, scene of guerrilla attacks on the transports, was burned by the Federals.

A month after his withdrawal, Farragut was back at his old anchorage below Vicksburg with his three heavy sloops-of-war, six gunboats, six steamers of the Mortar Flotilla, and sixteen mortar boats, in addition to transports and supply ships.

Three days were devoted to placing the mortar schooners in position and to preliminary bombardments to get the range. Although General Williams expressed a desire to cooperate by carrying the heights and spiking their guns, he was of the opinion that his force of thirty-two hundred effectives was too small to pit itself against an enemy garrison now estimated at ten thousand to fifteen thousand men. He and Farragut agreed that the Army should land a battery of artillery on the tip of the peninsula to engage the high batteries above the town. Twice the flag officer called his ship captains into conference for briefings on his general plan.

Farragut's plan called for the vessels to proceed up the river in two columns. In the starboard column nearest Vicksburg were the three heavy ships led by the *Richmond,* and in the port column were eight gunboats led by the *Iroquois.* The heavy ships were to be so widely spaced as to afford the gunboats ample shooting room without firing directly over the ships. The vessels were arranged as follows: [17]

PORT COLUMN—GUNBOATS	STARBOARD COLUMN—BATTLESHIPS
Iroquois (J. S. Palmer)	
Oneida (S. P. Lee)	
	Richmond (J. Alden)
Wissahickon (J. DeCamp)	
Sciota (E. Donaldson)	
	Hartford (R. Wainwright)
Winona (E. T. Nichols)	
Pinola (P. Crosby)	
	Brooklyn (T. T. Craven)
Kennebec (J. H. Russell)	
Katahdin (G. H. Preble)	

Farragut's battle instructions to his captains concluded with a clause which later gave trouble. After the vessels reached the bend in the river, four of the gunboats were to proceed upstream; "but should the action be continued by the enemy, the ships and *Iroquois* and *Oneida* will stop their engines and drop down the river again, keeping up their fire until otherwise directed." [18] By this Farragut evidently meant that his present attack was to be no mad dash to run the gantlet, as below New Orleans, but a more leisurely affair, in which the heavy ships would take time to demolish the enemy's batteries; and that during the battle they would either receive directions from the flag officer, or conform to the movements of the flagship, which occupied the center of the starboard column. Though Farragut explained his intention orally, it was not clearly understood by Captain Craven. Once at the captains' conference in the cabin and again on the *Hartford*'s quarter-deck, Craven asked the flag officer: "Is it your desire for me to leave any batteries behind me that have not been silenced?" And Farragut replied, "No, sir; not on any account." [19]

At 2:00 A.M. on June 28 Farragut hoisted two red lights at the *Hartford*'s mizzen. His fleet weighed anchor and set sail. Porter's mortar schooners, a division on either side of the river, let fly their thirteen-inch bombshells. As in the attack on the New Orleans forts, Porter, with the steamers of the Mortar Flotilla, moved upstream ahead of Farragut to attack the wharf batteries, while from the tip of the peninsula across the river General Williams's artillery (Nim's battery from Boston) hurled their projectiles against the batteries on the heights behind the town.

Thus, Farragut's ships and gunboats churned in stately procession up a watery aisle that was crisscrossed overhead by the lights of the mortar fuses that twinkled as the shells rolled over and over in flight. From Vicksburg's terraced batteries came the heavy explosions of columbiads—old-fashioned ordnance of the days of 1812, but still effective against wooden hulls. Farragut's battleships and the two leading gunboats were equipped with small pivot guns on their bows, his only guns that could be elevated to reach the highest enemy batteries. Until the fleet came abreast of the town, it could not use its broadside guns.

The *Hartford,* a mile behind the leading ships, opened fire at four-fifteen. Her broadside guns, triced up to give maximum elevation, let fly at batteries on a 190-foot ridge to the south of the town. To the surprise of Captain Bell, some of the *Hartford's* shells landed among those targets. A few could be seen against the morning sky flying over the ridge. Vicksburg's gunners, who scattered for cover when the fleet engaged them, returned to serve their guns the moment the ships turned their attention elsewhere. Many mortar shells burst too soon. And Captain Bell, unsympathetic toward this entire operation, noted that often both the mortars and the fleet "kept up a perfect hailstorm against the slopes where no guns are." [20]

The battery above the town raked Farragut severely when the flagship came alongside the city. "As we approached this fort," wrote Bell, "and when about half a mile below it, the sun rose a little to the right of it, red and fiery." Day brightening through the clouds of battle, Farragut could see that the *Richmond,* the *Wissahickon,* and the *Sciota* had already passed out of sight above the bend; while the *Brooklyn,* the *Katahdin,* and the *Kennebec* were behind him and still actively engaged. As the *Hartford* drove upstream, she was pursued by shot from two guns in the upper fort, "their shot striking astern and ricochetting over us and cutting our lower rigging severely." [21] Not two minutes earlier the flag officer had climbed down from a perch in the now shredded mizzen rigging.

Milling around in the narrow and crowded river and wrestling with the swift current beneath the city were the seven steamers of Porter's Mortar Flotilla: [22]

Octorara (D. D. Porter)
Miami (A. D. Harrell)
J. P. Jackson (S. E. Woodworth)
Clifton (C. H. Baldwin)
Westfield (W. B. Renshaw)
Owasco (J. Guest)
Harriet Lane (J. M. Wainwright)

Porter's steamers fought the wharf batteries and those near Vicksburg's hospital, which were commanded by Captain Todd, the Rebel brother-in-law of President Lincoln.[23]

About the time the *Hartford* was moving past Porter, the wheel ropes jammed on the *Octorara* and the flotilla leader drifted downstream among the other mortar steamers. During the confusion, several of these ex-ferryboats and double-enders were hit. The *Jackson*'s steering wheel was shattered. The *Clifton*'s boiler was ripped open, releasing clouds of steam which killed men in her magazine and drove others overboard. The *Westfield* was struck on her engine frame. Some of these vessels drifted into the line of fire of the *Brooklyn*. Shell from the latter burst off the port side of the *Octorara*.

Captain Craven of the *Brooklyn*, mistakenly understanding that Farragut did not wish him to pass above Vicksburg if any of the enemy's batteries remained unsilenced, dropped back, with the gunboats *Kennebec* and *Katahdin*. The flag officer, meanwhile, for hours after the passage of Vicksburg, worried himself sick over the fate of his rearmost ships. When at last he learned that they had suffered no casualties at all, but that Craven had misunderstood orders, he administered a reprimand and Craven resigned.

In the passage of Vicksburg, Farragut's ships suffered almost as heavily as in the run past the New Orleans forts. His personnel loss was sixteen killed and forty wounded. His ships, already battered by navigational hazards, received extensive injury in hull and tophamper.

Farragut had passed Vicksburg, but merely running by did not solve the problem. To Flag Officer Davis, who, on June 6, had beaten the Confederate river forces at Memphis, Farragut wrote that he needed Davis's ironclads as well as Halleck's troops in order to take Vicksburg. "I have only about 3,000 soldiers under General Williams associated with me, but they are not sufficient to land in the face of all Van Dorn's division and Beauregard's army. . . . I will await your answer with great anxiety. My orders are so peremptory that

I must do all in my power to free the river of all impediments; that I must attack them, although I know it is useless. . . ." [24] Writing to Halleck, who had now gained possession of Corinth, he urgently requested military assistance in capturing Vicksburg. "My orders, general, are to clear the river. . . . Can you aid me in this matter to carry out the peremptory order of the President?" [25] But Halleck did not respond, and Farragut's singlehanded naval attack failed. As Dave Porter forcefully expressed it in his report to his foster brother and flag officer: "Ships . . . cannot crawl up hills 300 feet high, and it is that part of Vicksburg which must be taken by the army." [26]

The seven units of Farragut's fleet that were anchored a few miles above Vicksburg now offered to the Confederates their fairest opportunity to repeat the exploit of the *Merrimack* against wooden ships.

The powerful Confederate ironclad ram *Arkansas* had just been completed up the Yazoo River, which emptied into the Mississippi a few miles north of Farragut's anchorage. Building the ram had been attended by incredible difficulties. Iron scrap and railroad rails had been gathered from all over western Tennessee and fabricated in Memphis. Before the impending Battle of Memphis, her builders had been forced to exchange the comparatively efficient machine shops of Memphis for a refuge at industrially primitive Yazoo City, seventy-five miles up the Yazoo River. The barge carrying the unfinished *Arkansas'* armor had sunk in the Yazoo and her plates had to be retrieved by divers brought in from a distance. Her commander, Lieutenant Isaac N. Brown, C.S.N., at swords' points with local authorities, had been compelled to apply to Jefferson Davis in Richmond in order to procure a crew for his vessel. If the *Arkansas* had sallied forth from its lair after Farragut's ascent above Vicksburg, it might have caught the Federal ships like sitting ducks. Farragut, cut off from his coal supply, had let his fires die down. The iron-plated Rebel, with steam up, maneuverable, might easily have surprised the wooden-hulled Federals at anchor without steam, and, plunging her cast-iron beak into their vitals, she might have scored a second Hampton Roads. But the *Arkansas* lost three precious days—and then Davis leisurely appeared with the river ironclads.

The opportunity for Confederate heroics seemed to have passed. The two fleets of Farragut and Davis were overwhelmingly superior. Farragut's heavy broadsides and Davis's armorclad invulnerability were both complemented by the speedy, maneuverable, and expendable Ellet Ram Fleet of fast riverboats equipped for ramming. Fire power, impregnability, and an ability to ram, were, however, qualities that were possessed by different ships in the Federal fleet, while the *Arkansas,* though greatly outnumbered, possessed within herself a fair measure of each of these fighting characteristics.

For fourteen days Farragut and Davis waited. Then they sent up the Yazoo a reconnaissance party consisting of the swift ram *Queen of the West,* the light gunboat *Tyler,* and the ironclad *Carondelet.* To their surprise and annoyance, the Federal scouting boats met the Rebel *Arkansas* charging downstream.

They turned and ran with the *Arkansas* hot in pursuit.[27] In the course of their running fight, both the *Carondelet* and the *Arkansas* grounded on a sand bar. The Confederate ironclad, being on the outside, got off first and continued her downstream run.

The *Tyler* and the *Queen* had no time to announce her approach before the *Arkansas,* firing bow guns and both broadsides, bludgeoned her way through the combined Federal fleets.

Both Farragut and Davis were unready in their engine rooms, with only low fires or none. Broadside after Federal broadside was unloaded against the slanted, tallow-greased iron sides of the intruder, but few shots left a mark. The *Arkansas,* after running the gantlet, took shelter under the guns of exultant Vicksburg.

The chagrined and humiliated Farragut the same night ran back down past Vicksburg. With him went two of Davis's boats, the ironclad *Essex,* under William D. Porter, and the light ram vessel *General Sumter,* under Henry Erben, whose assignments were to ram and closely engage the *Arkansas* in an effort to sink her. Again Farragut's passage was made under cover of mortar fire, this time with the mortars of Davis added to those below the Confederate stronghold. And Davis, with the *Benton* and other river ironclads, dropped down almost to the tip of the peninsula to afford gunnery support.

The passage down was made after nightfall. The wharf area, where the *Arkansas* was moored, was too dark, and eyes in the fleet were too blinded by gun flashes to pick out the Rebel ram. Farragut was depressed by a sense of frustration and failure. The *Arkansas'* humiliating dash through the fleets had exacted a toll of eighteen killed, fifty wounded, and ten missing.

In vain Farragut now tried to spur Davis into a cooperative daylight assault on Vicksburg in an effort to overwhelm the *Arkansas.* Farragut proposed to battle Vicksburg while Davis's ironclads destroyed the Confederate ram. "We know by experience," Farragut argued, "having twice passed these forts, that we can keep them well employed, so that you can have full play at the ram, and we will be able to help you occasionally." [28] Davis, however, leaned toward prudence. His unwieldly ironclads could not stem the current of the Mississippi without a tow, and wooden steamers capable of service as tugs could easily be sunk by Vicksburg's cannon.

When Farragut a short time later received Secretary Welles's authorization for him to leave Vicksburg and devote himself to the operations of the Gulf blockade, Farragut departed without regret. His ships required extensive repair, many of his men were ill, Farragut himself was suffering intermittently from "nervous fever." Of General Williams's thirty-two hundred men, only eight hundred were fit for service in mid-July; consequently he retired to Baton Rouge when the fleet went down. Flag Officer Davis, complaining that Williams's withdrawal made a close blockade of Vicksburg impractical, withdrew his vessels upstream to the mouth of the Yazoo.

The Confederate land attack of August 5 made Baton Rouge untenable for General Butler's meager forces, and the remnants of the Baton Rouge garrison were withdrawn after General Williams was killed in action. The ram *Arkansas,* in chronic difficulty with her engines, broke down a few miles above Baton Rouge. Here she was discovered and brought under fire by the U.S.S. *Essex,* under Captain W. D. Porter. After several hits had been scored upon her, she was set afire and abandoned by her crew.

In Washington Mr. Lincoln and his advisers seem to have had little real appreciation of the military situation on the lower river. Evidently they did not expect General Butler, with only enough troops for the occupation of New Orleans, to wage a land campaign from Baton Rouge to Vicksburg; otherwise they would have sent more troops to New Orleans at the outset of the New Orleans campaign. Nor, later, after Farragut had indicated the necessity for troops, were any sent. Mr. Lincoln seems to have relied a great deal upon the hope of uncovering much Union sentiment among the people along the rivers once his naval forces appeared on the river to give them protection. And he seems to have misjudged completely the implacable temper of the Confederate guerrillas which had made it necessary for Farragut to burn the towns of Grand Gulf, Mississippi, and Donaldsonville, Louisiana.

14.

Combined Attacks on Vicksburg and Port Hudson (Part One)

FOR MR. LINCOLN'S NAVY THE DEVELOPING SITUATION on the Western rivers in the latter half of 1862 required change of commanders, reorganization and increase of forces, and readjustment to new modes of attack.

The purely naval assault on Vicksburg had made the attractive headline: FARRAGUT'S SALT WATER FLEET JOINS HANDS WITH DAVIS'S RIVER IRONCLADS. But at best it had been only a gesture, impermanent and futile, which failed to shake Rebel control over Vicksburg. The military evacuation of Baton Rouge in August thrust Farragut back upon New Orleans as a base, and this, along with Davis's withdrawal to Memphis, was signalized by Confederate repossession of the Vicksburg to Shreveport railroad. Once again by rail the vital grain, beef and blockade-run supplies from Texas were hauled east to the peninsula opposite Vicksburg and ferried across the river under the protection of Vicksburg's guns. Confederate supplies also reached Vicksburg's wharves by steamer from Shreveport via the Red River. Below the mouth of the Red River at Port Hudson, Louisiana, at a location similar to Vicksburg's, the Confederates erected land batteries which defied the Lincolnite gunboats in the lower river.

Lincoln's problem on the Mississippi would have been greatly simplified had the Confederates merely clung to the strategic midsector of the Mississippi. However, just as in

Virginia, General Lee followed a defensive-offensive strategy in holding before Richmond while striking from the valley to menace Washington, so in the West the Confederates fought defensively at Vicksburg and Port Hudson while sending surprise cavalry raids deep into Union-held territory. In western Tennessee and Kentucky, General Nathan Bedford Forrest ("Get there fustest") and the wily raider, General John H. Morgan, destroyed Federal supply depots and interrupted use of the rivers in areas well behind the Union lines. If the Vicksburg and Port Hudson forts had converted the Middle West's extensive system of water highways into a landlocked lake, the occasional interruption of traffic by Confederate raiders and guerrillas tended to dry up that lake. Throughout the President's native Middle West, the crops of a second year piled up in warehouses. Newspapers begged the government to open the Mississippi to let the products of the great West reach hungry markets at New Orleans and beyond. Lincoln's party lost strength in the congressional elections, as Copperheads and defeatists like Vallandigham won the votes of purse-pinched farmers.

To meet the growing crisis, Lincoln's government reorganized the Western forces by transferring the gunboat fleet from the Army to the Navy. Despite the misgivings of Secretary Welles, who could not forget the *Powhatan* episode, David D. Porter, the youthful and energetic commander of Farragut's Mortar Flotilla, was jumped up to acting rear admiral and assigned to command the navy's new Mississippi Squadron. "Porter is but a Commander," Welles brooded in his journal. "He has, however, stirring and positive qualities, is fertile in resources, has great energy, excessive and sometimes not overscrupulous ambition, is impressed with and boastful of his own powers. . . . Is given to cliquism but is brave and daring like all his family. He has not the conscientious and high moral qualities of Foote . . . but his field of operation is peculiar and a young and active officer is required." [1]

To assure an adequate military force to operate down the

river with the fleet, Lincoln shifted several top generals and created a special army to be called the Army of the Mississippi. "Old Brains" Halleck, the snail-paced victor of Corinth, was called to Washington as general-in-chief and Grant was elevated to full command of the Army of the Tennessee, now operating in the northern part of the State of Mississippi. It was Lincoln's personal belief, apparently, that the existing armies in the West were needed precisely where they were, and that they had all they could do to handle the problems in their immediate fronts, plus nuisance raids in their rear by Forrest, Morgan, and the guerrillas. At any rate, Lincoln personally commissioned an energetic politician and fellow townsman, John A. McClernand, to recruit and organize the new Army of the Mississippi for joint action with the Navy against Vicksburg "to clear the Mississippi River and open navigation to New Orleans." [2] Lincoln's ill-considered appointment of McClernand hatched trouble for Army and Navy in the West. Neither Halleck nor Grant was consulted or even informed of it until conflicts of command jurisdiction arose. McClernand himself, nursing illusions of grandeur as "author and actual promoter" of the Vicksburg campaign and not above trading on his influence with the President, became in fact an incubus in the inner circle of Grant's commanders whose presence embarrassed the commanding general and made necessary a shift in his plan of campaign.[3]

In New Orleans, too, there was a shift of commanders. Farragut remained at the head of the Western Gulf Blockading Squadron, but General Butler, whose brusque treatment of pro-Secessionist foreign consuls had stirred up trouble for him in the State Department, had to yield his billet as military commander to another Massachusetts politician general, Nathaniel P. Banks. The latter took with him to New Orleans a small but welcome reinforcement of troops which could cooperate with Farragut against the Confederate stronghold of Port Hudson.

Although Stanton resisted the transfer of the river gunboats to the Navy, the War Department's unified control had encountered difficulties. Too often Western generals had tried to operate the gunboats like cavalry, and impractical orders had brought misunderstanding and friction. In view of the vast new chore of organizing and administering naval convoys on the Western rivers—a task made imperative by raiders and guerrillas—Lincoln sided with Secretary Welles and placed the two services on terms of equality. After October 1, when the gunboats of the Western Flotilla were transferred to the Navy, there appeared a doubt as to whether the unarmed craft of the Ellet Ram Fleet constituted gunboats in the sense named in the Congressional act. Admiral Porter, feeling his oats in his new job, ordered the Ellet rams tied up to the bank until the matter could be settled in Washington.

Since Stanton obstructed the transfer on the technicality that the Ellet vessels were not gunboats, the matter had to be threshed out in the Cabinet. "Stanton lost his temper, so we beat him," wrote Fox to Porter. "The cool man always wins. Let me impress upon you to be incontrovertibly right in case of a difference with the Army. The President is just and sagacious. Give us success; nothing else wins." [4]

During his first weeks at Cairo, the new navy base, Porter readied his fresh-water squadron for the forthcoming joint operations against Vicksburg.[5] Reducing army-recruited crews to proper naval ratings was ticklish business, though necessary in order to maintain the morale of the salt-water seamen who had joined the squadron. Establishing a hospital on shore relieved the makeshift gunboats of sufferers from routine maladies, but four hundred men debilitated by river fever had to be given medical discharge. Porter canceled the too-frequent sluicings of decks and ordered more extensive use of drying stoves. Frequent inspections required rugged recruits from cornfield and forest to wear their underflannels according to navy regulations.

Construction of new vessels and repair of old were pushed in the river towns from Cincinnati to St. Louis: shallow-draft ironclads secretly destined for Farragut in the Gulf, tinclads capable of floating "wherever the ground was a little damp," tiny dispatch vessels, and palatial headquarters craft like Porter's flagship the *Black Hawk*—a floating hotel with comfortable cabins for the admiral's staff, a piano in the wardroom, and stalls for cows and horses.

While waiting for General McClernand to recruit his army in Illinois, Indiana, and Iowa, Porter replaced the scored decks of the Pook turtles and fitted them with latest model Dahlgren guns. He established under Captain Henry Walke an advanced division of gunboats to patrol the Mississippi between Helena and Vicksburg, and another under Commander Le Roy Fitch to patrol the Ohio, Tennessee, and Cumberland Rivers. An epidemic of guerrilla attacks upon the river towns, which threatened the communications of the various armies, brought a flurry of army appeals for gunboat assistance. "There are so many generals acting independently of each other," Porter in late November declared, "that the whole American Navy could not comply with their demands." [6]

To free his hands for fighting at Vicksburg, Porter cracked down alike on Yankee traders and Rebel guerrillas. "There is no impropriety in destroying houses supposed to be affording shelter to rebels, and it is the only way to stop guerrilla warfare," reads one of Porter's general orders.[7] "Should innocent persons suffer it will be their own fault, and teach others that it will be to their advantage to inform the Government authorities when guerrillas are about certain localities." [8] Peacetime water-borne traffic with small Kentucky towns not garrisoned by Federal troops was suspended. Too many slippery Yankee traders flouted Treasury regulations and carried forbidden supplies to such places. Once there they were "robbed" at pistol point by conniving guerrillas. The admiral notified the Treasury agent at Memphis of his intention to stop all contraband. "The temptation to deal in contraband is very great just now, and there is no knowing how long the war may be prolonged if the trade is not arrested." [9] Guerrilla actions multiplied during low stages of water, when even shallow-draft wooden gunboats had difficulty navigating the sand bars in the Ohio. Porter ordered his patrol craft to impound all ferries so as to leave the guerrillas no means of crossing rivers and to destroy all small boats which might carry intelligence. All Rebel property was ordered captured. "That is the way to put down the rebellion. I am no advocate for the milk and water policy." [10]

In October when Admiral Porter and General McClernand had met in Washington, McClernand had set early December as the time when he expected to move on Vicksburg, and Porter had agreed to that date. By starting before the high-water season, the troops might thus have dry ground on which to land to the north of Vicksburg. Following their meeting, Porter had come west to the naval base at Cairo, McClernand had set up his recruiting headquarters at Springfield, and neither took advantage of the rail and telegraph connections between Springfield and nearby Cairo to communicate with the other. Porter knew that McClernand's recruits were passing through Cairo on their way to Memphis, where Grant's right hand, W. T. Sherman, was supervising their training as soldiers. From the papers Porter learned that McClernand was getting married. December arrived, with still no word from the honeymooning political general.

On December 14 Porter embarked down the river to support Sherman's attack on Vicksburg.

McClernand from Springfield telegraphed Halleck requesting orders to proceed down the river. Twenty-four hours later, having received no reply, he wired to Lincoln: "I believe I am superseded. Please inquire and let me know whether it is and shall be so." [11]

McClernand's telegrams brought clarification of a situation which for weeks had puzzled Halleck and Grant. On the eighteenth Grant at Oxford, Mississippi, received the President's orders to divide his forces into four army corps, one of which commanded by McClernand was "to form a part of the expedition on Vicksburg." [12] In turn Grant's telegram bearing these instructions did not reach McClernand for several weeks, because of wholesale enemy snipping of Grant's telegraph lines down the Tennessee River and the confusion incident to the Confederate capture of Grant's supply dump at Holly Springs. McClernand's orders to proceed down river were thus held up, so that he did not reach Vicksburg until the bell had struck at the end of the first round of fighting.

Porter reached Memphis on December 18. The river being very low, he had lost time by grounding on Island No. 23. Sherman, with twenty thousand men, embarked on forty-odd passenger steamers and was convoyed downstream by the gunboats. At Helena, twenty more paddle steamers with General Steele's thirteen thousand troops were added to the expedition.

The threefold plan of the joint operation involved Porter, Sherman, and Grant. A few miles above Vicksburg Porter was to sweep the lower Yazoo River of Confederate torpedoes and cover Sherman's landing. Already Captain Walke of the advanced gunboat division was busy removing torpedoes. The Yazoo flows into the Mississippi River about twelve miles north of Vicksburg, and the Chickasaw Bluffs, which bend to the right at Vicksburg, meet the Yazoo at Drumgould's Bluff about fifteen miles to the northeast of the Rebel stronghold. Upon the triangle bounded by the Mississippi, the lower Yazoo, and the line of hills between Vicksburg and Drumgould's, General Sherman was to disembark his troops and assault the Chickasaw fortifications. Sherman hoped to cross quickly the low country at the base of the hills, to scale the bluffs, and, getting in behind Vicksburg, to cut off the city's rail connection with Jackson. At Drumgould's the Chickasaw Hills touch the Yazoo and continue to fringe that generally north-south waterway as it bends in a graceful, scimitarlike curve, convexly toward the east. To insure the success of Sherman and Porter, General Grant—part three of the plan—with forty thousand troops, projected a march south from Oxford, Mississippi, on the comparatively high ground to the east of the Yazoo River. Here Grant would attack and try to force the Confederates to draw reserves from Vicksburg while Sherman and Porter stove in Vicksburg's back door.

The Confederates were well prepared to resist the backdoor assault. Between the Chickasaw Hills and the lower Yazoo lay a moat of marsh and drowned forest, crisscrossed by sluggish creeks and bayous. The country's half-dozen scattered plantations, so many islands of dry land reclaimed by dikes, were occupied by Confederate pickets and skirmishers. The few practicable roadways from the Yazoo to the hills were the man-made embankments around the bayous and a narrow corduroy road extending beyond Chickasaw Bayou, and these roadways were completely commanded by cannon emplaced on the Chickasaw Hills. The Yazoo River itself had been blocked by piles and sunken hulks at Drumgould's Bluff, and the entire lower river had been sown with torpedoes which, although crudely manufactured, were deadly.

While the Federal armada was steaming down the Mississippi, Porter learned of his first casualty from torpedoes. The ironclad *Cairo,* while sweeping for torpedoes, had been sunk by one in the lower Yazoo. Although her skipper, young Tom Selfridge, had run her injured bow onto a shoal, she had filled and skidded back into deep water, leaving only the tips of her funnels above water to mark her grave.

Porter and Sherman reached the mouth of the Yazoo on Christmas Eve, while the weather was yet dry and the water in the river at low stage. Porter sent gunboats to finish sweeping the Yazoo while Sherman burned three miles of railroad trestle west of Vicksburg. The heavy ironclad *Benton,* under Lieutenant Commander William Gwin, guarded, like a fire-spitting mother hen, the seven light-draft wooden steamers while they fished out the torpedoes. When Confederates fired on the Federals from an ambush on the plantation of the late Confederate General Albert Sidney Johnston, Gwin sent men ashore to burn the plantation house with its sugar refinery, sawmill, cotton gin, and quarters for three hundred slaves. The levee on the south bank, thirty feet above the low level in the Yazoo and covered by live oak, willow, and a tough matting of vines, afforded excellent cover for snipers.[13] The *Benton* answered the snipers with heavy rifled shot, which splintered trees and tore furrows in the bank but failed to rout the Confederates. Sherman sent several regiments of sharpshooters to ax their way through brush and brier and rout the snipers, so that the torpedoes could be cleared.

Two days behind schedule, Sherman landed his troops near Chickasaw Bayou. The delay enabled the Confederates to entrench along the crest of the hills between their forts. Confederate cannon now fended off most of Sherman's force as they tried to negotiate the bayou levees and the single corduroy road through the swamp. An heroic regiment which reached the foot of the bluffs was decimated by fire from the new trenches, and its survivors were penned in until nightfall under an overhanging cliff. During the second day of Sherman's maneuvers on shore, rain fell in sheets to mire down guns and horses. Brigadier General F. P. Blair's mount sank to the belly in the muck, and the general was compelled to slog ahead on foot.

Meanwhile, Porter, too far away to reach the hilltop batteries in Sherman's front, proceeded upstream to bombard Drumgould's Bluff. "My object," Porter reported, "was to draw off a portion of the troops from Vicksburg to prevent our ascent of the Yazoo." [14] After the channel had been thoroughly dragged, four ironclads and three wooden boats moved up and anchored behind a tree covered point across which they fired at Drumgould's.

The *Benton,* the most powerful ironclad and in the leading position, was too squat on the water for Commander Gwin to see over the trees. Rather than fire blindly, Gwin steamed beyond the curve and so moored his cumbersome craft that by pulling and slacking on her lines he could alternately fire bow and starboard guns. In this position, however, she was in plain view of the Confederates. The latter now directed all their fire upon the *Benton* and struck her repeatedly. Her slanted four-inch armor, greased with tallow, was proof against shot, but she had weak spots. Her funnels were knocked off; shot entered through her gunports and plunged through the lightly armored deck above her casemate. Inside the casemate one man was killed and eight were wounded. Throughout the unequal battle, Commander Gwin refused to enter the armored pilothouse, but exposed himself on deck to direct the *Benton*'s fire. "A captain's place is on the deck," he said.[15] Within minutes an enemy projectile glanced from the *Benton*'s casemate, struck Gwin, tearing off the muscles of his right breast and arm, and causing his death a few days later. After an engagement lasting an hour and a half, the gunboats retired downstream. The "old warhorse" looked feeble enough with funnels gone, steam down, and hobbling between two wooden paddle steamers, but, as Porter wrote, "the *Benton* . . . though much cut up, is ready for anything." [16]

Sherman's attack on the northern flank of Vicksburg was repulsed with a loss of two thousand men. The Confederates had enjoyed every advantage of position, while the Federals suffered every disadvantage—lack of roads, swampy terrain, heavy rains, failure of expected support from Grant. The rumble of railroad trains which Sherman's men heard behind Vicksburg had been caused by the arrival not of Grant's men but of Confederate reserves who had been released by the slackening of Grant's pressure further north. On the day of Sherman's departure from Memphis (and unknown to Sherman for more than a week), Confederate General Earl Van Dorn had captured Grant's base of supplies at Holly Springs, Mississippi. Synchronized with this had been strikes further north by Bedford Forrest, who had crossed the Tennessee, threatened Fort Pillow and Columbus with recapture, and caused the fearful Federal commander occupying Island No. 10 to roll his fifty-one heavy guns into the Mississippi River. The havoc had prevented Grant's carrying through his part against Vicksburg.

On the thirtieth, while yet ignorant of Grant's predicament, Sherman withdrew his men to the transports. Vicksburg, he conceded, was invulnerable to attack from the Yazoo swamps. Sherman proposed to Porter that they attack Drumgould's. The water level in the river was rising. They might remove the obstructions and, pushing up the Yazoo, join forces with Grant and attack Vicksburg from the rear. But the following day the move on Drumgould's was discouraged by a dense fog. While they waited in the fog, two other facts ended their tentative plan. A careless towboat captain rammed a coal scow and sank Porter's reserve of precious coal. All the transports and the light-draft wooden gunboats burned wood, replaceable from forests along the bank, but the ironclads were compelled to use anthracite. So cramped were their compartments that they could not carry more than a few tons at a time and had continually to be refueled from barges. Sherman, too, was embarrassed. His ammunition boat *Blue Wing,* while en route from Memphis, was captured by Confederate raiders and carried up the Arkansas River to a fort and cavalry base known as Arkansas Post. To make a quick expedition to capture that Rebel stronghold would at once eliminate a menace to river communications, relieve coal and ammunition shortages by placing the expedition closer to its sources of supply, and, most important in a political sense, remove the sting of the defeat at Chickasaw Bluffs. At the moment of Porter's and Sherman's decision to attack Arkansas Post, General McClernand appeared, bringing with him on board his headquarters boat his bride, her several maids, and quantities of baggage, together with newspaper men and politicians.

15.

Combined Attacks on Vicksburg and Port Hudson (Part Two)

McClernand was furious. Flashing the President's commission, he took over from Sherman the command of the army—his own personally recruited troops which the "crazy" West Pointer had run off with—and rechristened it "Army of the Mississippi." [1] He was still at the boiling point when he and Sherman later the same day boarded the naval flagship *Black Hawk* for a conference with Porter. It was near midnight and Porter, who had retired, received them in his nightshirt. Could Porter provide gunboat support for a joint attack on Arkansas Post? Porter could, indeed, but his gorge arose over McClernand's insolence toward Sherman. Sherman took Porter aside. "My God, Porter! You will ruin yourself if you talk that way to McClernand. He is very intimate with the President and has powerful influence." "I don't care who or what he is. I'll be damned if he shall be rude to you in my cabin!" [2]

Porter picked three of his best ironclads for the mission to Arkansas Post, and, to blank out the late frustration at Vicksburg, decided to go himself. Two angry generals and a naval commander now plowed up the Arkansas River to attack Arkansas Post. At intervals the vessels were tied up to the banks to cut firewood from the forest. To conserve coal, a pair of wood-burning transports towed each of the armored turtles, the *Baron DeKalb,* the *Louisville,* and the *Cincinnati.*

Along the river Confederate planters drove their hogs and cattle into the woods and either barged their grain upstream ahead of the invaders, or emptied it into the water as the gunboats hove in sight.

The Post of Arkansas, 60 miles above the mouth of the river and 117 below Little Rock, was situated in lowland with elevation barely above floodwater. Its defense work, Fort Hindman, had a casemated section of oak and railroad iron, mounting two nine-inch guns. Unlike the high gun nests at Vicksburg, this flat-country fort lay vulnerable to the horizontal fire of gunboats. Confederate Brigadier General Tom Churchill's five thousand men stood ready to fend off McClernand's thirty-two thousand and Porter's fleet.

McClernand's troops, commanded in the field by Sherman (XV Corps) and George W. Morgan (XIII Corps), after futile maneuvering through swamps in efforts to flank the Confederate entrenchments, made ready for a head-on assault across a cotton field. Porter's slanted iron walls were smeared with a thick coating of tallow to repel boarders. As was expected, the battle on Sunday, January 11, was a one-sided affair. Porter's turtles shot up the fort from close range and enfiladed the more distant trenches. During the action Porter circulated among the ironclads on a fast tug to cheer his men and take personal charge of firefighting when a blaze was reported to have broken out on board the *Cincinnati.*

The Confederates inside the fort endured the naval fire until their casemates had been battered in and their best guns dismounted. Then they shook out the white flag, and Colonel Dunnington personally surrendered to Admiral Porter, who scrambled ashore to receive the surrender. "You can't expect men to stand up against the fire of those gunboats," men of the garrison told Porter.[3] General Churchill, his trenches enfiladed by gunboats, surrendered under protest to McClernand. All told the Federal bag was 4,791 prisoners, 563 horses, and the unexpended remainder of the shot and shell the Johnny Rebs had captured in Sherman's ammunition boat the *Blue Wing*.[4] Inside the fort Porter found the *Blue Wing*'s mail pouches—empty.

McClernand's report, awarding the victory to himself and scarcely mentioning the Navy, was telegraphed from Memphis, and reached Washington ahead of Porter's, which was forwarded from Cairo. Mr. Welles, nettled by the slowness of naval communications, issued an order to speed them up. The good tidings from Arkansas Post offset several melancholy events. The celebrated Ericsson *Monitor,* en route to join Du Pont's force at Charleston, foundered in heavy seas off Cape Hatteras, and the Confederates regained Galveston, sinking the blockader *Harriet Lane* and burning the *Clifton* —vessels that had won distinction in Porter's Mortar Flotilla at New Orleans.

Meanwhile, McClernand's peremptory treatment of Sherman at Vicksburg and his pointing the Vicksburg attack forces away from its prime objective worried Lincoln and Halleck and alarmed Grant.

On the eleventh, before hearing of the victory at Arkansas Post, Grant at Memphis warned McClernand to abstain from all moves not connected with "the one great result, the capture of Vicksburg." "I do not approve of your move on the Post of Arkansas while the other is in abeyance. It will lead to the loss of men without a result. So long as Arkansas cannot reinforce the enemy east of the river we have no present interest in troubling them." [5] Through Halleck, Lincoln annulled McClernand's special commission. "You are hereby authorized," wrote Halleck to Grant on the twelfth, "to relieve General McClernand from command of the expedition against Vicksburg, giving it to the next in rank, or taking it yourself." [6] McClernand squawked to Lincoln: "I believe my success here is gall and wormwood to the clique of West Pointers who have been persecuting me for months." [7] Grant now made a personal inspection of McClernand's forces after their return to Milliken's Bend. He conferred with Porter and Sherman, as well as McClernand, and decided that he must himself assume personal command in this area.

"I found there was not sufficient confidence felt in General McClernand as a commander, either by the Army or Navy, to insure him success," Grant reported to Halleck. "This is a matter I made no inquiries about, but it was forced upon me. As it is my intention to command in person, unless otherwise directed, there is no special necessity of mentioning this matter. . . . Admiral Porter told me that he had written freely to the Secretary of the Navy, with the request that what he said might be shown to the Secretary of War." [8]

Happily Lincoln was resilient enough to admit a mistake. When McClernand made "political speech" protests against Grant's assumption of command on the river and his demotion of McClernand to the command of a single corps (XIII), Lincoln ignored them; and later, when Grant finally removed the President's fellow townsman for incompetence in the field, Lincoln accepted Grant's action.

What rendered the McClernand appointment unfortunate, however, was that it warped Grant's plan of campaign at the outset. "If General Sherman had been left in command here [on the river]," Grant explained to Halleck's aide, "such is my confidence in him that I would not have thought my presence necessary." [9] Grant's advance south from Oxford to the rear of Vicksburg might then have proceeded according to Grant's original plan, with Sherman and Porter standing ready to attack Vicksburg from its water side in conjunction with Grant's attack from the east. Indeed, after Grant had reduced McClernand, Sherman urged him to return to Memphis and proceed to Vicksburg via Oxford and Jackson, as he had at first planned. Intolerable rains had so flooded the country along the river that operations there for the next several months would likely be of doubtful value. But Grant had set his hand to the plough.

From January to April, Grant and Porter battled the Mississippi River and the flooded forest and river-bottom fields, through which they attempted to turn the flanks of Vicksburg, to bypass its frowning batteries, to blockade Vicksburg, and to interrupt the free use by the Confederates of the Red River highway.

A project in which Lincoln now showed renewed interest was the canal across Young's Point. Started by General Williams the year before, a finished canal at that time might have enabled transports, supply craft, and light-draft naval vessels to bypass Vicksburg. Halleck relayed Lincoln's wishes to Grant, and Welles wrote Porter urging full cooperation whenever the Army should set about the project in earnest.[10] Grant and Porter inspected the site. The upper end of the ditch they found to have been improperly located at an eddy in the river. They blocked out a new opening farther upstream where they hoped the current might be made to sweep directly into the canal. At Lincoln's suggestion, four idle dredging machines were brought down from St. Louis to assist the several hundred stump-grubbing Negroes and the five-hundred-man details of troops that were assigned from Sherman's corps which was encamped nearby on the levee. These machines worked nobly, until they neared the southern end of the ditch. Then the Confederates opened upon the dredgers with a new battery, which the soldiers christened "Whistling Dick." Work had to be suspended and the uselessness of the canal as a means of avoiding the enemy's cannon became apparent, for the Confederates had now extended their line of hilltop batteries down to Warrenton, some twelve miles below Vicksburg. Finally, the work of many weeks was ruined when the embankment caved in prematurely and the ditch was flooded with placidly swirling mud without a sufficient force of current to sluice it through the now useless canal. "Big Ditch," however futile as a means of bypassing Vicksburg, did cause the Confederates to spread out their forces and their heavy guns over a great length of territory, and it provided Grant's men with busy work at a time when they were restricted by floods to the levee itself and to crowded quarters on board transports.

Having had little faith in the canal from the start, Grant set in motion two expeditions to flank Vicksburg. One was an army effort to discover a route through the western lowlands, commencing with Lake Providence and moving through connecting bayous to the Red River. Had this passage proved feasible, Grant might have joined forces with General Banks and Admiral Farragut off Port Hudson. Confederate supplies from the Red River would have been cut off and the Army could have secured a foothold on the east bank of the Mississippi to operate from the south and east against Vicksburg. But after a thorough reconnaissance this route was abandoned.

A promising operation undertaken at the same time in early February was a joint army-navy expedition across the northern end of the Yazoo delta. Opposite the town of Helena, Arkansas, army engineers blasted the levee to flood an abandoned barge canal known as the Yazoo Pass. Through the Yazoo Pass, the Coldwater and the Tallahatchee, Porter and Grant proposed to send an expedition into the upper Yazoo River. If they could clear the Yazoo above the obstructions in the river and the hilltop batteries at Haynes's Bluff, they could at once cut off Vicksburg from its "granary" in the Yazoo delta and obtain a footing on the high ground east of the Yazoo, turning Vicksburg's right flank and besieging Vicksburg from the rear. The expeditionary force consisted of two river ironclads and eight light-draft rams and tinclads under Lieutenant Commander Watson Smith, and a division of troops under Brigadier General L. F. Ross.[11]

When the levee was blasted, the water, eight feet higher inside the river than in the old pass, gushed through in a muddy, roaring Niagara. "Logs, trees, and great masses of earth were torn away with the greatest of ease."[12] In a few hours the width of the cut in the levee grew to forty yards. The next morning it was eighty. Two weeks passed before the level outside approached that within the river, and the navy vessels, towing three barges of coal and followed by thirteen army transports, entered the pass.

Everything depended upon surprise and speed in the dash across the Yazoo delta to the undefended upper reaches of the Yazoo River. The Confederates, however, with spies in

Helena, had early got wind of the expedition and sent a working party of Negroes to fell timber across the route. Some trees could be bulldozed to one side by the ironclads. Others had to be towed out of the way by cable. The expedition had to send back two hundred miles to Memphis for six-inch hempen cables that would not snap under the strain. As the pass was only one hundred feet wide, branches from trees on either side frequently met overhead to form tunnels. The single-deck ironclads, being squat and low, could often sail under these vaulted roofs of the forest, but not so the towering transports, whose fancy, wedding-cake tiers of decks required the clearing of an aisle overhead. "Pioneer" companies skilled in the ax were brought up to perform this tedious labor, but their progress was retarded by the fact that they had little dry land to stand on, the forest floor being from one to eight feet under water.

Whenever one of the ironclads had to stop to coal ship, the entire line of vessels behind it came to a halt. When a transport developed engine trouble, smashed a wheel, or had its funnels knocked over by overhanging trees, the ironclads ahead of them also stopped.

Commander Watson Smith, unacclimated to duty on the river and physically unfit for this rough campaign, angered younger military and naval officers by his refusal to plunge ahead, leaving the transports behind. The result was that the expedition took two weeks to make the two-hundred-mile distance across the Yazoo delta. During this interval, the Confederates had built a cotton-bale fort to stop the invaders just before they reached the Yazoo.

Fort Pemberton was located near Greenwood, Mississippi, a few miles above the confluence of the Tallahatchie and the Yalobusha to form the Yazoo River. Block vessels were sunk at a right-angle bend in the Tallahatchie and a cotton-bale and earthwork fort, mounting an imported eight-and-one-half-inch Whitworth rifle and several lesser cannon, was built to stop the Federals. Ross's men on transports, strung out for over a mile behind the gunboats, were helpless to maneuver on land because of the depth of the surrounding backwaters. Everything now depended on the strength of the ironclads that spearheaded the line.

A week of desultory battle now occurred. The ironclads *Chillicothe* and *De Kalb,* side by side and operating only their bow guns, moved cautiously downstream toward the Confederate batteries. Lest they become disabled in their machinery and be swept toward the enemy by the current, they were managed by tow lines run out to trees on the river banks, by which they could be withdrawn up the river beyond the fort's range. In the initial skirmish, the casemate of the *Chillicothe* was penetrated by a sixty-eight-pound, steel-tipped shot from the fort. Next day the enemy made a bull's eye through a gun port, killing and wounding an entire gun's crew. Shot landing on the casemate dented it, sprang it, snapped off the bolt heads, and splintered the soft pine backing of the armor. Watson Smith spent several days patching the gun-port shutters and desperately leashing cotton bales around the outside of the casemate to protect its armor! His health broke and he was surveyed by a board of doctors and sent north, presumably in a dying condition, and the command was turned over to Lieutenant Commander James P. Foster.

With his ammunition expended and the *Chillicothe* sadly battered, Foster was ready to retire from the contest when the menacing explosion of a Confederate torpedo off the "Chilly Coffee's" bow hastened his decision. On the return trip to the Mississippi, the expedition met a force of ten thousand men sent by Grant to rescue them.

While the Yazoo Pass expedition was being undertaken, Porter, from his headquarters at Milliken's Bend, was attempting to break up the flow of traffic from the Red River to Vicksburg. Before dawn on February 2, he sent the *Queen of the West,* under Colonel Charles R. Ellet, dashing past Vicksburg with orders to ram in passing a merchantman at a Vicksburg pier. In the turbulent currents, the *Queen* missed her quarry at the wharf, but came through unscathed by the hundreds of Confederate shot hurled after her.[13] At undefended docks below Vicksburg, she destroyed quantities of cotton and food, and in the mouth of the Red River she burned three Southern steamers. A fortnight later Porter dispatched the first-rate river ironclad *Indianola* with sixty-days' provisions and two barges of coal. The *Indianola*'s fire power, added to the *Queen*'s speed in ramming, should be able to control the stretch of river between Vicksburg and Port Hudson. But this time the wheel of fortune creaked the wrong way. The *Queen* ran aground under enemy batteries. Ellet could not destroy her without burning to death his wounded, so she was captured. The Confederates now turned the captured *Queen* and their own fast steamer the *Webb* against the *Indianola*. Catching the Federal ironclad after dark, encumbered by barges, they stove her in by sinking her barges and ramming her first on one side and then the other. The *Indianola*'s angry guns were avoided by her nimble antagonists. She sprang a leak, was run aground, and captured.

At this point occurred the luckiest practical joke of the war. When word reached Porter's headquarters of the capture of the *Queen* and before the capture of the *Indianola* by the Confederates, one of Porter's officers suggested that a dummy monitor be sent down river to aid the *Indianola*. The idea appealed to the admiral. Paddle boxes bearing the motto: "Deluded People Cave In" were built on an old coal barge. A formidable Ericsson-style turret, logs painted black to simulate guns, and pork-barrel funnels with smudge pots completed the dummy. As the craft drifted past Vicksburg on the night of February 24, the enemy batteries saluted it with a lively fire, through which it floated complacently and without receiving a scratch. When the device ran aground on the lower side of the peninsula, Sherman's men gaily pushed it out again into midstream.

This night a Confederate salvage crew at work on the newly captured *Indianola* were panicked by word from Vicksburg of the passage of a "river monitor." To prevent recapture of their prize, they tried to burst its guns and touched off the vessel's magazines. When the joke became known a jeer arose throughout the South. "Laugh and hold your sides, lest you die of a surfeit of derision," howled the Richmond *Examiner*. "Blown up because forsooth a flat-boat or mud scow with a small house taken from the back yard of a plantation put on top of it, is floated down the river before the frightened eyes of the Partisan Rangers. A Turreted Monster! . . . The Partisan Rangers are notoriously more cunning than brave."[14]

Mishaps to the *Queen* and the *Indianola,* together with disquieting earliest rumors that the Yazoo Pass expedition had been checked by a cotton-bale fort, sent Porter and Grant on March 14 on a quick reconnaissance up Steele's Bayou. Opening into the Yazoo ten miles above the junction of Yazoo and Mississippi, Steele's Bayou, together with Black Bayou, Deer Creek, Rolling Fork, and Sunflower River, it was hoped, might open a zigzag route across the southern end of the Yazoo delta which would bypass the Confederate obtructions at Haynes's Bluff. A Federal naval force in the upper Yazoo beyond these obstructions could destroy Confederate river steamers, strike at Fort Pemberton from the rear, and cut off Vicksburg from the rich plantations of the area. More important, a military route across the lower delta would enable Grant to skirt around Vicksburg's right wing and besiege the city from the rear. After reconnoitering only 30 of the prospective route's 120 miles, Grant hastened back to the Mississippi to dispatch a supporting force under Sherman, while Porter forged ahead into the as yet unexplored reaches with five turtle-backed ironclads, four mortars, and four tugs.

Steele's Bayou, deep and wide and lined with cypress and moss-bearded live oak, offered easy sailing. But Black Bayou was a secondary, lateral waterway connecting with Deer Creek, practicable for dugouts but tough for 150-foot ironclads. Sometimes Porter's turtles had to ram and uproot trees to clear a channel. There were sharp turns that they negotiated only by bumping trees and bouncing themselves around, with only inches to spare. There were branches to be cut away overhead. The jarring of ironclads' ramming trees shook loose snakes, lizards, and weasels that had taken refuge from the backwaters. Seamen had to sweep these animals from the decks. Black Bayou was fringed with canebrakes and the first land the sailors had seen since leaving the Yazoo. Raiding a plantation, a party from the ironclad *Cincinnati* brought in chickens, hams, eggs, butter, bed quilts, and the like. In twenty-four hours of constant labor, the expedition squeezed through the four miles of Black Bayou into Deer Creek.

The stream here was wider and plantations were thick. Passing through this unspoiled region, the ironclad warships resembled roofs of cotton gins floating through the fields! Surprised owners set fire to their cotton and abandoned their houses. As cotton wharves were often placed opposite each other on either side of the narrow stream, the invaders frequently had to run the gantlet of these scorching braziers. Cheering Negroes crowded the river banks. "Bress de Lord, I's ready!" "De Lord and de Abolishuns dun set de darkeys free!" "Glory to de good Lord." Negroes followed the gunboats for hours, begging biscuit and tobacco, "which they eagerly eat, even when they had to pick it out of the backwater." [15] Some of these excited blacks may have been from Shelby's, the Dear Creek plantation where Mrs. Stowe had found her prototypes for Topsy and Uncle Tom.

For bulldozing trees or for knocking down bridges, Porter found the ironclads handily adapted. Not so, however, for dealing with willow withes in the upper stretches of Deer Creek. Here the lithe switches caught in the overhanging iron shields and had to be pulled up or cut off under water. In this tedious work the Negroes helped with a will, despite threats from their overseers.

Willow chopping slowed Porter's advance, and on Friday, March 20, the Confederates began felling trees a few miles ahead of Porter at the junction of Deer Creek and Rolling Fork. Porter sent a tug with a howitzer to drive back these woodsmen and a party of two hundred marines to entrench themselves upon an Indian mound located at the junction. Sherman, meanwhile, was hung up forty or fifty miles to the rear at Black Bayou, through which his towering transports were unable to follow Porter's low ironclads.

Confederate troops now arrived in considerable numbers and were reported felling trees behind Porter. By a contraband the admiral sent a distress call to Sherman written on tissue paper and wadded up in a tobacco leaf. A coal barge now sank behind him and obstructed the channel. Before superior numbers his marines and pickets fell back to the boats. Enemy sharpshooters closed in, taking cover behind logs and stumps. Porter had to close his gun-port shutters—they were masked anyway by the high banks of the creek—and rely solely upon the skill of his marine sharpshooters stationed in the protected pilothouses atop the ironclads' casemates.

Sherman made a forced march through canebrake and hip-deep swamp, his men lighting their way by candles and the short drummer boys carrying their drums on their heads. The rescue party relieved the beleaguered flotilla two days after the distress call was sent out. Sherman's men, muddy, rain-soaked, and covered with lint from cotton gins in which they had lately slept, were heartily cheered. The general himself appeared, riding bareback an animal picked up on a plantation. He found the admiral on the *Cincinnati*'s deck protecting himself from sharpshooters by a section of smokestack. In a dark moment the now joyful admiral had written instructions for destroying the ironclads.

With Sherman's aid the ironclads withdrew from their tight spot. The sunken barge was torn up and its load of coal was spread out on the bottom of the creek so the vessels could descend. Some of the retreating ironclads managed to salvage cotton as consolation prizes. The *Cincinnati* acquired 60 bales, averaging 450 pounds each. "The rebels follow and shoot at us," wrote a diarist on board the *Cincinnati*. "The negroes, too, are following closer to us than the whites, and they form a motley group indeed, of all ages and sexes, the lame, the halt, and the blind, as well as the stalwart and active. They are in all kinds of vehicles that can be conceived of, and on horses, mules, and afoot, in high glee—'going to freedom, sure,' they say. Some shout to the animals they are driving, 'Go 'long, dar, old fool hoss, don't know nothing; your's gwine to freedom, too.' The cotton gins and outhouses on Fore's plantation (4 miles above Black Bayou) are still burning. The gunboats are now turned around, bows downstream, and their speed is increased. At half-past 7 P.M. we reached Hill's plantation, and stayed over night. *Wednesday, March 25*—The Union troops are strewed all along the bank, cooking, jumping, wrestling, and upon mules' back (*in puris naturabilibus*)! forcing the animals to swim the creek, and endeavoring to climb a steep bank upon the opposite side; some twenty of them have already tried this feat and failed, still others try. Received orders to take on each of the gunboats 250 soldiers for transportation to the Mississippi. The soldiers are now slaughtering beef and mutton and cooking for their rations on the trip. . . ." [16]

On his return through Steele's Bayou, Porter learned that, during his absence from the neighborhood of Vicksburg, Farragut had passed the batteries at Port Hudson and communicated with Grant across the peninsula opposite Vicksburg.

The campaign against Port Hudson in the lower river had suffered from the Union commanders' having too much to do and too little to do it with. In addition to the New Orleans operations, Farragut managed the blockade of the Western Gulf from Florida to the Rio Grande. Banks had to administer martial law in New Orleans, threaten Texas, and politically reconstruct Louisiana. Since many of his green troops had never handled a musket before they arrived in New Orleans, it was March before Banks notified Farragut that he was ready to commence operations against Port Hudson.

Farragut, ever impetuous, started upstream at once. His

aims were to pass Port Hudson with as many ships as possible, to communicate with Grant and Porter at Vicksburg, to prevent the erection of new Confederate batteries at Grand Gulf, and to cut off Confederate supplies from the Red River. For greater maneuverability in the currents of Port Hudson's hairpin turn, Farragut leashed small gunboats to the port sides of three of his large steamers. During the attempted passage, the river ironclad *Essex,* too feeble in her engine power to ascend the river, was assigned a supporting position with the mortar boats below the batteries, while Banks's army was to assault Port Hudson from the rear. "The captains will bear in mind," ordered Farragut, "that the object is to run the batteries at the least possible damage to our ships. . . . I expect all to go by who are able, and I think the best protection against the enemy's fire is a well directed fire from our own guns. . . ." [17]

Farragut moved upstream at 10:00 P.M. on the fourteenth. The flagship *Hartford* was paired with the *Albatross,* the *Richmond* with the *Genessee,* the *Monongahela* with the *Kineo,* and last came the side-wheeler *Mississippi* without a consort. As the invaders approached, the Confederates set fire to piles of pitch pine along the river banks and arched the river with rockets to illuminate the Lincolnite targets. In this battle Farragut suffered greater losses than in the battle below New Orleans. The *Richmond's* steam line was cut and she, with her consort, failed to get through. The *Monongahela* grounded for thirty minutes. Her bridge was shot away and she was otherwise badly damaged before her consort the *Kineo* worked her free. The *Mississippi,* conned by her youthful executive officer George Dewey, grounded hard at the turn and had to be destroyed. Only the *Hartford* and her "little chicken" the *Albatross* made it past the batteries.

During the month that remained before Porter and Grant shifted their forces below Vicksburg, Farragut patrolled the river between Port Hudson and Vicksburg, and to the enemy denied access to his supplies from the Red River. This was perilous work, as the deep-sea *Hartford* might at any time

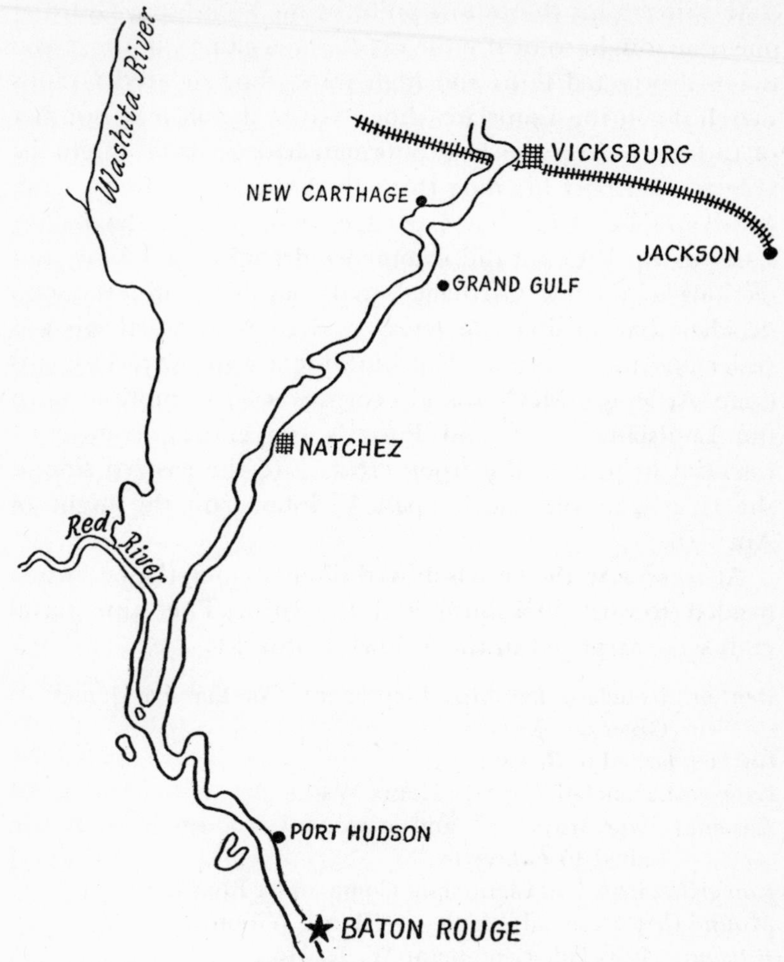

MIDSECTION OF THE MISSISSIPPI RIVER, showing Vicksburg and Port Hudson, which guarded the essential Confederate supply route through the Red River.

have been caught like the ill-fated *Indianola*. Of the two rams sent down from above as screening escorts, the *Lancaster* was sunk by enemy batteries during the passage of Vicksburg and the *Switzerland* arrived with a boiler punctured. Coal and naval stores, however, were drifted downstream to Farragut without mishap.

In shifting his troops to a point below Vicksburg, Grant at one time sought to utilize the experiences gained in the Yazoo delta. Protracted rains and high water long delayed Grant's march down the Louisiana shore. Given a sufficient number of tugs and barges such as Sherman had used, he might be able to transport his men through the drowned forest from Milliken's Bend to New Carthage, twenty-five miles below. Early in April Grant did commence dredging and axing out sections of a New Carthage canal, but his engineers soon decided that raising the levee road to New Carthage was easier and more certain than building a waterway. This was done. At length McClernand's corps was set in motion down the Louisiana levee, and Porter's cooperating ironclads—essential to protect the troop crossing to the eastern side of the river—ran the gantlet past Vicksburg on the night of April 16.

At 10:00 P.M. the vessels moved silently along the peninsula headed toward Vicksburg and the turn. The nine naval craft were arranged in the following order: [18]

Benton, ironclad, flagship, Lieutenant Commander James A. Greer
Ivy, tug, lashed to *Benton*
Lafayette, ironclad, Captain Henry Walke
General Price, captured and converted wooden side-wheeler, lashed to *Lafayette*
Louisville, ironclad, Lieutenant Commander Elias K. Owen
Mound City, ironclad, Lieutenant Byron Wilson
Pittsburg, ironclad, Lieutenant W. R. Hoel
Carondelet, ironclad, Lieutenant John M. Murphy
Tuscumbia, ironclad, Lieutenant Commander James W. Shirk

Three transports, the *Forest Queen,* the *Silver Wave,* and the *Henry Clay,* were placed in front of the *Tuscumbia* at the rear, and all ironclads save the *Benton* had coal barges in tow and were additionally shielded by piles of logs and wet hay.

Leading the column and skirting the dark woods of the peninsula opposite the town, the *Benton* was not detected until she reached the turn. Then, on the tip of the peninsula, a house was fired by Confederate pickets and on a hill beyond the city was lighted a calcium flare which directed shafts of blinding light on the river. The flagship was roughly whirled around by the current and came within forty yards of the wharves, so close that her captain could hear "the rattling of falling walls after our fire." [19] One after another the ironclads took their buffeting by batteries aloft and turbulent currents underneath. All ships came through with minor damage, save the transport *Henry Clay* which was destroyed by fire. All told only a dozen men were wounded. There was no one killed.

"It was a jolly scene throughout," Porter rejoiced next day in a letter to Fox, "and I reckon that the city of Vicksburg never got a better hammering. We all drifted by slowly, and opened on them with shell, shrapnel, and canister, as hard as we could fire. I was a little worried when I saw the *Henry Clay* on fire, but I soon saw that she was [an Army transport and] none of ours. . . . The scene along the river was beautiful—hundreds of little bunches of cotton all afire, from the *Henry Clay,* were floating down on the water, helping to light up what was already too light for us. These bunches of cotton followed us down the river, and when we anchored below Warrenton, it looked as if a thousand steamers were coming down." [20]

The protracted and unsuccessful maneuvering of Grant and Porter in the drowned forests around Vicksburg puzzled and annoyed President Lincoln. Lincoln was all for transferring from Charleston to New Orleans the army under Hunter and Du Pont's monitors to help open the river—that being the greatest present objective of the war; and, as Fox wrote Du Pont, the President was with difficulty restrained from that course.[21] Halleck relayed Lincoln's impatient queries and suggestions. Welles sent Porter a direct order to pass below Vicksburg and relieve Farragut—a message Porter did not receive until after he had already run the gantlet. To get a clearer picture of the complicated campaign, Stanton commissioned the journalist, Charles A. Dana, as a major in the volunteers and attached him to Grant's headquarters to make frequent and full reports of the situation.

Grant's troops having arrived at New Carthage, Porter on April 29 bombarded the Confederate batteries at Grand Gulf, preparatory to ferrying the troops across the river. It was a bitter fight lasting five and one half hours. The ironclads *Benton, Tuscumbia,* and *Pittsburg,* very much cut up, lost twenty-four killed and fifty-six wounded.[22] It was the navy's last solo performance in the Vicksburg campaign. Grant moved his troops a few miles further down the western bank and the Navy ferried them across at the undefended village of Bruinsburg.

In the final stages of the campaign Grant struck inland at Black River, Champion's Hill, and Jackson, maneuvering to prevent Joseph E. Johnston from joining forces with Pemberton in Vicksburg. On May 18 Sherman broke through to the river from the rear of the Chickasaw Hills positions that he had vainly assaulted last December, and Porter rushed up the Yazoo River to supply him with food and ammunition. Henceforth, the campaign became a regular siege, with trench warfare, sapping, and mining on the eastern military front. Throughout the forty days of the siege, the Navy rained thirteen-inch mortar shells upon the doomed city. Because the guns of the ironclads could not deal with Vicksburg's high batteries, Porter took fifteen eight- and nine-inch naval cannon around to his friend Sherman's sector of the front, where, manned by seamen, they directed their powerful blows against important positions of the enemy.[23]

General Banks invested Port Hudson on May 21 with twelve thousand men. On the twenty-seventh he launched an ineffective assault in which he lost one thousand killed and wounded, after which he remained quiescent until after the fall of Vicksburg.

By the end of June, the citizens of Vicksburg were eating mule meat under the name of "Confederate beef." On July

3 General Pemberton requested an armistice, and surrender was made on the Fourth.

Porter's telegraphed announcement reached Washington ahead of Grant's and was carried at once by Mr. Welles to the White House, where, as Welles's diary records the scene, Mr. Lincoln was "detailing certain points relative to Grant's movements on the map to Chase and two or three others, when I gave the tidings. Putting down the map, he rose at once, said we could drop these topics, and 'I myself will telegraph this news to General Meade [at Gettysburg].' He seized his hat, but suddenly stopped, his countenance beaming with joy; he caught my hand, and, throwing his arm around me, exclaimed: 'What can we do for the Secretary of the Navy for this glorious intelligence? He is always giving us good news. I can not, in words, tell you my joy over this result. It is great, Mr. Welles, it is great!' "[24]

Four days after Vicksburg, Port Hudson capitulated to General Banks. Farragut, as ordered by the Navy Department, now turned over to Admiral Porter the control of the entire river above New Orleans and went home for a well-earned furlough. The great campaign to open the Mississippi was completed. The Father of Waters flowed, in Lincoln's jubilant phrase, "unvexed to the sea."

16.

Du Pont and Dahlgren at Charleston

IN THE FALL OF 1862, WHEN LINCOLN SHIFTED commanders in the West, he was under pressure to make similar changes on the eastern blockade coast. During the year since the victory at Port Royal, Du Pont had preserved his reputation as the gracious, happy-ship commander of the South Atlantic Blockading Squadron. But now the war bugles sounded in the ears of the great ordnance inventor, John A. Dahlgren, and Dahlgren lusted to replace Du Pont in the forthcoming operation of ironclads against Charleston.

Du Pont had maintained a reasonably thorough blockade with the forces assigned to him, especially in view of the fact that the department had from time to time withdrawn certain of his best units to reinforce Farragut at New Orleans and for other temporary missions. Du Pont, however, was identified with the old wooden Navy, and Dahlgren—currently engaged in testing his huge fifteen-inch gun—was popularly rated, along with Ericsson, as representative of the new ironclad Navy.

In the obscure behind-the-scenes duel for command of the monitors against Charleston, Dahlgren enjoyed an exceptional position as unofficial naval aide to the President. From the outbreak of hostilities, the restless Lincoln was forever running to the Washington Navy Yard to see what Commander Dahlgren thought of the latest military or naval development.[1] Sometimes he would invite the slight, pale, scrupulously correct Dahlgren to accompany him on a brief outing on the Potomac. At times he would come simply to watch the test firing of a gun. Dahlgren's high forehead and delicately chiseled Teutonic features were set off by a thin shingle of sandy hair, crisply trimmed mustache, and electric sideburns. He was a thinker, and yet was human, too, his eyes flashing, nostrils dilating, as he warmed to a subject. He was the same age as Lincoln, as serious and austere as the President was jocular. The two were fit complements for each other. Lincoln, enjoying his company, invited him often to the White House, and found him a firm staff to lean upon on such occasions as the *Merrimack* scare when the Secretaries of War and Navy were at loggerheads.

Dahlgren's request to command the monitors was denied by Welles on the score that Dahlgren could not be spared from the gun factory.[2] In effect, this decision closed to the inventor the door to advancement in the navy line, since it was Welles's fixed policy to promote only on the basis of success in battle. Lincoln several times intimated to Welles that a letter from the department recommending Dahlgren would be favorably acted upon. But staunch Uncle Gideon was aware of Dahlgren's reputation in the service as a scholar who had spent twelve years before the war at his desk on shore, and he didn't think Dahlgren would be acceptable to the fleet as a battle leader. Certainly not to replace Du Pont. Accordingly, Welles called Du Pont to Washington, sounded him thoroughly on the subject of ironclads, and satisfied himself that Du Pont possessed the right brand of enthusiasm and fighting spirit. Du Pont was told to expect the ironclads as soon as they could be completed.

Lincoln now personally intervened to put Dahlgren's promotion through Congress so that Welles's own policy would not be vitiated, and Welles gave the new Rear Admiral Dahlgren appropriate duty as Chief of the Bureau of Ordnance, in addition to his work at the gun factory. The arrangement satisfied Dahlgren's desire for rank, but not his gnawing hunger for the test of battle. With that unappeased, he continued to fret at his specialized desk in Washington.

Du Pont, meanwhile, given to understand that he was expected to sail the ironclads past Fort Sumter and up to the wharves of Charleston—after the pattern set by Farragut at New Orleans—continued the usual routine of the blockade and waited for the ironclads to be completed and sent to him.

The *Monitor* and the *Galena* at this time were up the James River protecting McClellan's flank. They should be dispatched to Charleston, Fox promised Du Pont, as soon as Richmond fell. But Richmond stood, and, when McClellan withdrew from the peninsula, the thin-skinned *Galena* had been proved worthless. By the end of 1862 only the *Monitor* had been got off to Du Pont, and that vessel while on its way south on December 31, 1862, sank in a storm off Cape Hatteras. Later monitors in process of construction were to prove but slightly better in sailing qualities. Several after their maiden voyages from New York to Hampton Roads had to put into Washington's wooden-ship navy yard for repairs, whither both materials and workmen skilled in iron had to be rushed to them from Ericsson's establishment in New York. Sometimes such repair work was retarded by swarms of Washington officials eager to get a look at Ericsson's famous monitors. Captain Drayton, while his ironclad the *Passaic* was under repair, wrote a member of his family, "We are overrun with senators and members [of Congress] who won't be kept out, no regulations being considered to apply to those high functionaries, and on Saturday we had the President [,] Mr. Chase and some other important people, the former [Lincoln] went everywhere [;] crawled into places that Gerald or Henry would scarce have ventured in, and gave us a funny story or two in illustration." [3]

Long before the first ironclads reached Charleston, the newspapers were blaming Du Pont for the delay. Charleston was a difficult port to blockade. The sinking of the stone fleet in its main channels the first year of the war had only diverted the powerful currents of the harbor through other channels.

The city's defenders, foreseeing eventual attacks, had run lines of pilings, rope and chain obstructions, and torpedoes across the harbor's inner channels, and had greatly reinforced all the inner forts and sprinkled their outlying islands with new log-and-sand batteries to protect blockade-runners. At the beginning of the third year of war, with profits more fabulous than ever, the science of blockade-running was more highly developed. Long, gray craft with rakish masts and disappearing funnels had been built in Europe to elude and outrun the relatively unwieldy men-of-war outside Charleston's entrances. "I am kept pretty constantly upon blockade service, and hard and discouraging duty it is, off Charleston," wrote smart blockade captain John Downes. "I do not believe it possible to blockade the place effectually, and at times I am inclined to believe that with good pilots and judicious choice of time and opportunity, the blockade is but a trifling impediment in the way of steamers entering the harbor, painted lead color as they are; of a dark night, or a rainy one, they will pass, or can pass, within a few hundred yards without being detected, and, guided by signal inside the harbor, they almost invariably manage to avoid the blockading vessels. I would be glad if I could only impress upon you some faint notion of how disgusting it is to us, after going through the anxieties of riding out a black, rainy, windy night in 3 or 3½ fathoms water, with our senses all on the alert for sound of paddles or sight of miscreant violator of our blockade and destroyer of our peace, when morning comes to behold him lying there placidly inside of Fort Sumter, as if his getting there was the most natural thing in the world and the easiest." [4]

When the ironclads *Passaic* and *Montauk* reached the blockade base at Port Royal the middle of January of 1863, certain Confederate developments had already made it necessary for Du Pont to divert these first ironclads from the Charleston attack to other essential and pressing chores. The Confederate ironclad *Fingal,* with a more formidable engine than the *Merrimack,* threatened to drive off the wooden blockade ships from Warsaw and Ossabaw Sounds, or to release from her lair in the Ogeechee River the nimble blockade-runner *Nashville,* now converted into a commerce raider. Within Charleston two iron-plated rams were nearing completion: the *Chicora* and the *Palmetto State.* According to intelligent contrabands who escaped from Charleston to the blockaders, these vessels, 150 to 160 feet in length and equipped with old engines taken out of the steamers *Lady Davis* and *Aid,* could make four knots in smooth water. Four other ironclads on the stocks were being hurried along by the Confederates as rapidly as possible.

To his friend Commodore Theodorus Bailey, a veteran of New Orleans, Du Pont deplored the "morbid appetite in the land to have Charleston . . . the cradle of this wicked rebellion." He believed that had the government after Port Royal sent into this sea-island country one tithe of the Army of the Potomac, Savannah and Charleston might easily have toppled. "The difficulties have increased a thousandfold since then. English people who have been into Charleston call it a Sebastopol, and smile at the idea of its being taken. The Department thinks it can be done with a few monitors and talks of four. . . ." As for the department's idea of simply running past the forts *à la New Orleans,* if Du Pont had ever had faith in that plan, he cooled toward it when he returned to the realities of Port Royal. "You are aware there is 'no running by;' the harbor is a bog, or *cul de sac,* to say nothing of obstructions, which ironclads are much less serviceable in removing, as you know, than wooden vessels with their boats and appliances. I hope and believe we can do the job as well as most people. I shall certainly try." [5]

The most powerful of the Union ironclads in offensive strength was the armor-belted ship *New Ironsides.* Du Pont removed her anachronistic masts and spars, with which a conservative Bureau of Construction had equipped her, and sawed off her smokestack, which by an incredible blunder had been located immediately in front of the armored pilothouse! [6] The line of sight was now clear but the amount of gas and cinders thrown out from the stack and driven aft through the eyeholes in the pilothouse was enough to asphyxiate captain, pilot, and helmsman. The ship's heavy plate rendered her largely invulnerable, but her rudders were so flimsily bolted to her hull structure that her usefulness in battle was a question. Du Pont planned eventually to place her off Charleston to use her powerful Dahlgren guns against the Confederate ironclad rams. But the rams came out before the *New Ironsides* was ready.

On January 29, 1863, Du Pont's blockaders off Charleston crowded ashore and captured a blockade-runner carrying what was possibly the war's most important single cargo of contraband. Along with guns, arms, and ammunition, the crack British iron propeller, *Princess Royal,* was attempting to transport from Bermuda to Charleston two powerful steam engines for ironclads, together with expert machinists "to instruct the rebels in the management of new machinery and in the manufacture of steel-pointed projectiles." [7]

On the chance that they might recover the fabulous prize, which, the morning after her seizure, was riding outside the harbor with her captors, the Confederates gambled their two ironclads. At 4:00 A.M. on the thirty-first, the *Palmetto State* and the *Chicora,* taking advantage of a thick haze, sneaked out the Main Ship Channel and appeared suddenly under the starboard quarter of the blockader U.S.S. *Mercedita.* "She has black smoke. Watch, man the guns, spring the rattle, call all hands to quarters!" Captain H. S. Stellwagen, pulling on his pea jacket as he ran to the ladder, saw through the smoke a low boat which he took to be a tug belonging to the squadron. "Train your guns right on him and be ready to fire as soon as I order." Then he hailed: "Steamer ahoy! Stand clear of us and heave to! What steamer is that? You will be into us!" The stranger hallooed faintly from within his armored pilothouse and came on under the *Mercedita*'s counter. "This is the Confederate States ram ———" The name was choked off in the ram's impact, and her firing at the same moment exploded boilers and tore a hole five feet square in the port side of the Federal ship. Too close under to be menaced by the *Mercedita*'s gun, the ram demanded: "Surrender, or I'll sink you! Do you surrender?" [8] Stellwagen, without motive power and able to bring to bear nothing but muskets against his antagonist's shotproof hide, surrendered. Quickly the *Palmetto State*'s commander accepted from Executive Officer Abbot the parole of officers and crew and dashed away in company with C.S.S. *Chicora* to assault the next blockade ship, the U.S.S. *Keystone State*. It was after 5:00 A.M., and in daylight their second prey had time to slip her cable and commence firing to fend off these *Merrimack*-like twins. The *Keystone State* escaped after an hour's running fight, but received a crippling shot through her boilers just as her attackers gave up the chase.

The episode was humiliating enough for Mr. Lincoln's blockaders. The *Mercedita* surrendered. The *Keystone State* ran away. But to publish, as did General Beauregard and President Davis, that the blockade at Charleston was technically broken and that foreigners were now free to send vessels in and out of Charleston until a new Federal blockade should be cumbersomely instituted, was gasconade. At least eight Yankee blockaders were stationed off other near-by entrances to Charleston, and four of them—the *Augusta*, the *Quaker City*, the *Memphis*, and the *Housatonic*—arrived off the Main Ship Channel in time to trade blows with the attackers as they retired to the cover of shore batteries.

Following this incident, Du Pont insisted that the Navy Department send not just four monitors, but all they had. Welles and Lincoln had planned to send several monitors to Mobile. Welles deplored Du Pont's tendency to postpone the main attack. His perpetually calling for more ironclads reminded the Secretary of McClellan's calling for more troops. Lincoln jested about the monkey that kept asking for a longer and longer tail.

Du Pont's testing of the new ironclad *Montauk* resulted in the destruction near Fort McAllister of the Rebel raider *Nashville*. The *Montauk*'s commander—John L. Worden of

Monitor-Merrimack fame—had the good fortune to catch the *Nashville* aground just above the fort. Welles rejoiced over Worden's new victory, and in the press releases minimized the fact that, in returning downstream after blowing up the Confederate cruiser, the *Montauk* had herself been damaged by a torpedo.

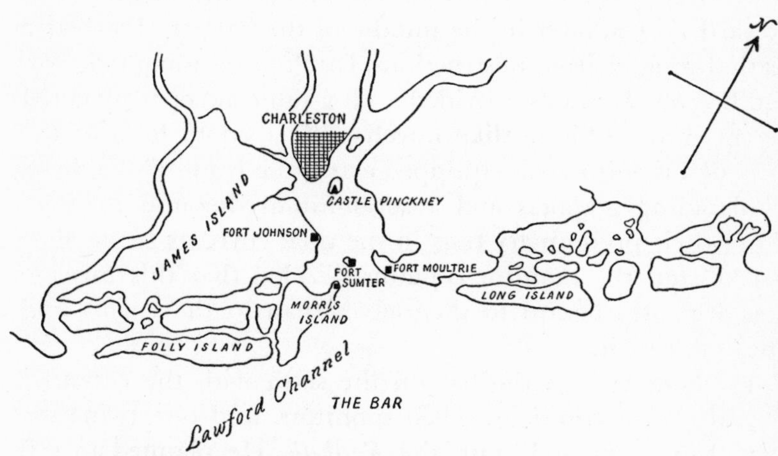

CHARLESTON HARBOR, a difficult area to blockade and the scene of attacks by ironclads under Du Pont and Dahlgren.

Du Pont, neither so certain or so enthusiastic as Fox about the ability of ironclads to deliver and absorb punishment, postponed the major attack for so long a time that Lincoln in April attempted to prod him into action.

Through Secretary Welles, Lincoln, on April 2, 1863, directed Du Pont after his present attack on Charleston to send all the ironclads that were in a fit condition directly to New Orleans, "reserving to yourself only two." [9] In the same mail Fox softened the blow by explaining that "the President was with difficulty restrained from sending off Hunter and all the iron-clads directly to New Orleans, the opening of the Mississippi River being considered the principal object to be attained." [10] To insure prompt action Lincoln dispatched these messages by dapper young John Hay, one of his personal secretaries.

Before Lincoln's special messenger arrived, Du Pont delivered his long-delayed attack upon Charleston. His Coast Survey party, escorted by a pair of monitors, marked the bar and set buoys along the Main Ship Channel which ran to the northwest, parallel to Morris Island and heading directly toward Fort Sumter in the middle of the harbor. To clear a path through harbor obstructions, Du Pont's leading monitor, the *Weehawken,* was provided with a mine sweeper invented by Ericsson. This raftlike novelty, V-shaped to fit over the bow of a monitor, was equipped across the front with a series of dangling grapnels and a seven-hundred-pound torpedo. After their preliminary tests in the tidal currents below Fort McAllister, the monitor captains decided that this torpedo was a greater hazard to themselves than to the enemy and they omitted it.

Du Pont crossed the bar on the sixth with the eccentric flagship *New Ironsides,* seven monitors, and one twin-casemated experimental craft, the *Keokuk.* He planned to sail around Fort Sumter, to engage its weaker northwest face, and, if possible, to get through the harbor obstructions to move on into Charleston. General David Hunter, whose troops had occupied Folly Island to gain command of two secondary approaches to Charleston, was poised to invade the southern end of Morris Island. But this first trial of the monitors was to be the navy's show.

Du Pont's forces, anchored inside the roadstead in the order of sailing, with the flagship in the center, were as follows: [11]

Weehawken, single-turret monitor, 2 guns, Captain John Rodgers
Passaic, single-turret monitor, 2 guns, Captain Percival Drayton
Montauk, single-turret monitor, 2 guns, Commander John L. Worden
Patapsco, single-turret monitor, 2 guns, Commander Daniel Ammen
New Ironsides, flagship, armor-belted, 16 guns, Commodore Thomas Turner

Catskill, single-turret monitor, 2 guns, Commander George W. Rodgers

Nantucket, single-turret monitor, 2 guns, Commander Donald M. Fairfax

Nahant, single-turret monitor, 2 guns, Commander John Downes

Keokuk, twin casemates, 2 guns, Lieutenant Commander A. C. Rhind

Each monitor carried an eleven-inch and a fifteen-inch Dahlgren gun. Against Du Pont's total of thirty-two guns, the Confederates had two major forts, Sumter and Moultrie, and a dozen satellite forts and batteries, collectively able to concentrate upon ships entering the harbor a heavier volume of fire than could be hurled upon any other spot in the world.

April 7, 1863. The early fog burned off to leave a day so clear that one could see beyond Fort Sumter the many steeples of Charleston. It was a balmy day, "flashing with the wings of countless butterflies." [12] At noon on the ebb tide, the most suitable stage of water for steering clumsy ironclads in a narrow channel, Du Pont signaled to get under way. As chains were being reeled in, the *Weehawken* at the head of the line fouled her anchor in the grapnels of her mine sweeper. The leading ship held up the line from 12:50 to 1:15 P.M. Then, one after another, the ponderous vessels got under way. It took thirty minutes for the four monitors ahead of the flagship to get started and another half hour for the four that followed. Inside the armor-belted flagship, with port shutters and overhead grating closed, it was almost pitch dark. Du Pont, in the crowded pilothouse, could be thankful that General Hunter had trained several of his sailors in the army's mode of signaling by semaphore, for otherwise the tightly closed ironclads were without means of communication. Nor, for want of correctional devices, was it possible for these primitive ironclads to carry compasses.

As the monitors came within range of Fort Sumter, it is doubtful whether any of Du Pont's sailors could see the people crowded upon the steeples and roofs of Charleston and along the neighboring shores. Some three dozen men all told, who were stationed within the pilothouses, could see the Confederate and state flags on opposite corners of Fort Sumter. The ironclads passed along the palmetto-skirted length of Morris Island without evoking the fire of batteries.

Not to ground the flagship in the narrow channel, Commodore Turner from time to time had a port shutter triced up and a lead dropped from the sill of the port. Too frequently for comfort, his heavy ship was found to be within a foot of scraping the bottom. Since the *New Ironsides'* armor belt protected only her midship section, Turner had sought to shield her wooden stem and stern by barricading vulnerable points with some six thousand sandbags. On her spar deck sandbags were laid over a spread of odoriferous green cow hides. All told the *New Ironsides* was as clumsy, unwieldy, and smelly as a barge, and her fragile steering mechanism was a constant worry to her skipper.[13]

At 2:10 the *Weehawken* reached the first obstructions. These were several rows of beer casks strung together by lines and extending across the harbor between Forts Sumter and Moultrie. Rows of pilings barred a passage between James Island and the Middle Ground. The *Weehawken*'s grapnels set off a Confederate torpedo which slightly lifted the ironclad's bow, but did no real damage. The *Weehawken* signaled: "Obstructions in my vicinity," and the line slowed down.[14]

At 3:05 Fort Moultrie and Fort Sumter opened fire.

The Federal ironclads were subjected to a terrific pounding by the forts, to which they could only reply in slow motion. As in Ericsson's first *Monitor,* gunners loaded and fired while their turrets revolved. Confusion developed as the monitors were crowded into the shell-splashed center of the cauldron. The comparatively tall *New Ironsides,* her black walls rising high above the squat monitors, responded so erratically to her helm that her pilot was compelled twice to throw out an anchor to escape collisions. The two monitors immediately behind her in line could not avoid bumping her, the *Nantucket* on one side, the *Catskill* on the other. At 3:25 Du Pont made the general signal: "Disregard motions of commander-in-chief," and kept his unmanageable flagship out of effective range so as not to hazard riding down the monitors.

As the battle progressed, each monitor came under intense fire for thirty or forty minutes. Du Pont could see through his glass the dark shot holes perforating the gaily painted smokestacks. Several turrets ceased to turn and had to be repaired under fire. The *Keokuk,* the last ironclad to come within the crossfire of the forts, fired only five shots at Sumter before her thin iron plates were riddled, and she hobbled out of action. At 5:00 P.M., on the advice of his pilots, Du Pont called off the action, intending to renew it on the morrow.

That night after anchoring, the captains of the ironclads came on board the flagship to report their experiences. They were men who had been carefully picked for this novel experiment and in them Du Pont had implicit faith. John Rodgers of the *Weehawken* jested grimly of the caprices of the mine sweeper. Sometimes, when the ironclad rose with the sea, the raft would fall. Rodgers never felt certain that it would not be washed upon his deck or caught beneath his vessel's overhang. The *Weehawken,* fortunately, had suffered no damage from the explosion of the Confederate torpedo. She had fired twenty-six shells at the forts and in turn had been struck by them fifty-three times. In spots her side armor was fragmented and the wood exposed. Of the cast-iron bolts which held her turret plates together, thirty-six had been snapped off and the turret somewhat weakened. Percival Drayton's *Passaic* had fired thirteen shells and received thirty-five hits. A shot landing at his turret's base had jammed together the rails of a gun carriage and put one of his two guns out of action. Vision through the eyeslits in the pilothouse was so restricted and battle smoke was so dense that Drayton thought it a great piece of luck that no one had grounded or been sunk by collision.

And so on down the list—too little striking power of their own, too high a vulnerability to overwhelming fire from the forts. Worden's *Montauk,* firing twenty-seven shots, received fourteen hits, no great damage. But after testing the enemy's fire and observing the obstructions, Worden believed that Charleston could not be taken by the ironclads now present, and that a continuance of the attack would have spelled disaster. The *Patapsco* got off ten shells, received forty-seven hits, and had one gun disabled. The *Catskill* fired twenty-two shells, was struck twenty times, and suffered no injury. The *Nantucket* hurled fifteen shells, and had one gun put out of action. Commander Donald Fairfax was "disappointed beyond measure at this experiment of monitors overwhelming strong forts." [15] John Downes of the *Nahant* threw fifteen shells in exchange for a pounding which jammed his turret and disarranged his steering gear. Broken boltheads hurtled like dumdum bullets inside the *Nahant*'s pilothouse. The cast-iron pellets knocked out pilot and quartermaster and fatally fractured the skull of helmsman Edward Cobb—who was the sole fatality of the day on board the ironclads. The *Keokuk* got off three shells before being completely riddled herself.

That the ironclads were mechanically unequal to the tough work cut out for them seemed so clear that Du Pont decided not to renew the attack. All night the *Keokuk's* people struggled to keep their vessel afloat, but the large and ragged apertures along her water line could not be plugged with any materials available. At 8:20 A.M. she sank off the lower end of Morris Island in seventeen feet of water. Du Pont sent the sunken vessel's skipper, Lieutenant Commander A. C. Rhind, to Washington to report the failure of the attack and Du Pont's decision not to renew it. On the way, Du Pont's messenger passed Lincoln's, John Hay, who on the ninth arrived off Charleston and delivered his dispatches to Admiral Du Pont.

By letter from his secretary, Lincoln learned the opinion of the ironclad skippers that in their attack on Fort Sumter they had attempted the impossible.[16] While they had been in action only forty minutes, most of the vessels had suffered broken boltheads and slightly indented armor plate, but these trifling damages had frequently sufficed to put a monitor out of action. A shot landing near the base of a turret could spring the mechanism of a gun carriage and blank out a gun. A bolthead rolling under the deck could scotch a turret. Fleet Captain George Rodgers gave Hay his opinion that the monitor fleet could not have survived a full hour of fighting. Du Pont was convinced that to run past the fort was to risk entanglement in the harbor obstructions and possible capture by the enemy, and thus even loss of local control on the blockade coast. Du Pont had positively declined to accept the latter risk.

Lincoln visited the army's front in Virginia in order to glean the earliest news from Richmond newspapers. Commander Rhind, with Du Pont's brief report and Rhind's own eye-witness narrative of the sinking of the *Keokuk,* did not reach Washington until five days after the battle. Welles took the naval officer at once to the White House. Both Welles and Lincoln had hoped, as discouraging newspaper reports came in, that the attack on the seventh had been an exploratory demonstration, feeling out the situation and preliminary to a main assault to come later. They were dismayed to learn that Du Pont considered it as final and a defeat. Rhind's story fell on unsympathetic ears. The *Keokuk* was not a monitor, and, thought Welles, its loss had "stampeded, disgusted, and wholly upset" its skipper. Why Du Pont had sent Rhind home "to howl," Welles bitterly surmised, was "to strengthen faith in himself and impair faith in the monitors." [17]

Above all things the immense psychological value of monitors must not be dissipated. Within the month the frightened Confederates below Vicksburg had destroyed a captured ironclad when Porter's dummy monitor had come in sight. Moreover, if Du Pont abandoned the attack now, the jubilant Confederates might shift their troops elsewhere—against Grant at Vicksburg, or the Army of the Potomac in Virginia. Du Pont must be made to hold his ground.

On April 13 Lincoln telegraphed Du Pont: "Hold your

position inside the bar near Charleston, or if you shall have left it, return to it, and hold it till further orders. Do not allow the enemy to erect new batteries or defenses on Morris Island. If he has begun it, drive him out. . . ."[18] And the next day, fearing that Du Pont and General Hunter might interpret the presidential order as a reprimand, Lincoln amplified his thoughts in a private note written jointly to the two commanders. "No censure upon you or either of you is intended. We still hope that by cordial and judicious cooperation you can take the batteries on Morris Island and Sullivan's Island and Fort Sumter. But whether you can or not, we wish the demonstration kept up for a time for a collateral and very important object. We wish the attempt to be a real one (though not a desperate one) if it affords any considerable chance of success. But if prosecuted as a demonstration only, this must not become public or the whole effect will be lost. Once again before Charleston, do not leave till further orders from here." [19]

Du Pont, meanwhile, had returned all monitors to Port Royal to repair their battle damage and get them ready, according to the earlier orders he had received, to be sent to Farragut in the Gulf. A quarrel between Du Pont and General Hunter had arisen over withdrawal of monitor support for troops on Folly Island. Another controversy grew out of the bad press reports. The Baltimore *American* attacked Du Pont in a slanted narrative of the Charleston affair, and Du Pont traced it to a writer who had been given hospitality on board a navy-chartered steamer. Du Pont's request to publish his detailed dispatches was refused by Welles, because to do so would officially blast the reputation of the monitors. Du Pont exchanged formal polemics with the Secretary. His sense of personal injury loomed in his own mind larger than the President's orders to renew the demonstration off Charleston. Not only did the discouraged officer make no move to carry out Lincoln's order, he did not even acknowledge its receipt. Worst of all, his want of energy at Charleston permitted Confederate divers to salvage the two long eleven-inch columbiads from the sunken *Keokuk.*[20] On June 3, therefore, Welles detached Du Pont.

Dahlgren, whom the President had long wished to favor, now succeeded to the command of the South Atlantic Blockading Squadron. Welles bucked and squirmed in disapproval of Dahlgren's use of personal influence with Lincoln. At first, the Secretary insisted that Dahlgren retain control over gunnery developments and accept temporary command of ironclads under Admiral Foote, but Foote's sudden death deprived Welles of his only suitable alternate, and Dahlgren, Lincoln's favorite, won preferment by default. At the same time another engineer, Major General Quincy A. Gillmore, replaced Hunter.

Charleston operations under the Dahlgren-Gillmore team followed the slow tactics of attrition and siege. With monitors supplying artillery, giving flank support, and enfilading enemy positions, General Gillmore landed on the southern end of Morris Island and fought his way north. His conquest of Fort Wagner at the upper end of the island cost him two months of arduous effort and the loss of sixteen hundred men.[21] Dahlgren's cooperating monitors suffered from the fire of various supporting forts as well as from that of Wagner.

When, on September 7, Fort Wagner was suddenly evacuated, the Union commanders were surprised and unready for their next move. Both Dahlgren and Gillmore, each acting in ignorance of the other's plan, hastily launched boat expeditions in an effort to seize the pile of rubble that once was Fort Sumter. If they could overpower the remnants of its garrison, the mound of broken brick could still be used as gun platforms against forts remaining in enemy hands. Under its friendly guns, the Navy might remove the harbor obstructions so that Dahlgren might yet fulfill Du Pont's grand dream of sailing in silently to the wharves of Charleston.

Four hundred sailors from the fleet were sent as a landing party to assault Fort Sumter. Towed close under the crumbling walls of the fort, they were here discovered by Confederate picket boats and brought under fire by Fort Moultrie.

Many of the seamen had difficulty finding a place to land. Others who scrambled up the pile of rubble on the southeast face ran into a sheet of musket fire. The attackers were thrown back with the loss of 130 killed, wounded, and captured.

Although Dahlgren's health often confined him to his bed even when General Gillmore came to the flagship for conferences, he clung to his job afloat with determination. As Welles had predicted, some older officers and friends of Du Pont were displeased with Dahlgren's appointment, and their complaints erupted from time to time as newspaper censure of his slow progress at Charleston. Dahlgren's refusal to place his naval storming party under Gillmore's control, as the general requested, strained relations between admiral and general. In October two of Gillmore's subordinates visited Welles to denounce Dahlgren "as incompetent, imbecile, and insane." The canny Secretary bridled as always when any part of the Navy came under fire from the Army, and noted that Dahlgren was "neither a fool nor insane." "Both Dahlgren and Gillmore are out of place; they are both intelligent, but they can better acquit themselves as ordnance officers than in active command." [22]

After the Federal forces occupied Fort Wagner, Charleston was no longer the happy harbor for blockade-runners that it had been. Henceforth, Gillmore's long-range bombardment of Charleston from the swamps of Morris and James Islands and the maneuvering of Dahlgren's ironclads inside the harbor channels sealed the starvation blockade at this important point. The Federal fort at the mouth of the harbor also penned in Charleston's ironclad rams so that they were able to take no further part in the war. Like his predecessor Du Pont, Admiral Dahlgren chose not to risk barging through Charleston's channel obstructions for fear Confederate forces might capture a disabled ironclad and turn it against the blockade fleet of wooden ships.

The final year of desultory naval blockade at Charleston was punctuated by the exploits of Confederate semisubmersible torpedo boats. These "Davids," so-called because built to fight Goliaths like the *New Ironsides,* were cigar-shaped cylinders, six feet in diameter and forty to fifty feet long, powered by man-driven propellers and armed with sixty-pound torpedoes. Several of these fragile craft sank during practice maneuvers. One exploded a torpedo under, but failed to sink, the *New Ironsides,* and lost all its own crew but the man on deck who had guided her. Another, which sank the wooden blockader *Housatonic,* followed her victim to the bottom with her entire crew.

Under the circumstances, Dahlgren and Gillmore could not very well press for a clear-cut military decision. Their battle, indeed, like that of the Confederate defenders was primarily political. Lincoln craved victory over Fort Sumter and Charleston because these objectives had become symbols of Secession. And the Confederates were similarly motivated to retain these positions.

Charleston remained impregnable behind its forts, its harbor obstructions, and its sea-island moats until General Sherman's fateful march to her undefended back door.

17.

The Red River Campaign

IN A FEW YEARS THE UNITED STATES GOVERNMENT would be able to send a general to Paris with instructions to get his legs under Napoleon's mahogany conference table and tell him to clear out of Mexico. But in midsummer of 1863 Lincoln could only register a quiet diplomatic objection to France's new puppet empire in Mexico, however flagrantly its establishment violated the Monroe Doctrine.

After the victories at Vicksburg and Port Hudson had opened the Mississippi River, Secretary of State Seward suddenly became alarmed over the situation in Texas. The Confederates had recaptured Galveston in January of 1863 and since that hour there had not been a foot of ground in all of Texas under Federal control. At Cabinet meeting on July 31, Seward whispered to Lincoln, Stanton, and Welles his fear that the French Emperor might try to get control of Texas, and urged "the immediate occupation of Galveston." Welles was disgusted with Seward's secretiveness. He thought the subject should be openly canvassed by the entire Cabinet, since directly or indirectly it concerned all of them, but being a diffident person he said nothing, and in the afternoon met again with Seward and Stanton in Halleck's office. Here Welles advocated striking Indianola, Texas, in place of Galveston. "Where," asked Halleck, "is Indianola? What are its advantages?" "In Western Texas," replied Welles. "It is much nearer the Rio Grande and the Mexican border, consequently is better situated to check advances from the other side of the Rio Grande; the harbor has deeper water than Galveston." [1] Welles, had the exigencies of the blockade in mind and did not relish another investment of slender military resources in Galveston. Halleck rubbed his elbows as usual when puzzled over what to do, and said he had just written General Banks and wanted his reply before deciding. That evening in his diary Welles, understanding the matter to have been left undecided, entered an acid comment: [2]

> This is a specimen of the management of affairs. A majority of the members of the Cabinet are not permitted to know what is doing. Mr. Seward has something in regard to the schemes and designs of Louis Napoleon; he cannot avoid communicating with the Secretaries of War and the Navy, hence the door is partially open to them. Others are excluded. Great man Halleck is consulted, but is not ready,—has received nothing from others, who he intends shall have the responsibility. Therefore we must wait a few weeks and not improbably lose a favorable opportunity.

While the War and Navy Departments reached no immediate decision on where to strike in Texas, Halleck, prodded by Seward, got off a directive leaving that decision up to General Banks:

> There are important reasons why our flag should be restored in some point of Texas with the least possible delay. Do this by land, at Galveston, at Indianola, or at any other point you may deem preferable. If by sea, Admiral Farragut will cooperate.
>
> There are reasons why the movement should be as prompt as possible.[3]

This directive was sent on August 6 by telegraph through General Grant at Vicksburg, and thence by special messenger to Banks at New Orleans.

Banks received it on the fifteenth. At once he set aside his long-laid plans for cooperating with Farragut against Mobile and began preparations for an amphibious movement upon Sabine at the southeastern corner of Texas, which was the nearest point to New Orleans. Banks was justified by the meagerness of his forces in seeking the cheapest and quickest means to fulfill his instructions. In this, however, he failed to reckon either with Confederate defense works at Sabine, which repelled his quickly organized attack, or with General Halleck's growing personal preference for an amphibian expedition into northeastern Texas along the line of the Red River.

Before Banks received Halleck's first directive, the general-in-chief was writing a second. "That order," Halleck explained, "as I understood it at the time, was of a diplomatic rather than a military character, and resulted from some European complications, or, more properly speaking, was intended to prevent such complications." [4] He was not changing the original order; i.e., Banks was still free to choose the place and manner of attack, but he was anxious for Banks to know that he himself favored the Red River route rather than an assault on the coast. "If it is necessary, as urged by Mr. Seward, that the flag be restored to *some one point* in Texas, that can be best and most safely effected by a combined military and naval movement up the Red River to Alexandria, Natchitoches, or Shreveport, and the military occupation of northern Texas." [5]

A few weeks later when Grant suggested a quick stab from Natchez against Kirby Smith through Monroe, Louisiana, Halleck saw a chance to tie in Grant's move with Banks's. "Your plan," wrote the general-in-chief to Grant, "will agree very well with the line of operations suggested to General Banks, viz: to ascend the Red river to Shreveport and move on Marshall, Texas." Grant was directed to confer on this matter with General Banks. "The government is exceedingly anxious that our troops should occupy some points in Texas with the least possible delay." [6]

Banks, meanwhile, free to make his own decision, landed forces at Aransas Pass near Corpus Christi and at Brownsville, the great Confederate blockade-running base at the mouth of the Rio Grande. The route via the Red River, he explained to the general-in-chief as tactfully as he could, involved an extended march over territory deficient in food and fodder with water-borne supplies uncertain because of low water in the Red River. "The rivers and bayous have not been so low in this State for fifty years, and Admiral Porter informs me that the mouth of the Red River and also the mouth of the Atchafalaya, are both hermetically sealed to his vessels by almost dry sand-bars, so that he cannot get any vessels into any of the streams." [7] Regardless of the routes taken or areas seized, Banks had now carried out the government's injunction to plant the flag on Texas soil.

The diplomatic objective achieved, Halleck might have dropped his idea of a thrust into Texas via Alexandria and Shreveport had it not been for the situation in Arkansas. Like Louisiana, Arkansas was in process of becoming a reconstructed state; i.e., a new state government was being organized by Unionists and "reconstructed" Rebels who were taking the President's oath of allegiance. That this civil process should be menaced by the activities of Confederate General Kirby Smith gave Halleck so much concern that he ordered Grant to aid Steele in the occupation of Little Rock. "If Steele and Banks succeed," Halleck wrote Grant on September 9, "all trans-Mississippi must return to the Union." [8]

Halleck obtained from the Navy Department assurance that Admiral Porter would cooperate as soon as the stage of water in the Red River would permit it. The river gunboats would be needed to smash Fort De Russy in the lower reaches of the river, to convoy transports and commissary boats, and to deal with any shore batteries or ironclad rams that the Confederates might have near Shreveport.

As the months rolled by, Shreveport loomed ever more important on Halleck's map in Washington. The Rebel capital of the State of Louisiana was important in view of the President's efforts to reconstruct the state. It was the chief Confederate military depot for the southwest. In Federal hands it would become a superb base for operations against Texas.

In far-away Washington, Halleck confined himself to suggestions and occasional directives that commanders on the ground consult one another with a view to collaborating. He himself never drafted an operation order for the campaign up the Red River. Banks in New Orleans finally came to accept the general-in-chief's views as "the government's instructions," and so, eventually, did the other participants. As the plan was finally worked out by the various collaborators, Banks with seventeen thousand men, reinforced by ten thousand under A. J. Smith temporarily detached from the Army of the Tennessee, would march up the line of the Red River, accompanied by Admiral Porter's gunboats. Near Shreveport they would be joined by Steele with ten thousand, marching direct from Little Rock. The combined Federal force of thirty-seven thousand men would then rout the Confederates' twenty-five thousand under Kirby Smith, Dick Taylor, and Sterling Price. Shreveport would become the Chattanooga of the West. The Confederacy east of the Mississippi would be separated by a wide band of Union-held territory from the remnants of the Confederacy in the West.

Halleck's failure to draft an operation order left Banks in the unsatisfactory military role of "first among equals," who could make suggestions but not issue commands to his associates from other military departments. The Navy, of course, was a completely free agent, coordinate with the Army, to be tactfully reasoned with rather than ordered.

Not only was there a complete absence of unified command, the associated leaders were motivated by a variety of aims rather than by a single clear-cut military objective.

A. J. Smith's force was on temporary "loan," its main objective being participation in Sherman's Atlanta campaign. After thirty days, Sherman stipulated, A. J. Smith would have to return to the main operations east of the Mississippi.

In addition to their military problem, Banks and Steele were promoting civil government. Elections were scheduled in the hinterland of Arkansas and Louisiana, as new territory was brought within the Union lines.

Moreover, the rumored two hundred thousand to three hundred thousand bales of precious cotton along the Red

River cast borealis lights over the whole country. Banks's commissary officers were provided with quantities of rope and bagging against expected seizures of cotton. Admiral Porter's seamen, flushed with recent captures of prize cotton up the Ouachita River, dreamed of even greater windfalls up the Red River.

Accompanying the expedition, in spite of Banks's restrictions, were civilian speculators, river pilots, captains of steamboats chartered as transports or supply craft, representatives of state or welfare organizations having troops in the expedition, and the like. Most prominent among civilian speculators was the Honorable Samuel L. Casey of Kentucky, who the previous December had presented to President Lincoln a scheme for bringing out Red River cotton from behind the military lines. Casey had a brother-in-law who was a Confederate colonel under Kirby Smith, and through him, presumably, had made some arrangement with the Confederate authorities. The pass which Lincoln gave to Casey authorized him to ascend the Red River with as many as three "inferior stern-wheel steamboats . . . taking in tow any number of barges, scows, flats." He was to go "without money and without cargoes outgoing, and only with crews to navigate the whole, and necessary provisions for himself and said crews," and was to be given safe conduct "on his return to our lines . . . with any cargoes he may bring." [9] At the height of the military campaign, this curious document in Mr. Lincoln's holograph, when presented to Porter and Banks, gained admission to the expedition-crowded Red River for Casey and his friends and his miscellaneous vessels.

Porter marshaled eighteen gunboats at the mouth of the Red River the first week in March, 1864, twelve of them ironclad. Since the fall of Vicksburg, the river ironclads had seen little action, and Porter was anxious to unlimber their guns against Fort De Russy. The Red River had now risen enough to float them in the lower river below Alexandria, but whether they could ascend above that city depended upon the river's reaching a high-water stage as in a normal year.

Though Admiral Porter professed great faith that the needed rise would occur, he was to be proved in this instance a mistaken optimist.

After A. J. Smith's twenty transports joined the squadron on the eleventh, Porter sent the ironclad *Eastport,* under Captain S. L. Phelps, up the river to clear a channel through the rafts and driftwood obstructions near Fort De Russy. Smith's men landed and marched in back of the Confederate fort to attack its undefended side in conjunction with a bombardment by the ironclads. To Porter's annoyance Fort De Russy's garrison surrendered to A. J. Smith without a fight. "Colonel De Russy, from appearances, is a most excellent engineer to build forts," Porter reported to Welles, "but does not seem to know what to do with them after they are constructed. The same remark may apply to his obstructions, which look well on paper but don't stop our advance. The efforts of these people to keep up this war remind one very much of the antics of Chinamen, who build canvas forts, paint hideous dragons on their shields, turn somersets, and yell in the faces of their enemies to frighten them, and then turn away at the first sign of an engagement. It puts the sailors and soldiers out of all patience with them after the trouble they have had in getting here." [10]

A. J. Smith covered the remaining distance to Alexandria on foot, flanked on the right by Porter's overwhelming force. In the lower reaches of the Red River, Porter's men tumbled several hundred bales of cotton onto navy coal barges, while two of his fast tinclads (the *Lexington* and the *Ouachita*), sprinting ahead, reached Alexandria in time to see the last of a fleet of Rebel transports disappear over the "falls" or rapids into the upper river. A Confederate ferryboat which had grounded had been set afire to prevent its falling into Federal hands.

At Alexandria, Porter's seamen emptied warehouses of cotton. While waiting for Banks's army, which had been delayed for ten days by torrential rains west of New Orleans, the sailors fanned out over the countryside and brought in cotton from plantations. Sometimes these naval machinists put disused gins into operation, and ginned and baled their captured cotton, using old ships' awnings as cover material. "Jack made pretty good cotton bales," boasted the admiral.[11] When Banks's wagon trains came in, the skylarking seamen borrowed army mules, painted them with navy initials two feet high, and hauled cotton from a distance. Confederate government cotton, stenciled with "C.S.A." on one end, was marked "U.S.N." on the other. Where ownership was doubtful, ingenious tars labeled their bales: "C.S.A.-U.S.N." The late-arriving Army regarded the profitable cotton-raiding pranks of the seamen with the jaundiced eye of envy. An army officer only half in jest inquired of the admiral whether the initials on prize cotton meant "Cotton Stealing Association—United States Navy." Others, more direct, asked General Banks to arrest the sailors. "Make war upon them, upon the ground that they are engaged in a business which does not belong to the Navy at all."

"Admiral Porter," replied Banks, "is, doubtless, acting under instructions from the Navy Department, and it is not my business to interfere with him." [12]

Banks had other worries. There was the election at Alexandria with its oratory, flagwavings, and firecrackers. In this political business, the Army took pains not to interfere. On the twenty-seventh, the day after his army arrived, Banks received by special messenger a curt note from Grant. The newly appointed Lieutenant General frowned upon Banks's diversified activities west of the Mississippi. "Should you find that the taking of Shreveport will occupy ten or fifteen days more time than General Sherman gave his troops to be absent from their command, you will send them back at the time specified . . . even if it should lead to the abandonment of the main object of the expedition." [13]

Banks was ten days behind schedule, but even had he arrived on time he could not have moved forward any quicker because of low water over the falls at Alexandria.

During the past two weeks, the contrary river had been

rising a few tantalizing inches a day. The Federal hospital boat *Woodford,* which attempted too soon to go up over the falls, was wrecked.

Porter dragged the heavy *Eastport* above the rapids. The process took two days, while transports and lighter craft passed around her up the swirling channel. On the twenty-eighth Banks set out overland for Natchitoches and Porter sailed upstream for the neighboring village of Grand Ecore, about a third of the distance between Alexandria and Shreveport. The gunboats were accompanied by Kilby Smith's brigade on transports and a host of commissary craft. Some of the heaviest of the chartered supply boats, which Porter had expressly forbidden to ascend into the upper river, came anyway. For the all-important cotton their civilian owners and pilots ignored commands and navigational hazards alike. Confederate forces hovering in the offing just ahead of the Federal invaders put the torch to cotton. General Banks's angered quartermasters, their boats piled with useless ropes and bagging, blamed the Navy. The Rebels would not have burned their cotton, said they, had the Navy not begun confiscating it. Their fallacious reasoning assumed that Southerners preferred for the Federal Army to get it.

After Banks's election routine had been repeated at Grand Ecore and Natchitoches, the combined expedition set out for Springfield Landing, a hundred miles further on and about forty miles from Shreveport. Again their routes diverged. Banks moved on the comparatively straight, narrow road through pine forests. Porter's waterway, narrower than ever, writhed and twisted about on itself. Around its sharp-angle turns the reluctant ironclads sometimes had to be coaxed by tugboats at bows and sterns. Snags and sand bars that threatened the squadron would normally have been covered to a safe depth by the spring floods. But it was not so this year. Nature favored the defense in this campaign, as the depth of water in the upper river sank disastrously.

Porter was four days making a hundred miles. Fortunately he was stopped near Springfield Landing by a channel block, consisting of an old steamer loaded with bricks and sunk across the stream. While Porter was examining the cynical invitations to the Yankees that had been posted on the hulk and was considering how best to blast it out of his way, there appeared a young cavalry officer in blue with news that Banks had been badly defeated near Mansfield, Louisiana, and was now falling back to Grand Ecore.

With heavy hearts Porter and Kilby Smith reversed course to bump back down the snaggy stream. Several army transports grounded and had to be towed. One such was discovered to have been filled to the rails with molasses, tar, turpentine, and other produce that had been loaded at Alexandria! General Kilby Smith's headquarters boat towed one of Porter's shallow-draft monitors.

Near Coushatta the transports were attacked by Confederate infantry under General Jack Green.[14] At the ambuscade the river banks stood high above the pilothouses of the flotilla so that sharpshooters could annoy the ironclads as on Deer Creek in the Yazoo country. However, the hurricane decks of the transports were higher off the water, and Kilby Smith's men, shielded by bales of cotton and hay and sacks of oats covered with wet soldiers' blankets, returned the fire of the attackers.

Up to the brink of the river dashed the Confederates, exhilarated by their recent victory over General Banks and fortified by canteens of Louisiana rum. Boat howitzers mowed down wave after gray wave of these reckless zealots. Their leader, General Green, was decapitated by a cannonball as he galloped across the field, and his horse streaking on with headless rider made a gory splash against a somber backdrop of pines.

General Banks dug trenches around Grand Ecore and waited here for ten days while Porter attempted to save the *Eastport*. This heaviest ironclad to ascend the upper river, having been left below the shallows at Grand Ecore, had come above them to protect the Army and had been caught by the fall in depth. The unwieldy *Eastport,* after having been dragged over part of the rapids, ran on a torpedo which opened a small hole in her bottom. In addition, she scotched hard on a log jam. Although her case appeared hopeless, Admiral Porter made a quick trip to Alexandria in the tin-clad *Cricket* to get steam pump boats, but in the end he was compelled to explode her guns and blow up her magazines.

During these anxious days at Grand Ecore, Banks received another warning from Grant that A. J. Smith's men should be promptly returned to Sherman. Banks now determined to abandon the expedition. When Porter learned that, prior to his defeat, Banks had allowed his advance cavalry to be separated from his infantry support by eight miles of wagons on a narrow trail through a dense forest, he lost all faith in his capacity as a general. "I cannot express to you my entire disappointment with this department," Porter wrote Sherman. "You know my opinion of political generals. It is a crying sin to put the lives of thousands in the hands of such men, and the time has come when there should be a stop put to it." [15] Porter, goaded by fear that the general might retreat at any moment and leave the fleet stranded, unburdened himself angrily and at length to Secretary Welles. "I do not see why a fleet should not have the protection of an army as well as an army have the protection of a fleet. If we are left here aground, our communications will be cut off and we will have to destroy the vessels. I do not intend to destroy a row boat if it can be helped, and if the proper course is pursued we will lose nothing." [16]

Not only the military were unhappy at Grand Ecore. The Honorable Samuel E. Casey, with the President's special permit, lost a barge load of choice cotton, which was seized by the Army to piece out a pontoon bridge.

Although Banks was not at this time aware of it, his turning back from Shreveport did not in the least disconcert General Steele. That general had insuperable problems of his own which shortly forced him to retire upon Little Rock.[17]

Banks's retreat to Alexandria carried him away from the shores of the Red River and left the Rebels free to harass fleet and transports. The winding and twisting about of the river enabled the Rebels to fire on passing steamboats and, by hurrying across narrow necks of land, to hit the boats again at the next turn in the river. Near the mouth of the Cane River, the Confederates established an artillery ambush which seemed particularly vindictive toward the navy's pump boats, which were crowded to overflowing with families of fugitive Negroes. Porter himself ran past this nest of hornets in the tinclad *Cricket*. During the passage the little craft, receiving thirty-eight hits, lost fifteen in killed and wounded out of a crew of fifty.[18] Porter was forced to use Negroes to man the guns and, when the vessel's captain and pilot were disabled, he himself took the wheel and steered her beyond the zone of fire.

Over the falls at Alexandria the water was only three feet, four inches deep, and the ironclads required seven feet. "If General Banks should determine to evacuate this country," Porter wrote Welles, "the gunboats will be cut off from all communication with the Mississippi. It can not be possible that the country would be willing to have eight ironclads, three or four other gunboats, and many transports sacrificed without an effort to save them. It would be the worst thing that has happened this war." [19]

The Navy feared that Banks would desert the fleet. Captain T. O. Selfridge, Porter's second in command, was told by army officers that General Banks had said that the whole cost of the naval part of the expedition would not equal the cost of the subsistence of his army for one day. But by the time of Banks's return to Alexandria, Grant had heard of the peril to the fleet and had ordered Banks to keep A. J. Smith until the fleet got out.

At one of the darkest moments in the navy's history, Lieutenant Colonel Joseph Bailey of the Fourth Wisconsin Cavalry proposed to construct a dam to release the imprisoned fleet. The admiral did not believe it could be done but was willing to try anything. Banks assigned three thousand men, and between two hundred and three hundred wagons to do the work. As he was desperately short of forage, the time he could remain at Alexandria was limited and the work had to be pushed day and night.

The rapids at Alexandria consisted of two stretches of rocky "falls" a mile apart, the channel between them filled with rugged rocks. Bailey constructed a dam below the lower falls.[20] Several pioneer regiments felled pine trees to make cribs for brick and stone. All the neighboring steam mills were torn down for material. Teams moved in every direction. Flatboats were built to bring down stone from quarries up the river. After sections of the dam had been built out from either side of the river, four navy barges filled with brick were sunk in midstream between the sections.

In eight days of working the water had been raised sufficiently to allow three of the lighter vessels to cross the upper falls and come down and be ready to pass when a sluiceway was opened in the dam. In another day the water would be high enough to float the other vessels over the upper falls. But now the pressure of the water became so great that two of the barges were swept prematurely downstream out of the sluiceway. Seeing this accident, the admiral jumped on a horse and galloped to the upper falls to order the *Lexington* to attempt a passage. The vessel came over just in time, then steered for the opening in the dam, where, in the turbulent waters, destruction seemed to await her. "Thousands of beating hearts looked on anxious for the result," wrote Porter; "the silence was so great as the *Lexington* approached the dam that a pin might almost be heard to fall. She entered the gap with a full head of steam on, pitched down the roaring torrent, made two or three spasmodic rolls, hung for a moment on the rocks below, was then swept into deep water by the current and rounded to, safely into the bank. Thirty thousand voices rose in one deafening cheer, and universal joy seemed to pervade the face of every man present." [21]

The accident to the dam dropped the water level and prevented the heavier ironclads from crossing the upper falls, but Colonel Bailey and his frantic workers built wing dams out from either bank just above each of the falls so as to raise deep flumes of water. In desperation the Navy stripped off the two-inch side armor from the river ironclads, tugged it upstream, and dumped it in quicksand. Guns were taken out of the ships and carried on heavy army caissons to be mounted below the falls. Some cannon of antiquated pattern Porter destroyed.

On May 11 the *Mound City,* the *Carondelet,* and the *Pittsburg* were dragged through the upper flume. The channel was very crooked and too narrow for comfort but they made it. Next day the *Ozark,* the *Louisville,* and the *Chillicothe* were brought through. With hatches battened down, the six ironclads one at a time plunged into the lower flume. "The passage of these vessels was a most beautiful sight," Porter reported.[22] They unshipped a few rudders and chafed minor holes in their hulls, but came through with the loss of only one man swept off a tug.

The anticipated trouble getting over bars in the lower river, which the naval squadron had dreaded, did not materialize. Very high backwaters of the Mississippi raised the level in the Red River all the way from its mouth 150 miles upstream to Alexandria.

From uncertain beginnings in the suggestions of General Halleck, the Red River expedition had blundered into the hinterland of Louisiana, poorly equipped for the military work it was expected to perform, badly managed, and terribly buffeted by bad luck on the water. From its worst predicament, Mr. Lincoln's Navy had been extricated by the labors of a brilliant young army engineer. The sorry debacle which overtook General Banks in the piny woods had been relieved by the heroic engineering victory of the Army and the indomitable, hard-bitten courage of the men of Mr. Lincoln's Navy.

During this troubled campaign, Lincoln had found a new general to replace Halleck, and upon General Grant the Red River episode's many lessons in the conduct of amphibian operations were not lost.

18.

Mobile Bay

After the capture of New Orleans in April, 1862, Farragut wanted to push on at once to Mobile. He wished to strike while the Confederates were still groggy from loss of their chief city and before they had had time to build up the defenses of this second most important port on the Gulf. For this reason, after the capitulation of the New Orleans' forts he sent the Mortar Flotilla into the Gulf to await his coming. "Mobile is so ripe now," Commander Porter insisted, "that it would fall to us like a mellow pear." [1] At this juncture, however, Lincoln vetoed Mobile and rushed Farragut's deep-sea warships five hundred miles inland in a singlehanded naval effort to seize Vicksburg. When Farragut returned from Vicksburg to New Orleans, battered and sore after his unequal encounter with the Confederate river ironclad *Arkansas* and his fruitless battles with snags and shoals, his ships were in no condition to attack the greatly strengthened Mobile forts, nor was General Butler at New Orleans able to assign any of his meager forces to cooperate against Mobile.

Bargain-rate conquests on the Texas coast now beguiled Farragut's blockaders. Without the loss of a man, Galveston, Corpus Christi, and Sabine City were seized by blockaders who found carrying on their blockade work inside of harbors less onerous and more effective than outside. Their fancied safety, however, was fool's gold. Without adequate troops to garrison their easily captured cities, the snug-harbor blockaders shortly found themselves surprised, captured, burned, sunk, or driven out.

No cheap victory was possible and none was attempted at Mobile. The main channel into Mobile Bay was guarded by two brick forts of approximately the same vintage as the forts below New Orleans. Fort Morgan on Mobile Point was a three-tiered pentagon, in general appearance resembling Fort Sumter; while on Dauphin Island to the west of it was the smaller Fort Gaines. Northwestward beyond Fort Gaines lay Fort Powell, built on a shellbank to cover the lesser entrances from Mississippi Sound into Mobile Bay. Just inside the main entrance of the bay was an irregular pocket of deep water three miles wide and eight miles long. Only the far end of this pocket was outside the range of the gatepost forts that flanked the main channel. Beyond this pocket lay a body of water too shallow for Farragut's battleships. These shallows, varying up to fifteen miles in width, extended about thirty miles northward to the city of Mobile.

Tantalizing information came through to the blockaders in an unending stream. Vessels sent to Mobile by General Butler to procure flour for the starving people of New Orleans brought information on the lack of military preparations after New Orleans fell. Fugitive Negroes told of their feverish work upon the several fortifications. Confederate draftees, deserting from the forts themselves, supplied Farragut an accurate picture of developing Confederate defenses. Fort Morgan had held only a handful ("two fire companies") in April of 1862. By August, its garrison had swelled to seven hundred men, and they had mounted a total of seventy-nine guns.[2] The place was now so strong as to require a regular military investment.

In the fall of 1862 Farragut's preparations to attack Mobile with wooden ships were categorically discouraged by Washington. McClellan had been outgeneraled again. Lee had invaded Maryland. British-built cruisers had eluded the diplomatic dragnet and put to sea, to be armed in neutral waters for raids on the high seas against United States commerce.

There were, Gustavus Fox explained informally to the restless admiral, not enough ships to allow him an adequate force to attack Mobile. Crippled vessels were limping into Northern navy yards faster than they could be repaired, and, to aggravate the shortage, the department had been compelled to set up a new West Indian Flying Squadron under Commodore Charles Wilkes to try to catch the Confederate raiders *Alabama* and *Florida*. Mobile would have to wait. "We don't think you have force enough," wrote Fox, "and we do not expect you to run risks, crippled as you are. . . . my opinion is that wood has taken risk enough, and that iron will be the next affair." [3] As for the new monitors expected by the end of the year, they were earmarked for Charleston. As soon as Du Pont captured Charleston, Fox promised, ironclads should be sent to Farragut.

So Farragut with his wooden ships established as close a blockade as possible and waited—for two years. Du Pont fought his unprecedented battle against forts in Charleston Harbor and was replaced by Dahlgren. The unending bombardment of the Citadel of Secession may have been important in building Northern morale, as Lincoln evidently believed, but it tied up the ironclads and kept them from fulfilling a valid military objective at Mobile. In the summer of 1863 Farragut went north for needed rest.

For two years following the fall of New Orleans the Confederates made sport of the blockaders off Mobile. When blockade-running became too hazardous to risk sending out thirty-one kegs, each containing five thousand dollars in specie to pay interest on their debt to British creditors, citizens of Mobile persuaded a venal English consul to ship the kegs as British property to Havana on board a British warship.[4] Of course, when the trick was exposed, Her Majesty's Government disavowed the act and discharged the consul, but the specie was not returned. From Mobile, raiding parties sailed out through shallow Mississippi Sound—Farragut always had too few light-draft blockaders to control this sound. At the mouths of the Mississippi River, the raiders hid themselves and like pirates pounced upon unsuspecting merchant craft. Twice when their prizes were too heavy to bring home through the sound they entered via the main channel, quietly eluding the blockade fleet. Commander John N. Maffitt, C. S. Navy, plagued by yellow fever and neutrality regulations, hoisted an English ensign over his British-built cruiser *Florida* and headed toward Mobile Bay. The blockaders were so anxious not to precipitate a foreign war that they permitted the intrepid stranger to ignore their challenge until it was too late for their random shots to sink him. The senior blockading officer was cashiered by Lincoln for timidity or want of judgment.

When Farragut returned to the Gulf in January of 1864, the need for action against Mobile was more urgent than ever. The Confederates had been pushing the construction of ironclads not only to defend Mobile but to assume the offensive and break the blockade. It was a time when all around the blockade coast the Confederates were improvising ironclads. In the sounds of North Carolina the ironclad ram *Albemarle* was taking shape. Charleston and Savannah were riveting railroad iron over heavy wooden casemates. Far inland, at Selma, Alabama, the ironclad *Tennessee* was under construction, with three courses of wrought-iron plates, two inches thick.[5] The *Tennessee* was built on the lines of the *Merrimack,* only shallower, more manageable. Confederates claimed she would surpass the *Merrimack* in power. In addition there were three other gunboats at Mobile: the *Selma,* the *Gaines,* and the *Morgan*. These, with their heavy wooden casemates painted black and tallow-greased, were described to Farragut as ironclads by deserters who claimed to have worked on them. Supervising construction at Mobile and preparing actively to advance against Farragut's blockaders was Admiral Franklin Buchanan, the South's ranking naval officer and the experienced first commander of the *Merrimack*.

It was the report that the *Tennessee* was finished that had brought Farragut back from his furlough, impatient, chafing at delay, almost ready to plunge into Mobile Bay without an iron ship. There was the chance that he might catch "Old Buck" at the embarrassing moment, when his powerful ironclad, minus its guns, fuel, and ammunition, was being floated on caissons across Dog River Bar into the deep water of the bay. Farragut would have taken that chance had it not been for the fact that his own heavy ships could not navigate the shallow upper reaches of the bay, and Farragut's few light-drafts were fragile matchboxes by comparison with the Confederate ironclad.

What Farragut urgently needed was a light-draft monitor for the shallow-water work at Dog River Bar. The Navy Department, indeed, had foreseen his requirement months ago and had ordered twenty such craft.[6] Only half as deep as the first *Monitor,* yet having the same invulnerability and striking power, these craft had been designed to ferret out enemy ironclads and destroy them on their stocks. Ericsson had approved their plans, and Chief Engineer Alban C. Stimers had been placed in charge of the project. Unfortunately, Stimers had tried to incorporate in the new models too many good suggestions which added weight to the finished product, and—disastrously as it turned out—he failed to check a young assistant's mathematical calculations for buoyancy. In consequence, when the first ship of the class was launched at Boston, it nearly sank. It was impossible without swamping the miserable craft to load on board its guns, shells, ammunition, and fuel. Lincoln's Navy Department salvaged as best they could, by stripping off armor and converting the bad lot into expensive and not very useful torpedo boats. This fiasco in naval construction deprived Farragut of the specialized force that had been intended for him.

In his extremity, Farragut, in January 1864, applied to Porter on the Mississippi for the loan of two monitors. "If I had them, I should not hesitate to become the assailant instead of awaiting the attack. I must have ironclads enough to lie in the bay to hold the gunboats and rams in check in the shoal water." [7] And at the same time he appealed again to

Secretary Welles urging that with a single ironclad and the cooperation of five thousand troops to isolate the forts, he could destroy all of Buchanan's forces afloat. The threats of Confederate propagandists that Old Buck would not only sink Farragut and raise the siege of Mobile Bay but also sail on to liberate New Orleans served to keep the occupied city in a state of alarm. "If the Department could get one or two of the ironclads down here it would put an end to this state of things and restore confidence to the people of the ports now in our possession." [8] Welles responded by earmarking for Farragut two single-turret monitors built in New York (the *Tecumseh* and the *Manhattan*) and two twin-turret river monitors (the *Chickasaw* and the *Winnebago*) in St. Louis. These vessels, although already launched, would require four or five months to finish and another month for towing and repairing en route to Farragut off Mobile.

From January to July, 1864, Farragut waited for the monitors. As a diversion in favor of General W. T. Sherman's operations in central Mississippi, he bombarded Fort Powell for two weeks. Because of shallowness of the water he could barely bring his mortar schooners within the extreme range of three miles of his target, and then, recoiling under the vertical firing, their hulls were driven a foot deep into the bottom mud. Once upon returning from an inspection trip to the coast of Texas, Farragut found only two small vessels off Mobile. Where were the other eleven of the thirteen ships assigned to this station? Two or three at a time might expect to be absent for repairs or coal at Pensacola Navy Yard, but Farragut now learned that his blockade captains had become so interested in prize money that they were taking time off from their stations to convoy all the way to the admiralty court in Key West the numerous petty cotton schooners captured while trying to run the blockade. "There appears to be no consideration for anything but capturing blockade runners," rasped Farragut in reprimanding the senior officer off Mobile, "totally ignoring the fact that the great object of the Government is to prevent the egress of the ironclads and other gunboats. . . . The capturing of the blockade-runners, although important as crippling the enemy in the sinews of war, is nevertheless of little consideration as compared with the close blockade of the port to prevent ingress and egress of vessels of war." [9]

Operations at Mobile suffered, one is driven to believe, because Farragut was no politician. He needed a few ironclads and a few thousand troops. Certainly, in the important business of persuading Washington to give him the necessary forces, he could not in the spring of 1864 hold a candle beside such officer-politicians as Admiral Porter on the Red River or Admiral Dahlgren in Charleston Harbor. Farragut was treated like a commander on a foreign station whose needs were less than urgent. Secretary Welles respected him as a modest, forthright, and daring officer who could be depended on to carry through a difficult campaign. But he answered Farragut's persistent pleas with temporizing and delay. To detach a few ironclads from Porter and Dahlgren was a thought that apparently did not occur to Mr. Welles. It might have—had Farragut's relations with that influential dynamo Gustavus Fox been as chummy as Porter's, or if Farragut's acquaintance with Mr. Lincoln had been as personal and intimate as Dahlgren's.

Farragut's chances of obtaining military support improved in the spring of 1864 when Grant took over from Halleck the general direction of the Federal armies. The new general-in-chief's first act was to remove General Banks from command of armies in the field. Since Lincoln refused to recall Banks from the Department of the Gulf, Grant had to make shift by creating the so-called Military Division of West Mississippi for General E. R. S. Canby, leaving Banks his former title and vague administrative duties in New Orleans. In effect Grant regarded Canby's post as a sort of receivership charged with salvaging Banks's scattered and (after Red River) dispirited army. Grant, moveover, insisted upon considering Texas and the entire area west of the Mississippi River from a military point of view, and applied a policy of retrenchment in the West and concentration upon military theaters in the East. Grant's recall of outlying garrisons like that at Matagorda, Texas, disturbed those Unionists who, having disclosed their loyalty during the Federal occupation, were now thrust back among hostile Confederate neighbors, but Grant elected to consider only the cold military facts of his situation.

In General Canby, Farragut found a willing and businesslike collaborator. Canby planned to move upon Mobile in July when Farragut's ironclads would arrive. And there was sound military reason for him to hold to his plan. Not only was Mobile itself a vital objective. The attack on Mobile would create a diversion in support of General W. T. Sherman's campaign against Atlanta.

Early in July, however, Grant transferred the bulk of Canby's army to Virginia to replace heavy losses in the Army of the Potomac. The reduction of Canby's force canceled any formal, full-scale military campaign against the city of Mobile, but both Canby and Farragut were willing to limit the military objective to the forts in the lower bay. As finally agreed, Farragut would run past the forts into the lower bay and deal with Buchanan's fleet, while a small detachment under Brigadier General Gordon Granger would land on the beaches to close the back doors of Forts Morgan and Gaines, cutting their communications with Mobile and rendering secure Farragut's communications with the outside across Dauphin Island and Federal Point.

Since May, the ironclad *Tennessee* had been maneuvering in the lower bay with the gunboats *Selma, Gaines,* and *Morgan.* Farragut, reconnoitering on board a small warship, descried Buchanan's blue flag. From Fort Gaines on Dauphin Island three rows of pilings extended eastward across the shallows toward the main channel. In the channel itself a red buoy about a mile west of Fort Morgan marked the eastern end of a mine field, in which almost daily a Confederate vessel could be seen planting "torpedoes." Farragut's ships would have to sail to the eastward of this buoy in a channel directly under Fort Morgan, the enemy's strongest fort.

Farragut planned to enter the harbor on a full tide, wooden ships leashed in pairs so that a crippled ship could be assisted by its yokemate and drifted in on the tide. Smaller gunboats were leashed to port sides of battleships to shield them from the fire of Fort Morgan. To starboard and ahead of the double column, the ironclad monitors would advance in single file to draw the fire of the fort away from the wooden-walled ships. Inside the harbor the monitors would deal with the *Tennessee,* light gunboats would run down enemy gunboats, wooden battleships would use their heavy guns to support the army against the forts and, if necessary, would ram the *Tennessee.*

His long-awaited monitors reached Farragut by the end of July, after repairing at New Orleans and Pensacola and after laborious towing. The *Tecumseh,* under Captain T. A. M. Craven, the last to arrive, was forced to remain an extra forty-eight hours in the navy yard at Pensacola. Her tardiness chagrined Farragut, for the army contingent under General Granger had arrived on schedule and proceeded on August 3 to land on Dauphin Island behind Fort Gaines. Had not Craven been a personal friend and scheduled to lead the line of monitors, the impetuous admiral would doubtless have launched his attack without the *Tecumseh.* The delayed monitor, towed by the battleship *Richmond,* arrived off Mobile Bay a few hours before the battle.

Farragut's line-up in the fog before daybreak on August 5, 1864, was as follows: [10]

I. Monitor Division

Tecumseh, single-turret, Captain Tunis A. M. Craven
Manhattan, single-turret, Commander J. W. A. Nicholson
Winnebago, twin-turret, Commander T. H. Stevens
Chickasaw, twin-turret, Lieutenant Commander George H. Perkins

II. Wooden Ship Division

Brooklyn, Captain James Alden

Octorara, Lieutenant Commander C. H. Greene

Hartford, flagship, Captain Percival Drayton

Metacomet, Lieutenant Commander James E. Jouett

Richmond, Captain T. A. Jenkins

Port Royal, Lieutenant Commander B. Gherardi

Lackawanna, Captain J. B. Marchand

Seminole, Commander E. Donaldson

Monongahela, Commander James H. Strong

Kennebec, Lieutenant Commander W. P. McCann

Ossipee, Commander W. E. LeRoy

Itasca, Lieutenant Commander George Brown

Oneida, Lieutenant C. L. Huntington

Galena, Lieutenant Commander C. H. Wells

The fog cleared and the ships got under way by 5:45 A.M. They were well prepared. Farragut had given orders to remove all unnecessary gear from decks and masts. Chains had been hung over the sides, and vital parts of the ships had been made snug with sandbags and sacks of coal and ashes. At the Pensacola yard, where Farragut had developed a modest metal-working shop, boiler iron had been bent around the stems of several of his heavy ships to render them more effective as rams.

In placing the *Brooklyn* and the *Octorara* at the head of the double column of ships, Farragut had yielded, on advice of his captains, the position of greatest danger—which, as an old-fashioned sea dog, he considered a perquisite of his rank. The *Brooklyn,* his captains insisted, had four guns in the bow which would be useful during those long minutes when the ships would be head on toward the enemy and unable to use their broadside guns. Farragut, missing the lead position, climbed into the port main rigging of the *Hartford* to get a better view. Captain Drayton, remembering the slight touches of gout and vertigo from which the sixty-three-year-old admiral suffered, sent Quartermaster Knowles up the ratlines to pass a small rope around the admiral to steady him.

At 6:47 A.M. the *Tecumseh,* the leading monitor, touched off a challenging shot toward Fort Morgan, and at 7:06 Morgan replied. Quickly now puffs of smoke and the blasting roars of battle arose from the fort, the shore batteries outside the fort, and the decks of ships. On swept the file of wooden ships, harnessed two and two. They overhauled the slower monitors. Although cruising under low steam pressure to minimize possible damage from exploding boilers, they were borne forward with speed by the flood tide. The *Brooklyn* and the *Octorara* led the line, with Farragut's *Hartford* and *Metacomet* immediately following.

As the *Tecumseh* reached the area of gravest danger between Fort Morgan and the minefield, she sighted in the bay ahead the C.S. ironclad ram *Tennessee* and the gunboats *Selma, Gaines,* and *Morgan* moving out from behind Federal Point. Captain Craven, eager to close with the *Tennessee* as quickly as possible, shifted the *Tecumseh*'s course toward the Confederate terror. The new course carried him across a corner of the minefield, to the left of the red marker buoy. The *Tecumseh* ran onto a torpedo.

"After you, pilot," Captain Craven stood aside to allow Pilot John Collins to go first up the ladder, and in a matter of moments the *Tecumseh* sank.[11]

Collins stepped up and out into the water, the ship falling away beneath him. Twenty-one other sailors scrambled from the stricken ironclad's hatches during these precious seconds before she turned turtle and sank, carrying to the bottom her courteous skipper and ninety-two other officers and crewmen.

When the *Tecumseh* went down, the *Brooklyn,* under Captain James Alden, had just hauled up behind the monitors and had come under hot fire from the fort. The *Brooklyn's* lookout at this crucial juncture reported shoal water. The vessel was hugging the shore under Fort Morgan, and, as the smoke cleared up a little, Captain Alden saw "a row of suspicious looking buoys . . . directly under our bows." [12] He gave the order to back up and clear these obstructions.

Farragut, on the next ship in the line, instantly perceived the danger of his own ship and the vessels following him awkwardly crowding in confusion behind the pair of stalled leaders, inside the critical shell-splashed arena between fort and torpedo field. Captain Drayton's position was on the *Hartford's* deck beneath the admiral's perch in the rigging. Captain Jouett, of the side-wheeler *Metacomet,* was standing on his vessel's starboard paddlebox under, and within earshot of, the Admiral. "Oh God," Farragut whispered, "shall I go on?" And it seemed to him that an inner voice commanded: "Go on!" Farragut's hail was answered from the *Brooklyn* with a warning of torpedoes ahead.

"Damn the torpedoes! Four bells! Captain Drayton, go ahead! Jouett, full speed!" [13]

Jouett reversed the *Metacomet*'s paddlewheel. The *Hartford* and the *Metacomet,* hausers straining and sidewalls chafing, waltzed about sharply to port, sailed past the *Brooklyn* and the *Octorara,* and directly ahead across the minefield. As they came to the spot where the *Tecumseh* had disappeared, Farragut had Jouett drop a boat to pick up survivors. At the same time, on the parapets of Fort Morgan, Confederate General Richard L. Page—a one-time shipmate of Farragut's—ordered his gunners not to fire on the lifeboat.

"I steamed through between the buoys where the torpedoes were supposed to have been sunk," Farragut reported to Welles. "These buoys had been previously examined by my flag lieutenant J. Crittenden Watson, in several nightly reconnaissances. Though he had not been able to discover the sunken torpedoes, yet we had been assured by refugees, deserters, and others of their existence, but believing that from their having been some time in the water, they were probably innocuous, I determined to take the chance of their explosion." [14]

From the moment of the *Hartford*'s turn to the left, she was able to deal heavy blows from her starboard broadside. The *Brooklyn* and the *Octorara,* righting themselves, fell into Farragut's wake and the remainder of the line followed through in good order. The Confederate ram *Tennessee* at 7:50 lunged toward the *Hartford,* missed, and merely exchanged a broadside before the flagship ran clear of its path. The Confederate gunboats *Selma, Gaines,* and *Morgan,* more maneuverable than their iron consort, were able during Farragut's approach to cross his T and send a number of raking shots down the length of his deck. But the stingers of these nimble wasps were soon drawn. At 8:02 Farragut cast off the *Metacomet.* Jouett churned water in pursuit of the *Selma,* and, having shallow draft, was able to follow his prey into shoal water and capture her. Later ships were not so prompt as the flagship in cutting loose their gunboat consorts, so that the *Morgan* and the *Gaines* escaped to the protection of Fort Morgan. Here the *Gaines,* heavily injured by the fire of the fleet, was destroyed, but the gunboat *Morgan* after nightfall outran Farragut's cruisers and made her way up the bay to the city of Mobile.

All of Farragut's wooden ships succeeded in running the gantlet and anchored with the flagship four miles above the forts. They were at breakfast, and had scarcely begun to think of how they would deal with the *Tennessee* when they saw that vessel pouring black smoke and driving up the bay toward their anchorage. Old Buck had decided to settle the issue promptly.

On each ship was an army signalman for communicating with General Granger's force on shore. Farragut now used military personnel, they being quicker than navy flag signals, to order his ships to attack the oncoming *Tennessee,* both by gunfire and ramming, bows on at full speed. This time Farragut chose as his personal vantage point the main rigging near the top, and again a protective rope was passed around him.

The *Monongahela,* under Commander Strong, twice crushed her nose against the shell of the great iron turtle. Without inflicting any apparent damage to the *Tennessee,* she tore away her own boiler-iron prow and sprung or shattered the butt ends of her planking on both bows.

The *Lackawanna,* under Captain Marchand, making good speed, struck the ram a heavy right-angle blow at the after end of the casemate. As both ships recoiled from the impact, several of the *Tennessee's* crew thrust their heads through her ports and used "opprobrious language," provoking the *Lackawanna's* marines to drive them back inside with a rain of holystones and spittoons.

The *Hartford,* under Captain Drayton, was the third vessel to ram. Unable to slip the anchor cable because of a jammed shackle pin, Captain Drayton had quickly hauled it clear of the water, and, without taking the time to "cat and fish" it on board, had sailed head on toward an enemy who was also making directly for the *Hartford.* Had the two flagships collided bows on, it is possible that Buchanan's ironclad might have thrust itself so deeply into the vitals of Farragut's wooden ship as to sink it and be herself swamped by her victim. At the last minute Buchanan swerved to one side and the two ships scraped each other. As they ground past, the *Hartford's* broadside of nine-inch solid shot bounded off the slanted, greased casemate not more than eight feet away. Because of injuries to guns and port shutters, the *Tennessee* had but two serviceable guns in broadside, and these tore through the *Hartford's* berth and spar decks and even into the hold where her wounded were. The long *Lackawanna* misjudged the quickly shifting positions and, in heading back for another blow at the enemy, crashed into the *Hartford,* forward of the mizzen. Farragut scurried down from his perch in a minute and over the side to see what damage he had suffered. Cut down to within two feet of the water line, he ordered another run against the ram. But at this moment the *Tennessee* struck her colors and raised the white flag. The *Ossipee,* under Commander Le Roy, having too much headway, backed engines but could not avoid giving a glancing blow to the stricken vessel.

Admiral Buchanan, wounded in the leg, sent his sword to the flagship in token of surrender. Farragut, with permission from General Page in Fort Morgan, dispatched all the wounded, both Union and Confederate, to Pensacola and buried his dead on shore. Heavier than in any of his previous battles, Farragut's losses totaled 150 killed and 132 wounded. Of these 93 had been drowned in the *Tecumseh*.[15]

Fort Powell, the shellbank fort at the entrance to Mississippi Sound, was blown up by her own men the night after the battle, her garrison escaping to the mainland. Two days later, after being shelled by the monitor *Chickasaw* and hemmed in by General Granger, Fort Gaines on Dauphin Island surrendered. General Granger next shifted his few troops to Federal Point, where following a fortnight of bombardment and siege, Fort Morgan also capitulated.

News of Farragut's victory reached the North via the Richmond *Sentinel.* General Butler at Bermuda Hundred, Virginia, first spotted the news in a Richmond paper exchanged by troops at the front. Alone in his tent Butler voiced three cheers for Farragut and telegraphed the clipping to Mr. Lincoln.[16] When Mr. Welles a day later carried official navy news to the White House, he was disappointed that the President did not again throw his hat into the air as after Vicksburg. "News of Farragut's having passed Forts Morgan and Gaines was received last night," reads the entry in Uncle Gideon's diary, "and sent a thrill of joy through all true hearts. It is not, however, appreciated as it should be by the military. The President, I was sorry, spoke of it as important because it would tend to relieve Sherman. This is the narrow view of General Halleck, whom I tried to induce to make a joint demonstration against Mobile one year ago. He has done nothing new and only speaks of the naval achievement as a step for the army. . . . I regret that from constant daily intercourse he should be able to imbue the President at times with false and erroneous notions." [17]

Once military operations had been started at Mobile Bay, they were continued, even though operating only on a shoestring. All blockade-running activities, of course, had been completely eliminated. The city of Mobile itself held out grimly until after Appomattox.

19.

War on the High Seas

GIDEON WELLES HELD A TAUT REIN. GOOD MANagement with him a fetish, he prided himself on the smooth running of his establishment in contrast with the War Department or the Department of State.

In no phase of its diversified activity, however, was Lincoln's Navy so bewildered, so torn between conflicting objectives, so harassed by other departments and so plagued by angry outcries of public opinion as in its conduct of the war on the high seas. Confederate commerce raiders threatened the Navy Department's basic concept of attrition warfare through steady, unremitting pressure of the starvation blockade. Time and again the "Rebel-pirates," as Mr. Welles called the Confederate commerce raiders, would appear off Boston, Sandy Hook, or the Virginia capes to burn and sink Yankee merchantmen. Commerce destruction was often secondary in the minds of these raiders. Uppermost was their dream of scattering Yankee blockaders in pursuit of the destroyer. Since the Confederate States had no navy to dispute Lincoln's command of the sea, their object was by shock, by ruthless blows to the pocketbook, to force the Northern merchant to bring pressure upon his government to divert blockade vessels to the chase and relax the jugular-vein grip of the blockade.

In this psychological tussle, the Confederate "sea pirates" were pitted against the tough and stubborn will of a Puritan giant. "Uncle Gideon" was not insensitive to public opinion.

But whenever the best interests of the country—as Welles understood these—demanded that the Navy Department take a beating in the public press rather than bend before the breeze, Secretary Welles suffered that beating in dignified silence, and let off steam in his diary. Gideon Welles's fixed idea was that the essential work of his department was maintenance of the blockade. Against this fixed idea, Confederate cruiser warfare was destined to spend itself in vain.

Among the merchant vessels seized and converted into warships by the Confederate Government in the early days of the war, the *Sumter* and the *Nashville* were the first to win fame as commerce raiders.

For a month the C.S.S. *Sumter,* under Captain Raphael Semmes, played cat and mouse with the Federal blockaders off the Pass à L'Outre entrance to the Mississippi. Then, on June 30, 1861, while the watchdog was momentarily yelping after a blockade-runner, the *Sumter* put to sea.[1] The embarrassed Federal captain of the battleship *Brooklyn,* not a dozen miles off, dropped his less important prey, but after a short chase was outdistanced by the smaller and speedier *Sumter*.

This first Confederate wolf to escape into the open sea made a rich haul among the unsuspecting Yankee sheep in Gulf coast commerce. Into the south Cuban port of Cienfuegos, Semmes brought seven prizes. He might have destroyed them on the high seas, he explained to the officials, but part of their cargo was owned by Spaniards. Would not the Spanish captain general permit him to sell his prizes here? In groping for a decision through the devious intricacies of belligerent and neutral rights, the Spaniard might have acceded to Semmes's request had it not been for the vigorous representations of the United States consul. Semmes's prizes were released to the American consul and restored to their owners. Another fat Yankee merchantman, the *Abby Bradford* of New York, Semmes sent under a prize crew to New Orleans. Recaptured by Lincolnite blockaders, she never reached her Rebel destination.

Denied the usual rewards of naval prize by Federal diplomatic intervention and Federal command of the sea, Semmes henceforth removed their passengers and crews and put captured vessels to the torch. When his own ship, a 501-ton former passenger packet, became over crowded, he disembarked prisoners in an out-of-the-way West Indian port or else converted a suitable prize vessel into a cartel ship. Usually he placed such a ship under ransom bond, the ransom money to be paid six months after the Confederate States obtained independence. Food and general stores he took from his victims, weather and sea permitting. Semmes captured the provision ship *Daniel Troubridge* of New Haven at a time when his own beef had soured and his bread had filled with weevils. His crew spent a busy day throwing overboard Connecticut woodenware and carrying her stores of pork, beef, hams, flour, bread, and crackers in boats across to the *Sumter,* along with a plentiful supply of live pigs, sheep, and geese.

As for coal, the *Sumter* had no access to a coaling base in the Confederate States and was essentially a ship without a country, dependent upon foreign charity for her essential life-giving motive power. Fortunately for Semmes the ports he visited were under colonial officials of countries generally hostile toward the United States and predisposed to favor the Confederacy. "A belligerent ship of war cannot increase her armament or her crew in a neutral port, nor supply herself with ammunition," argued Semmes before the colonial officials; "but with these exceptions she may procure whatever supply she needs." [2] Against Semmes, the United States agents tried to buy up all the coal in the port, to charter all the lighters by which coal could be conveyed on board, or to bribe coal handlers to swamp the loaded lighters in the harbor. But in spite of these devices the *Sumter,* in each case after considerable sea-lawyering on the part of her captain, was allowed to take on coal at Cienfuegos, Curacao, Trinidad, Paramaribo, Maranham, and Martinique.

In all, the *Sumter* captured eighteen merchantmen out of ports from Philadelphia to Maine. Of these, seven were released to their owners by the captain general of Cuba, two were recaptured from prize crews, two were released on ransom bond as cartel ships, seven were burned.

News of the "Rebel pirate's" depredations precipitated upon Lincoln and his Navy Department frantic appeals from insurance company officials, merchants, mayors of coastal cities, and governors. Welles weathered the storm with such a degree of serenity that newspapers dubbed him "the Rip Van Winkle of the Navy Department," and demanded that Lincoln dismiss him and appoint a more active Secretary. Welles's answer to the *Sumter* was primarily to tighten the blockade. He rebuked Captain Poor of the *Brooklyn* for allowing the *Sumter* to escape through the blockade, sent a few ships to various cross roads of traffic both in Europe and in the West Indies, and allowed a few blockaders, while en route north for repairs, to make short cruises in search of the marauder. Lieutenant David D. Porter in the *Powhatan,* picking up a hot scent, chased the *Sumter* as far as the coast of Brazil. In Martinique one of Welles's cruisers, the *Iroquois,* under Commander James S. Palmer, surprised the *Sumter* and kept her under surveillance for a week before the Rebel slipped out one black night through an unguarded channel.

Crossing the Atlantic, the *Sumter* procured in Cadiz a few essential dockyard repairs, then, after capturing two American prizes, she put into Gibraltar. Englishmen in Gibraltar were at this moment so highly incensed over the *Trent* case that Semmes hoped to be allowed to make a complete overhaul in an English dockyard. But in this he was frustrated. His boilers broke down so completely that he could not risk leaving Gibraltar, and there were no repair facilities here. Then he was hemmed in by the three Federal ships—the *Kearsarge,* the *Tuscarora,* and the *Ino*—which had been assigned to this strategic intersection.[3] When to these misfortunes was added Yankee tampering with his crew to persuade them to desert whenever he allowed them to go ashore, Semmes abandoned the *Sumter* and was shortly given command of the *Alabama.* The first Confederate commerce raider, hors de combat and manned by a few caretakers, continued for several months to be blockaded in Gibraltar. Eventually she was sold at auction to a Liverpool dealer who converted her into a blockade-runner.

The *Nashville,* the South's second high-seas raider, was a fast coastal side-wheeler whose unbraced weather deck could support only two midget brass twelve-pounders. Her single cruise as a raider, to Europe and back, was made over unfamiliar routes to avoid capture. This timid Rebel encountered no Yankee naval ship and captured only two merchantmen. But the fact that with her great speed she was able to run the blockade at will gained very unfavorable publicity for Mr. Lincoln's Navy. Frank Leslie's *Illustrated Newspaper* printed a cartoon depicting Sinbad Lincoln wading down the blockade coast, bearing on his shoulders Gideon Welles as "the Old Man of the Sea." [4] Significantly in the offing was a sketch of the raider *Nashville.* Following the *Nashville*'s run through the blockade to Beaufort, a comic artist for *Harper's Weekly* drew the hirsute Secretary reclining on rocks labeled WASHINGTON and BEAUFORT, reading from a paper a fortnight old: " 'The Rebel Steamer *Nashville* run the Blockade at Beaufort on Thursday last.' Well, I declare! This is too bad! Really, if George doesn't send me the New York Papers more regularly, I'll have to subscribe for them myself." [5] Beneath the secretary's knees, the cartoonist showed the *Nashville* sliding through the strait, while between his carpet slippers a spider wove a peaceful web.[6]

At the height of her fame in the spring of 1862, the Confederate Government diverted the speedy *Nashville* from cruiser service into running essential contraband materials through the blockade. Eight vessels of Lincoln's Navy were at one time expressly detailed to capture her and, according to the Richmond *Enquirer,* a reward of two hundred thousand dollars was offered for her capture.[7] Eventually, as heretofore noted, she was destroyed in the Ogeechee River by the monitor *Montauk*—to the delight of Mr. Welles who had been lampooned on her account.

The second and most important phase of Confederate commerce raiding—operations of the British-built *Florida* and *Alabama*—was initiated by Secret Agent James Dunwody Bulloch. None of Bulloch's acts was ever really secret. When he landed in England, he was shocked to find that his mission had been fully exposed in the newspapers, and later, whenever he made a move, he found that American consuls and Minister Charles Francis Adams were fully informed and able to protest to the British Government in advance of his acts. Bulloch, engaging a lawyer to locate loopholes in British neutrality law, let contracts for building the two famed cruisers. The contract for the *Florida* he gave to W. C. Miller and Sons, Liverpool. The senior partner of this company, a former naval constructor in the Royal Navy, owned a scale drawing of a British gunboat which was used for the *Florida*.[8] The contract for the *Alabama* was let to the Lairds of Birkenhead Ironworks. In his dealings with the shipwrights Bulloch avoided all mention of the purpose to which the vessels would be put. The senior Laird, as a member of Parliament, might have been embarrassed otherwise.

American consuls and Minister Adams, however, somewhat heatedly pointed out that Bulloch's bankers, Fraser, Trenhold and Company, were well-known Confederate agents and that the vessels under construction, while not actually fitted with guns, had portholes and deck bolts for securing gun carriages. To these diplomatic objections, Bulloch, prompted by his advocate, could truthfully rejoin that the mere *building* of a ship (whatever its purpose) was no offense against British law, that only *arming* and *equipping* were forbidden. As soon as he could get the ships to sea, Bulloch hurried the *Florida* to the Bahamas, the *Alabama* to the Azores, there to fall in with peaceful merchantmen bearing their armament, ammunition, and crews. So long as he installed guns, loaded ammunition, and shipped his seamen *outside* of English waters, Bulloch trusted that he was safe. Bulloch was not too scrupulous as to method, but was a bold, brash manipulator who conceived it as his patriotic duty to get the ships and did so. He took pride in the fact that there was nothing to compromise the pacific character of his vessels when they left their cradles; despite the fact that hammock nettings, gun ports, and general appearance indicated their ultimate purpose.[9] Registered as English ships, in the names of Englishmen, commanded by Englishmen, bearing regular official numbers, their tonnage marked upon the combings of their main hatches as directed by the Board of Trade, they had been made perfectly secure against capture in this early stage before they were armed. Lest Minister Adams's protests might succeed in stopping the *Alabama* in spite of all his precautions, Bulloch arranged a party on board the spanking new craft and a trial spin in the Mersey. A few hours later the ladies and gentlemen were brought back to the dock in other boats, while the wily *Alabama* disappeared in the direction of the Azores and her colorful career on the high seas.

By this time Gideon Welles had grudgingly detached several cruisers from the blockade and sent them prowling the sea lanes to and from such strategic traffic intersections as the English Channel, Gibraltar, Capetown, and Bahia, below the bulge of Brazil. When news arrived of the *Alabama*'s first captures, Welles increased the number of search vessels, not by depleting the blockade but by chartering additional vessels, such as the fast liner *Vanderbilt,* from the merchant service.

He also created a West India Squadron. If he could remove from the blockade squadrons the temptation to leave their monotonous beats for the carefree excitement of needle-in-the-haystack cruises, he might thereby tighten the blockade itself. Welles also required a suitable billet for the troublesome Commodore Charles Wilkes, of *Trent* case fame. Wilkes's home was in Washington and, being an accomplished courtier, he had the ear of Lincoln and Seward. For months after the seizure of Mason and Slidell he had been assigned no duty; then Wilkes's James River Flotilla, organized to cooperate with McClellan, was left without a purpose when the Peninsula campaign was abandoned. Partly to give the headstrong and fidgety commodore something more fruitful to do than lecturing Lincoln and Seward on naval matters, Mr. Welles on September 8, 1862, organized the West India Squadron, and with Lincoln's blessing appointed Wilkes to command it.

The new squadron with which Wilkes was to protect American shipping from the depredations of the British-built cruisers *Alabama* and *Florida* was a scratch lot. To three of the best of the river flotilla—the *Wachusett,* flag, the *Sonoma,* and the *Tioga*—Mr. Welles added four of the least useful gunboats from the blockade squadrons—the *Dacotah,* the *Cimarron,* the *Octorara* and the *Santiago de Cuba.* "While exercising your rights as a belligerent," Welles cautioned Wilkes, "you will respect the rights of neutrals, always avoiding to give unnecessary offense while asserting the authority and enforcing the duties of your command." [10] As danger from the *Alabama* and the *Florida* was "pressing and imminent," Wilkes was hurried to sea with less than half his ships.

At Bermuda, which scarcely lay within his province, Wilkes became so infuriated with the British officials' want of courtesy toward himself that he engaged them in a protracted and acrimonious correspondence. His presence in the port with three United States ships—one of whom always anchored outside "in the fairway" in readiness for a chase—deterred a large number of blockade-runners from putting to sea. There was one tense moment when a British man-of-war swooped down to within half-pistol shot of Wilkes's flagship *Wachusett* and, like a challenging cock, glared for several minutes in drum-taut silence. Wilkes reported these affronts at length. When finally forced by shortage of coal to move on to his allotted cruising area, he began at once to bombard the Navy Department with pleas for more ships, a barrage that only ended eight months later with his recall. Gideon Welles had no intention of reinforcing Wilkes, was adamant about it, and soon became convinced that Wilkes was more interested in collecting prize money through seizure of blockade-runners than he was in concentrating upon catching raiders in the strategic traffic intersections of the West Indies.

Meanwhile, Raphael Semmes of the *Alabama* was disturbing the country, and especially the Navy Department. "November 4, Tuesday. Further news of the depredations of the *Alabama*," reads Welles's diary. "Ordered *Dacotah, Ino, Augusta,* etc., on her track." And a month later: "The Rebel steamer *Alabama* was at Martinique and escaped the *San Jacinto*." "December 29, Monday. We had yesterday a telegram that the British pirate craft *Alabama* captured the *Ariel,* one of the Aspinwall steamers, on her passage from New York to Aspinwall, off the coast of Cuba. Abuse of the Navy Department will follow." [11] Semmes had hoped to catch a homeward-bound California treasure ship to replenish his funds, since he could not sell prizes. The *Ariel,* however, was outward bound, and yielded a mere eight thousand dollars in U. S. Treasury notes and fifteen hundred dollars in silver. As there were seven hundred souls on the *Ariel* and it was impossible to crowd them on board the one-thousand-ton *Alabama,* Semmes disarmed the 150 marines on board, took their parole, and released the ship under ransom bond.[12]

After the *Florida* had run past the blockaders into Mobile Bay, the British humor magazine *Punch* had tossed off a limerick: [13]

> There was an old fogy named Welles,
> Quite worthy of cap and of bells,
> For he tho't that a pirate,
> Who steamed at a great rate,
> Would wait to be riddled with shells.

After completely outfitting herself at Mobile and signing on an all Southern crew, the *Florida* came out under cover of a January norther and, crowding on both sail and steam, outraced Farragut's blockaders. The *Florida* now prowled the sea lanes along the Antilles, while the *Alabama*—notified through captured papers of General Banks's projected descent on Galveston—swept westward to the Texas coast.

Posing as a blockade-runner, Semmes lured away from the group of naval ships off Galveston the U.S.S. *Hatteras,* under Lieutenant Commander Homer C. Blake. Ten miles off shore the *Hatteras* hailed, "What steamer is that?" "Her Britannic Majesty's ship *Vixen."* [14] The *Hatteras* lowered a boat to board her when Semmes dropped the mask, identified his vessel as the Confederate steamer *Alabama,* and fired a broadside. The Federal, a side-wheel converted merchantman of eleven hundred tons, answered the fire and attempted to close and board, but her bottom was foul with seaweed. The Rebel, having superior speed, kept clear of the *Hatteras* and shot her to pieces. With his walking beam shattered and his vessel on fire in two places, Commander Blake continued firing, hoping to disable the *Alabama* and attract the attention of the fleet off Galveston. But at length his magazines had to be drowned and his port guns heaved overboard to keep afloat. Blake fired a gun to leeward in token of surrender. Semmes took off her survivors, and within ten minutes the *Hatteras* went down.

Meanwhile, the *Hatteras'* small boat, which had been lowered before the action commenced, rowed back to the fleet. As the dread news rippled eastward and northward, it set up fresh tensions around the blockade coast. A flurry of commands fanned out from Gideon Welles's desk. "The *Florida* has escaped from Mobile, and the *Alabama* has destroyed the *Hatteras* off Galveston." [15] Pictures of the raiders were distributed, identical except that the *Florida* had two funnels and the *Alabama* but one. Welles even relaxed his rule and drew a temporary reinforcement for Wilkes of three ships from Admiral S. P. Lee's inactive North Atlantic Blockading Squadron. The *Vanderbilt* was ordered to cruise off Brazil until her skipper obtained assurance that the *Alabama* had left the West Indies, then she was to proceed to the Cape of Good Hope, Helena, Cape Verde, the Canaries, Madeira, Lisbon, and the Azores.

With speed both the *Florida* and the *Alabama* departed from the Gulf and Caribbean areas, making few captures and steering wide around Federal ships in the main channels. Wilkes at this troubled period captured so many blockade-runners as to call attention to his want of success in seizing the raiders. He also made the blunder of detaining the *Vanderbilt,* commandeering her, in fact, for use as his flagship, the *Wachusett* being in need of repair.

To Welles now came Seward complaining of Wilkes's action in Bermuda. Through the sluggish channels of diplomacy the English had protested. Welles thought the British unduly fussy. Wilkes, he wrote in his diary, "has not committed the indiscretions toward neutrals which I feared he would, and of which he is charged." [16] But when Welles learned that Wilkes had detained the *Vanderbilt* and that the *Alabama* had been sighted off Brazil about the time the *Vanderbilt* might have been there to intercept had his orders not been interfered with, he dispatched the colorless Admiral J. L. Lardner to replace Wilkes.

Wilkes was set down in the Secretary's black book as "erratic, impulsive, opinionated," and as having a disinclination to obey orders that "do not comport with his own notions." "His special mission, in his present command, had been to capture the *Alabama.* In this he had totally failed, while zealous to catch blockade-runners and get prize money. Had he not been in the West Indies, we might have captured her, but he has seized the *Vanderbilt,* which had specific orders and destination and gone off with her prize-hunting, thereby defeating our plans." [17]

Both the *Florida* and the *Alabama* were now bound for distant and safer waters. But off Brazil the most brilliant daredevil cruise of the war was begun. The *Florida* put Lieutenant Charles W. Read on board a prize with twenty-four petty officers and men. "Savvy" Read, twenty-three, Naval Academy 1860, and a veteran of the New Orleans battle, mounted two boat howitzers on board the prize brig *Clarence* and sailed north. Off Cape Henry on June 12, by feigning distress, he got aboard of, and captured, the bark *Tacony* and two schooners.[18] As the *Tacony* was better suited to his purpose, he shifted his guns to her, burned the *Clarence* and the schooner *M. A. Shindler,* and shifted the latter's passengers to the *Kate Stewart,* which he bonded as a cartel.

As soon as the *Kate Stewart* touched the dock in Philadelphia, the *Tacony's* dispossessed merchant skipper telegraphed news of Read's fresh depredations to Washington. It was Saturday. Fox was Acting Secretary in Welles's absence over the week end. Over the Secretary's name identical orders went out to navy yards in Philadelphia, New York, and Boston to charter or seize half a dozen moderate-sized fast vessels, put on board of each a dozen men, plenty of small arms, and one or two howitzers, and send them out "in various directions . . . within the next forty-eight hours." [19] Monday morning the economy-minded Welles smirked over Fox's extravagance, but allowed the order to stand as it had gone out in his name. Together with Admiral Lee's vessels, about two dozen ships in all were dispatched after the *Tacony.*

During the next fortnight, while cruising north along the coast, Read burned or bonded nineteen sail, two of them being Atlantic passenger steamers: the *Isaac Webb,* from Liverpool to New York, with 750 passengers, and the *Shatemuc,* from Liverpool to Boston with immigrants. Off Boston on the night of June 24 he captured the fishing schooner *Archer,* and, to elude the gunboats now scouring the coast for him, he shifted his howitzers to the *Archer* and burned the *Tacony.*

Being short of ammunition, he entered Portland harbor, captured the revenue cutter *Caleb Cushing,* and was making off with her when the aroused citizens of Portland sallied out in two steamers to hem him in against the coast and capture him.

The *Alabama* remained at sea a total of twenty-three months. After sinking the *Hatteras,* she proceeded to the coast of Brazil, the Cape of Good Hope, the Straits of Sunda, the China Sea, and the Bay of Bengal. Then she doubled back to the Cape of Good Hope and Brazil, thence to the English Channel and Cherbourg, France. All told she burned fifty-

#110 11-28-2005 7:12PM
Item(s) checked out to Hibbitts, E.H..

TITLE: Mr. Lincoln's navy.
BARCODE: 31836000219501
DUE DATE: 01-02-06

TITLE: Four years in the Confederate Nav
BARCODE: 31836000219519
DUE DATE: 01-02-06

TITLE: Blockade runners of the Confedera
BARCODE: 31836001435320
DUE DATE: 01-02-06

TITLE: The Confederate privateers, by Wi
BARCODE: 31836001445098
DUE DATE: 01-02-06

three merchantmen, released nine on ransom bond, sold one, and sank one man-of-war, the *Hatteras.*[20] By June 11, 1864, when she dropped her anchor in Cherbourg, she was mechanically a tired ship, creaky from her seventy-five thousand miles by sail and steam, and in desperate need of a dockyard overhaul. Three days later, while Semmes was negotiating with the reluctant government of Napoleon III, the U.S.S. *Kearsarge,* under Captain John A. Winslow, appeared. The United States consul in Cherbourg and Minister Dayton in Paris, while interposing with the French foreign office to thwart Semmes's permission to refit, had also summoned the *Kearsarge* by a telegram to Flushing, Holland. Warily, lest the long-sought Rebel again give the Federals the slip, Winslow did not drop anchor, but, after feasting his eyes upon the *Alabama* from a distance, sailed back outside the harbor. He intended to be hampered by no twenty-four-hour rule in case Semmes should come out. During her two years in European waters away from the real war, the *Kearsarge* had been carefully groomed for combat. Chain cables had been hung up and down her sides to protect her engines, and these had been so well concealed by an outer layer of planking that Semmes and his officers, through their glasses, had been unable to detect it. Winslow summoned other ships to come to his aid in case of a protracted blockade, but this proved unnecessary.

Semmes, perhaps divining that the French at this late date would allow him nothing more than emergency fuel, resolved Winslow's doubts by a courteous, old-fashioned challenge to a duel. In the note, written to A. Bonfils for relay through the United States consul, Semmes informed Winslow "that my intention is to fight the *Kearsarge* as soon as I can make the necessary arrangements. I hope these will not detain me more than until tomorrow evening, or after the morrow morning at furthest. I beg she will not depart before I am ready to go out." [21]

"The combat will no doubt be contested and obstinate," Semmes predicted in his journal, "but the two ships are so equally matched that I do not feel at liberty to decline it." [22] Semmes placed his several dozen chronometers, specie, and ransom bonds, trophies of the chase, on board the English yacht *Deerhound,* took on coal, and entertained on board a party of ladies.[23]

About 9:30 A.M. on June 19, 1864, the *Alabama* steamed out of the harbor, accompanied by the *Deerhound* and the French cruiser *Couronne.* Sightseers with glasses lined the French shore. A party of ladies witnessed the fight from the *Deerhound's* deck. The *Couronne* stopped at the three-mile limit to make sure that neutral French waters would not be violated.

The *Kearsarge* moved out to sea six or seven miles beyond the breakwater, then rounded to and steamed toward the *Alabama.* At 11:10, the *Alabama* opened with a broadside at twelve hundred yards. Semmes evidently hoped to settle the fight with his long guns, but Winslow closed the range to nine hundred before opening the *Kearsarge's* port broadside. The two ships now steamed in circles around a common center, firing their port guns. In statistics the antagonists were equally matched, each having the same tonnage and about the same power in guns.

During the sixty minutes that the battle lasted, the *Kearsarge* received a hundred-pound shell which lodged in her sternpost and failed to explode. The impact raised the transom frame and bound the rudder so hard as to require four men at the helm. Shell after shell splintered the *Kearsarge*'s false sidewall, spent itself against the chain armor, and plopped harmlessly into the water. Semmes, perceiving their failure to penetrate the *Kearsarge,* now alternated shells with solid shot. After an hour of dueling, the entirely unprotected *Alabama* had large holes punched out along her water line. With his boilers extinguished, Semmes tried to make sail and escape to the French coast, some five miles distant, but his stricken ship began to settle, the muzzles of his guns to dip into the green water. Semmes hauled down his colors and dispatched a boat to announce his surrender. In another twenty minutes the *Alabama* plunged to the bottom.

The *Deerhound,* lying near, was now hailed by Captain Winslow and asked to assist in rescue of survivors. "For God's sake do what you can to save them." [25] Winslow's two seaworthy boats—others had been shot up—garnered sixty-one prisoners. The *Deerhound* picked up Captain Semmes and forty-one others and—to Winslow's astonishment—hightailed it for the English coast, without surrendering to Winslow the prisoners.

The defeat of the British-built raider, with British guns and crewmen, by the Yankee-built *Kearsarge,* with Yankee cannon and Yankee seamen, was heart-warming to Gideon Welles.[26] But Semmes's escape left a sour aftertaste, for Welles in the last year of the war still clung to his initial theory that the South's almost legendary scourger of the seas was a common pirate. Lincoln, whose sense of humor sometimes puzzled Mr. Welles, expressed a desire for the unexploded Rebel shell from the *Kearsarge*'s sternpost and out it was cut, together with a sizeable chunk of the sternpost itself, the whole neatly packaged and forwarded to the White House as a souvenir of the chief battle fought by Mr. Lincoln's Navy on the high seas.

Including six months in the dockyard at Brest, the *Florida*'s active career lasted from January, 1863, when she escaped from Mobile, to October, 1864, when she was illegally captured in the neutral harbor of Bahia, Brazil. During fifteen months of cruising, she destroyed thirty-three vessels, varying from fishing schooners worth only a few thousand up to the *Jacob Bell,* a China trader loaded with silks, tea, and spices, and valued at $1,500,000. Four ships she bonded. If to these are added captures made by her brilliant junior officer, C. W. Read, in *Clarence-Tacony-Archer,* her grand total comes very near to the *Alabama*'s, and her ending, certainly, was more spectacular.

Entering Bahia on October 4, 1864, she discovered there the black-hulled U.S.S. *Wachusett,* waiting like a spider.[27]

Technically, by the rules governing belligerents in neutral ports, she was safe from violence within the harbor, and, when one belligerent vessel departed, the other was compelled to remain at anchor for twenty-four hours before following her. The *Florida*'s skipper, Captain C. M. Morris, C. S. N., felt sufficiently secure to withdraw the powder charges from his guns and to spend his nights on shore. But he reckoned without Commander Napoleon Collins of the *Wachusett*.

The commander of Charles Wilkes's former flagship shared Wilkes's views on the efficacy of quarter-deck decisions, as well as Wilkes's contempt for the rights of those Latin American neutrals who extended hospitality to Confederate raiders but lacked the military strength to protect them within their harbors. In Bahia there was one small Brazilian gunboat, behind which the *Florida* anchored, and a fort. The United States consul came on board the *Wachusett* with a tale of violation of Brazil's neutrality by the *Alabama*. Urged by the consul, Commander Collins decided to sink the *Florida* regardless of consequences.

Accordingly, at 3:00 A.M. on the seventh, he slipped his cable and rammed the raider. The blow cut down her bulwarks and carried away mizzenmast and main yard, but left her hull uninjured. Small arms fire from the *Florida* was answered by two unauthorized cannon shot from the *Wachusett,* which flew wild but induced the *Florida*'s junior officer on board to surrender. Collins now quickly towed the *Florida* out of the harbor, and was trailed a few miles by the Brazilian gunboat, which fired three shotted guns but missed her target.

The first British-built raider to be captured, together with the brusqueness of her seizure, caused excitement in Washington. Senator Sumner, of the Foreign Affairs Committee, and Secretary of State Seward wanted to release her at once to the Brazilian Government. Welles staunchly demurred. "If we have injured Brazil, let us make reparation, full and ample," Welles argued wryly. "If she has injured us, let her do her duty also, in this respect. So far as her majesty is disturbed by our taking a sneaking thief, whom she was entertaining, by the throat . . . let all proper atonement be made." [28] Welles suggested to Seward that the prisoners captured on the *Florida* be tried as pirates, but Seward shrank from that extreme.

In Hampton Roads a transport ran into the *Florida* "by *accident*" and caused her to founder, but not before samples of her British cannon had been shipped to the Washington Navy Yard. The *Florida's* prisoners were lodged in Fort Warren in Boston, and, to appease the State Department, Commander Collins was courtmartialed and sentenced to be dismissed from the service—a sentence which, diplomacy having been satisfied, Uncle Gideon quietly disapproved and set aside.

The direct losses inflicted upon the United States merchant marine by all the Confederate raiders amounted to about 244 ships.[29] In money this approximated the $15,000,000 damages paid by Great Britain in the *Alabama* claims soon after the war. But such a sum does not cover the hundreds of ships that were laid up in port or shifted to foreign registry for fear of capture. Nor does it account for the transfer of American maritime trade to neutral bottoms. The virtual disappearance of the United States flag from merchant shipping on the high seas can be credited, first, to the failure of Lincoln's State Department to stop the release of British-built cruisers to Confederate agents and, second, to the fearful exigencies that made it so difficult for Lincoln's Navy either to pen these cruisers in port or to capture them.

20.

The Finish at Wilmington

AT WILMINGTON, NORTH CAROLINA, MR. LINCOLN'S Navy came nearer to failure than at any point on the entire three thousand miles of blockaded coast. After the fall of New Orleans, the Confederates heavily fortified this seaport of Richmond. Closer to Richmond than either Charleston or Mobile, it was also nearest to all three of the most important blockade-running centers—Halifax, Bermuda, and the Bahamas. After Charleston had been sealed by Dahlgren and Gillmore, and Mobile by Farragut and Canby, Wilmington became the only major Confederate port through which the armies fighting in Virginia could be supplied. Extraordinary means were taken to defend it. Vessels were especially built to run the blockade at this point. The *Bat,* of Liverpool, for instance, was a sleek greyhound designed for speed—230 feet long, 26 feet beam, 9 feet deep. Outbound in her cigar-shaped hull, she could stow 850 bales of priceless cotton and, coming in, similar quantities of material essential to the Confederacy. Her two double-oscillating engines, generating 180 horsepower, drove her a phenomenal 15 knots to enable her to run circles around the heavy blockade ships with their cumbrous freight of naval cannon. Blockade-runners held to such regular schedules into Wilmington that even British papers friendly to the North speculated as to whether Lincoln's blockade officers were corrupt and conniving to prolong the war. During the last two months of greatly intensified activity against Wilmington, between

October 26, 1864, and January 1865, the Confederates obtained through this port 8,632,000 pounds of meat, 1,506,000 pounds of lead, 1,933,000 pounds of saltpetre, 546,000 pairs of shoes, 316,000 pairs of blankets, half a million pounds of coffee, 69,000 rifles, and 43 cannon, while cotton to pay for it was shipped out.[1]

On the map the situation at Wilmington resembled that at Mobile. The city lies on the Cape Fear River, about twenty-eight miles inland from its furthest entrance. Wilmington, but six miles from the ocean, is accessible from a number of inlets on both sides of the two mouths of the river. The two entrances into Cape Fear River are seven miles apart and separated not only by Smith's Island but by a shoal which extends for ten or twelve miles out into the Atlantic and renders Cape Fear one of the main hazards to traffic along the coast. Off each of the entrances there was an outer and an inner shoal. The southern entrance was protected by Fort Caswell on the mainland opposite Smith's Island, and the northern, called the New Inlet Channel, most frequently used by blockade-runners, was protected by a formidable series of log-and-sand fortifications built during the war and known collectively as Fort Fisher.

On the lower tip of Federal Point, the Confederates built a mound of sand sixty-five feet high, upon which they placed two heavy British cannon to command the New Inlet Channel as it enters the lower river. Through the outside shoals this channel was frequently shifted about by storms and currents, but generally it ran for some distance parallel to the flat, shrub-clad sand dunes of the coast. North of the Mound Battery was erected a series of palmetto-log-and-sand bombproofs and traverses about one hundred yards back from the beach. These extended northward along the shoreline for a mile, then made a right-angle turn and continued westward across the peninsula to the river. The fort was shaped like a gigantic letter L. Across its shorter land face, it was reinforced against infantry assault by a field of mines connected by wires to galvanic batteries within the fort and by a row of palisades to shield sharpshooters. Lengthy Fort Fisher, along with several smaller batteries further up the coast, afforded refuge and security to the speedy runners that raced past the blockaders.[2] Even injured blockade-runners always tried to get through to beach themselves rather than be captured, as the fort's garrison had developed salvage to a fine art, a single cargo frequently being worth the price of the vessel itself.

The activities of Lincoln's Navy Department against Wilmington fell into three phases: (1) the period of indecision and reconnaissance under Admiral S. P. Lee, (2) the first expedition against Fort Fisher under General B. F. Butler and Admiral D. D. Porter, which turned into a fiasco through want of cooperation between the Army and Navy, and (3) the final successful assault of Fort Fisher by Porter and General A. H. Terry.

The first commanders of the North Atlantic Blockading Squadron, Stringham and Goldsborough, failed to recognize the strategic importance of Wilmington. They could hardly otherwise have frittered away their amphibian expeditions against Hatteras Inlet and Roanoke Island when the same attack forces (in the early days before Fort Fisher was constructed) might have seized Wilmington. Admiral Sam Phillips Lee, who succeeded to the command of this squadron in September, 1862, and held it until October, 1864, was frank enough to admit that Wilmington was not being satisfactorily blockaded, and sufficiently astute to perceive that joint army and navy action to seize Wilmington was both necessary and essential.

Lee, however, could not cut the Gordian knot. Priding himself on the prompt attention he gave to routine details, he was smothered by them. Merely handling the correspondence of a squadron of a hundred vessels was a time-consuming chore. This correspondence consisted of assignments of vessels, reassignments due to breakdowns, repairs, absences for refueling, provisioning; reports of blockade-runners chased, destroyed, captured; distribution of consular information on vessels to look out for; reports, endless reports, trivial and major, for the Secretary.

To the routine of the blockade was added confusion over trading permits. After Lincoln lifted the blockade of Beaufort, North Carolina, and organized loyal state governments in Virginia and North Carolina—or rather in the thin slivers of tide-water coastline under Federal control—a complex tangle of problems arose, involving issuance of trading permits by army officers, navy officers, Treasury officials, and the carpetbagger governors. S. P. Lee's blockade squadron was specifically charged with interdicting all traffic to and from enemy-held territory. Yankee merchantmen, posing as army sutlers, obtained clearances for the reopened port of Beaufort, and then, when blockaders were not looking, sneaked into Rebel-held inlets near Wilmington to dispose of contraband at fabulous prices. During several months before the interdepartmental confusion was clarified, Gideon Welles stood pat on enforcing the letter of his blockade even against the United States Army. A gunboat was actually anchored in the shadow of Fortress Monroe to prevent the Army from disembarking here the lumber, potatoes, onions, and tar they had purchased in Rebel-held territory. General Dix, enraged, appealed to the President against this blockade of his fort by a gunboat of Mr. Lincoln's own Navy, and the matter was finally straightened out.

From the start, S. P. Lee realized that Wilmington could not be satisfactorily blockaded and would have to be captured. Even with three cordons of blockaders outside of each entrance into Cape Fear River, Lee found it impossible to prevent vessels from going in or out. "It is greatly to our mortification, after all our watchfulness," reported Captain B. F. Sands, Lee's senior officer off Cape Fear. "None can be more vigilant than we are—the officer of the watch, with the quartermaster, always on the bridge, lookouts on each bow, gangway and quarter. For myself I never pretend to turn in at night, and am frequently on deck during the night inspecting the lookouts in person, taking what sleep I can get in my clothes, ready for a moment's call." [3]

Wilmington, however, could not be taken without the help of a cooperating army. Its entrances were shallow and tortuous, its channels shifting and, according to reports of intelligent contrabands and others, obstructed in such a way as to bring an intruder under cross fire from the forts. Admiral Lee needed an army to land on Federal Point between Fort Fisher and Wilmington, to besiege Fort Fisher in conjunction with a naval attack.

In December of 1862, when ironclads were being made ready for Du Pont's attack on Charleston, there was a possibility of their stopping at Cape Fear long enough to enter the river and assail Fort Fisher from the rear, while the wooden fleet bombarded its sea face and an army under General John G. Foster assaulted its land front. Lincoln, Welles, and Fox became quite excited about this plan, but the *Monitor* foundered off Hatteras and Admiral Lee's reconnoitering party found the bars at Cape Fear to be six inches too shallow to float the *Passaic* and the *Montauk,* so the proposal had to be given up.

Lee now devised several other projects. He tried to induce General Foster to march directly on Wilmington from his position at New Berne in Pamlico Sound. Also, he suggested a military landing on Smith's Island and building a fort there across from Fort Caswell, but the Confederates garrisoned the island first. It was S. P. Lee's misfortune always to know what could be done, but never to be quite able to do it. Gideon Welles, after many months of fruitless effort to get Halleck to contribute a military force, finally authorized Lee to go ahead without an army, if he felt he could accomplish anything.[4] Lee sent numerous reconnaissance parties inside the channels at night. A small boat expedition under the daredevil Lieutenant William B. Cushing ascended the Cape Fear River to within a few miles of Wilmington, examining river obstructions, dodging enemy batteries, and even capturing a courier with dispatches from Fort Fisher. Had not the light-draft monitors proved to be failures, Lee might have sent these inside the river and captured Wilmington. But he never launched a purely naval attack, and was unsuccessful in his cogently reasoned pleas for military help.

After Farragut's victory in Mobile Bay, when Fox appealed to Lieutenant General Grant for military cooperation against Wilmington, Grant told him plainly that he would assign an army to the job provided the Navy would replace Lee with a more energetic naval commander.

Welles shared Grant's opinion that Lee was not the man to make the necessary bold assault. "He is true and loyal, prudent and cautious. Farragut would take the place three times while Lee was preparing, and hesitating, and looking behind for more aid." [5] To make the shift as palatable as possible to Lee and his family—S. P. Lee being a son-in-law of Welles's old friend F. P. Blair, Sr. and brother-in-law of Lincoln's postmaster general, Montgomery Blair—Welles ordered an exchange of places between Farragut and Lee. He had no sooner dispatched the order, however, when he received from Farragut an application for leave of absence. The aging admiral had experienced a letdown after Mobile Bay, was troubled by gout and vertigo, and wanted rest. Welles instantly canceled Farragut's new assignment—"a life so precious must not be thrown away"—and called David D. Porter to Washington for consultation. "Admiral Porter is probably the best man for the service, but his selection will cut Lee to the quick. Porter is young, and his rapid promotion has placed him in rank beyond those who were his seniors, some of whom it might be well to have in this expedition. But again personal considerations must yield to the public interest." [5] The ebullient Porter, having lately escaped from the Red River with almost a whole skin, preferred to remain on the Mississippi, but Porter—Welles's diary notes—"repeated what he has heretofore said—that he had been treated kindly by the Department, and if I ordered him to go over Niagara Falls in an iron pot he should obey the order." [6] With Grant's enthusiastic approval—Grant and

Porter having pulled in harness at Vicksburg—Welles shifted Porter to the North Atlantic Blockading Squadron, and forged ahead with the Wilmington plans, the shutting off of all Rebel communication there being regarded as "paramount to all other questions,—more important, practically, than the capture of Richmond." [7]

But if Wilmington was the main objective of the Navy, this was not true of the Army. Grant's chief preoccupations continued to be the Confederate army before Richmond and Sherman's situation at Atlanta. Wilmington, so far as the commitment of troops was concerned, remained a secondary consideration.

When Grant first agreed to send troops to Wilmington, it was with the understanding that the object be kept secret. He would detail a force from Virginia to sail under sealed orders for Port Royal, South Carolina, between Wilmington and Charleston. At the latter location Gillmore and Dahlgren were called on to exert themelves and create the impression that Charleston was to be attacked. The blow at Wilmington was to be a surprise, a sneak play, to be cheaply won with the expenditure of only a few thouand troops. But late in September news of the proposed Wilmington expedition leaked to the press, and Grant, keeping his own counsel, deferred the attack.

Under Porter the squadron acquired a new tautness and reckless energy. Crews when turned out at night, Porter ordered, "must not wait to dress themselves, but get to quarters with their clothes in their hands." [8] To the daredevil Cushing, the new admiral promised promotion in grade if he sank the Rebel ram *Albemarle* near Plymouth, North Carolina, and he instructed Commander W. H. Macomb, in charge of operations in the sounds, to outfit his boats with proper grapnels so that, if the ram appeared, he could crowd in upon her from every side, "lay her on board," and fight it out hand to hand. "Even if half your vessels are sunk you must pursue this course." [9] On a dark night Cushing headed up the Roanoke River in a fast new steam torpedo boat, equipped with a torpedo fastened to the end of a long spar. By the light of campfires on shore he found the Confederate menace berthed inside a pen of logs. Cushing crowding on steam, swept wide around, and charged toward the log pen, sledding his vessel up on to the logs. Then, utterly oblivious of the Confederates on board the ram, who sprang their rattle, fired muskets, and trained their big gun directly at him, Cushing coolly lowered his torpedo-tipped spar, worked it forward under the *Albemarle*'s overhanging armor, and exploded it beneath her wooden hull. At the same instant the ram's cannon was fired and Cushing dived into the water to make a nerve-tingling escape down the river. Macomb, not waiting for orders, pushed his gunboats up the river and retook the town of Plymouth before the Confederate panic subsided.

Porter hailed Cushing's "absolute disregard of death or danger" as the spirit he wished to see prevail in the squadron.[10] Macomb and Cushing were both promoted. Lincoln recommended, and Congress passed, a vote of thanks for Cushing. To cap the climax, Porter raised Cushing to the command of his flagship for the forthcoming Fort Fisher campaign.

By mid-October the Navy was on its toes to go ahead with the campaign, but week after week passed and Grant, who controlled all the Federal armies, neglected to assign a military force to collaborate. Finally on the twenty-eighth Gideon Welles protested officially to Lincoln. "Every other squadron has been depleted and vessels detached from other duty to strengthen this expedition. The vessels are concentrated at Hampton Roads and Beaufort, where they remain, an immense force lying idle, awaiting the movements of the army. The retention of so many vessels from blockade and cruising duty is a most serious injury to the public service, and if the expedition can not go forward for want of troops, I desire to be notified, so that the ships can be relieved and dispersed for other service . . . the autumn weather so favorable for such an expedition is fast passing away. The public expect this attack and the country will be distressed if it be not made; to procrastinate much longer will be to peril its success."[11] Lincoln, usually quick to intervene to patch up quarrels in the midst of a campaign, was often, as now, reluctant to interfere at the start. He declined to prod Grant, as Welles requested.

But the Navy was shortly rescued from its predicament by General B. F. Butler, now serving on the Richmond-Petersburg front, from whose army the troops for Fort Fisher were to be drawn. Butler, after reading about a recent powder magazine explosion in England, suggested to Fox that a shipload of powder detonated near Fort Fisher might temporarily stun its garrison and ease the way for a Federal assault. It was a period of new weapons and tactics, and the idea of a ship torpedo had not been tested. Ordnance experts opposed the scheme; one ridiculed it, comparing to it the firing of feathers from muskets. But the Navy went ahead with the powder boat, in the belief, apparently, that by accepting General Butler's novel idea they would get the troops.

At New Orleans Porter had slighted Butler by excluding the military from the ceremony when the forts were surrendered to the Mortar Flotilla, and Butler had retaliated by causing a staff member, Engineer Godfrey Weitzel, to make a detailed map of Fort Jackson to prove that it had not been seriously damaged by Porter's mortars. As it chanced, the division of Butler's troops which Grant picked to cooperate with Admiral Porter at Wilmington was under the immediate command of Godfrey Weitzel, now a fledgling major general.

While the powder boat was being prepared, the bitter recollections of New Orleans were outwardly suppressed. There were social functions at Fortress Monroe and on the flagship, and staff officers spoke guardedly of the *entente cordiale* between the general and the admiral.

Early in December, Grant, learning that Confederate General Bragg had withdrawn from Wilmington to face Sherman at Savannah, ordered the Wilmington expedition to get off at once, with or without the powder boat. By courtesy, the general-in-chief's orders were sent to Weitzel through his immediate superior, General Butler. Butler hurriedly procured the army's share of powder to be loaded on the ship torpedo, and the expedition was embarked in the James River on December 8 and moved down to Hampton Roads. For five days the expedition's sailing was further delayed by storms in the Atlantic. The powder boat, with its dangerous freight and complicated detonating mechanisms, had to be towed to Beaufort, the fleet's advanced base.

During these three days of waiting in Hampton Roads, Porter learned that Butler himself had embarked with the troops. It was the first indication he had had that the general intended to go on the expedition. To Fox, Porter wrote: "Butler has just put his troops on board the transports in all the rain and storm, and is now in a great hurry to get off. I believe the troops are all negroes, and I don't expect much of them. I believe Butler is going himself to look on or direct—he had better leave it to Weitzel." [12] The *entente cordiale* evaporated, and there was no meeting of minds on how the expedition was to proceed. "General Butler did come on board my vessel one night in Hampton Roads," Porter later told the Committee on the Conduct of the War, "with General Weitzel and Colonel Comstock, and asked me if I had a map of Cape Fear river, and I said I had. They asked my opinion, and I gave my opinion of what I thought was the best way to go to work. They made no remarks whatever, but went into a far part of the cabin and there consulted together. After they got through their conversation, they got up, bade me 'good evening,' and went off. That was the only consultation I ever had with them." [13] Butler told Weitzel his reason for going with the expedition was to "see that this powder-boat is exploded properly." [14] Butler's situation was complicated. While the expedition was being prepared, Weitzel, suffering from a sense of inferiority, had confided to Butler his belief that the latter had promoted him more rapidly than his ability and experience warranted. Butler explained to Grant that his motive in going was "to take the responsibility off General Weitzel." [15] In any case, he went.

As a result of poor staff work, there was needless confusion over the place of rendezvous near Wilmington. The naval forces rendezvoused first in Beaufort, seventy miles north of Wilmington, while the military hovered fifty miles to the southward off Masonboro Inlet. Three days of good weather were lost before Butler finally located Porter, then below the horizon twenty-five miles off the coast of Cape Fear. By this time the transports had to go into Beaufort for fuel and water. Storms locked them in port for several days. It was necessary to postpone the explosion of the powder boat. When, finally, the admiral felt he could delay no longer, he sent a messenger, allowing time for Butler's troops to reach the scene eight or ten hours after the explosion. But the messenger's boat, arriving off Beaufort at night, was prevented by a storm from crossing the bar and could not deliver Porter's message until the next morning, some hours after the powder boat had been exploded. Butler, seventy miles away from Fort Fisher, interpreted this as a deliberate slight to the Army on Porter's part.

The powder boat, towed close in toward the beach and anchored, would have made a fine prize for the Confederates to capture had Commander A. C. Rhind depended on its clockwork devices for igniting its fuses. Before he left the ship, Rhind built a fire in its after compartment, and it was this blaze, possibly, which, twenty-two minutes after schedule, set fire to her powder and exploded and burned her like a giant firework at 1:40 A.M. on December 24. Men in the fleet twelve miles away saw a column of flame shoot up and heard four distinct explosions. The effect of the powder boat upon Fort Fisher, however, was nil. Some of the Confederate garrison believed that a blockade-runner had blown up.

Butler, alerted by the admiral's late message, reached the scene the next afternoon. Under pleasanter circumstances, he might have enjoyed the noise and spectacle of the fleet bombardment which was now in progress. Five commodores commanded the several divisions of the armada, disposed on great arcs out from the fort, each hammering away at its own specified segment of the mammoth target.

With the aid of navy boats, Butler managed to put on shore between 2,100 and 2,300 of his 6,500 men, before a gathering storm and worsening surf moved him to halt the disembarkation. General Weitzel and Engineer Comstock scanned Fort Fisher's parapets from close range. Returning, they reported to General Butler that only two out of seventeen guns on the land face of the fort had been dismounted. Through Weitzel and Comstock, General Butler now urged Admiral Porter to run past the fort into Cape Fear River; but the Admiral replied that there was not water enough and suggested that Butler's troops storm the fort.

Butler now decided to re-embark the troops and return to Hampton Roads. He believed (1) that Fort Fisher was not materially damaged, (2) that it was impossible to get food and ammunition ashore through the present high surf, and (3) that the fleet, in case of a protracted storm, would have to beat out to sea in order to avoid being driven ashore and wrecked. Although Grant's instructions had specified that if a landing was effected the troops should entrench themselves on the peninsula, Butler arrogated to himself the right to interpret Grant's language. To effect a landing, he explained later to the Committee on the Conduct of the War, "requires something more than to land 2,500 men out of six thousand, five hundred, on a beach with nothing but forty rounds in their cartridge boxes, and where their supplies would be driven off the first storm." [16] Accordingly, Butler re-embarked his troops, or all but about six hundred of them who could not be got off the beach because of the twelve-foot surf. These he left for the Navy to recover two days later and returned to Hampton Roads.

Admiral Porter's amazement and chagrin shortly turned to disgust and violent anger. He wrote sizzling dispatches to Secretary Welles, who published them to defend the Navy and generate popular enthusiasm for the Wilmington operation. Welles and Fox took Porter's letters and couriers to Lincoln, who listened sympathetically but insisted on deferring to General Grant's wishes. Stanton, when approached by Lincoln, readily agreed to give up Butler, but questioned whether Porter was any better—"spoke of him as blatant, boisterous, bragging, etc." [17] But both Welles and Fox supported Porter, who, for all his faults, had demonstrated superiority as a fighting commander.

Grant sided with them, replying to their telegraphed appeal that he would immediately organize another expedition to be sent under sealed orders to Wilmington. To Admiral Porter General Grant wrote, "Hold on, if you please, a few days longer, and I will send you more troops, with a different general." [18]

Grant returned the same troops that had sailed on the first expedition, along with an added force of fifteen hundred men, eight thousand in all, under Brevet Major General A. H. Terry. The second expedition, having sailed under sealed orders, arrived at Beaufort on January 8.

Porter was there to meet the new general. Terry came aboard the flagship "instantly" for the full and free conferences that General Grant had specifically ordered. Porter gave Terry copies of his own general orders, covering the naval attack procedure, and had Terry's general military orders printed for him on the flagship's presses. Violent gales penned the expedition in port until the twelfth, on which date the naval vessels formed in three lines, with the transports in company, and steamed down the coast to within ten miles of Fort Fisher.

Early on the fourteenth the gunboat division, selected to cover the landing of the troops, ran close in and shelled the woods. The transports moved inshore. At 9:00 A.M. the small boats of the division, with sailors at their oars, began putting the troops on shore. The surf was heavy, but the men—chiefly the same white and Negro troops who had been here before—took their ducking cheerfully, and by 3:00 P.M. the last man and the last box of provisions was put ashore. "Everything seemed to betoken great energy on the part of General Terry," commented navy Captain Breese in charge of landing operations. Terry shoveled a trench across the peninsula as a safeguard against attack from Wilmington, and shifted into position to assault Fort Fisher.

Meanwhile, Porter sent Commodore Radford with the ironclads to anchor one thousand yards off the corner of the fort. These sturdy craft (the *New Ironsides,* the *Saugus,* the *Canonicus,* the *Monadnock,* and the *Mahopac*) concentrated their heavy fire against the land face of Fort Fisher, splintering the palisades, dismounting guns, pitting the parapets with a smallpox of shellholes, packing the muzzles of guns with sand, and cutting the wires leading to the fort's land mines. On arcs opposite the sea face of Fort Fisher was stationed the most powerful battleship force ever assembled. They were in four divisions and contained sixty-two ships.[19] Their deep-throated bombardment continued throughout the day of the fourteenth.

On January 15, the day of General Terry's supreme effort, a landing party of two thousand sailors and marines from the fleet went ashore to spell out the last full measure of cooperation by sharing in the assault itself. The incident was pure plagiarism lifted from old storybooks, but Porter was grimly determined that this second grand effort should not fizzle. "The sailors will be armed with cutlasses, well sharpened, and with revolvers. . . . When the signal is made to assault . . . board the fort on the run in a seamanlike way." [20]

When General Terry at three o'clock gave the signal to attack, Porter shifted his naval fire away from the land face. The naval party under Captain K. R. Breese raced toward the seaward corner of the fort, while Terry rushed around the other end of the fort's land face. The navy men flashed cutlasses in the sun and popped their pistols, but found the going heavy in the deep sand. Lieutenants S. W. Preston and B. H. Porter, two of the admiral's aides, were killed at the front of the charge. Enemy sharpshooters mowed down several dozen before the remainder broke and fled down the beach or burrowed into the sand. While the seamen's assault failed, it occupied the attention of the defenders while General Terry's troops gained entrance into the fort.

Terry's soldiers—black as well as white—grappled desperately from one traverse to another. From 3:00 until 10:00 P.M. the battle raged. As long as daylight lasted, the ironclads, anchored near the shore, kept up their steady pounding of the bombproofs just ahead of the fighting Federal troops. Finally, at ten, Terry's rockets announced victory and the entire fleet erupted with cheers, steam whistles, blue Costons, and rockets. At long last Fort Fisher had fallen. The port of Wilmington was sealed to blockade-runners. The work of Mr. Lincoln's Navy was all but complete. Richmond was doomed.

During the final months Mr. Lincoln enjoyed pleasant personal associations with Farragut and Porter—the two foremost naval fighters developed during the war.

Farragut had been brought to Washington as president of the Naval Promotion Board. Although the assignment was expected to give him rest and enable him to recoup his strength, it involved endless "dissipations" at the dinner table which, in the opinion of Captain Drayton, risked the admiral's life as much as his battles. Farragut's dryly witty ex-fleet captain cautioned Mrs. Farragut not to permit her husband "to run wild, and get back to the late hours which through constant lecturing I thought to have somewhat broken in on." [21] Farragut, however, Drayton wrote a friend on January 21, 1865, "lives in society from morning to night, and seems to enjoy the excitement. He and his wife went to the opera with the President and lady the night before I came away." [22]

Late in January, while Porter was operating with the Army against the city of Wilmington, the Confederate rams in the James River broke through Dutch Gap to threaten Grant's supply base at City Point. Commander W. A. Parker shifted his double-turreted monitor *Onondaga,* he said, "to obtain an advantageous position," but his move looked like flinching to General Grant, who promptly telegraphed Washington to have Parker removed. Lincoln summoned Farragut from the Hotel Willard and packed him off to the James the same night to take whatever steps were necessary. The emergency had passed, however, before Farragut's special train reached Annapolis. Welles supplanted Parker by telegram, overwhelming forces were rushed up from Hampton Roads, and the Confederate rams retired above the barrier. In the final throes of the long contest, both Southern and Federal forces were on edge.

In January F. P. Blair, Sr., and Montgomery Blair went to Richmond to feel out the grounds for an early peace, and in February Lincoln with Seward met the Confederate Peace Commissioners at Hampton Roads in an unsuccessful conference. Toward the end of March, the President accepted Grant's invitation to visit the front and remained with army and navy officers until after Richmond had fallen.

On the morning of March 28 Lincoln conferred on board the *River Queen* with Grant, Sherman, and Porter. His chief concern, testified Admiral Porter, was to secure the surrender of the Confederate armies without further loss of life, and to that end he desired liberal terms to be offered. "Let them surrender and go home," Porter quoted Lincoln as saying. "They will not take up arms again. Let them all go, officers and all, let them have their horses to plow with, and, if you like, their guns to shoot crows with." [23]

When Grant began his final push at Petersburg and Richmond, Lincoln sent the *River Queen* to return Mrs. Lincoln to Washington and for two days accepted a small cabin on Porter's flagship, the *Malvern*. The navy's job was now finished, and Porter was happy to spend the next week escorting the President. "Uncle Abe is having a good time down here," Porter reported to Fox on March 28, 1865, "and would have had a better one had he come alone. Mrs. Lincoln got jealous of a lady down here, and rather pulled his wig for him. We put him through the Navy and did all we could to make him forget the cares of office, for which he seems grateful." [24]

Lincoln positively refused to accept the admiral's cabin and spent the first night in somewhat cramped quarters. Porter had his carpenters enlarge the cabin and on the following morning Lincoln came out smiling, "A greater miracle than ever happened last night; I shrank six inches in length and about a foot sideways!" [25]

On the night of April 1, forty-eight hours before Richmond was evacuated, Mr. Lincoln, sitting on the upper deck of the flagship off City Point, turned to the admiral and asked: "Can't the Navy do something at this particular moment to make history?" Porter reminded him that the Navy by simply being here was holding Richmond's river flotilla in check. "But, can't we make a noise?" [26]

Porter, accordingly, sent Commander William Ronckendorff up the James River to direct the monitors to open fire on the Rebel works above Howlett's Battery. As soon as the moon went down they were to send off rockets, burn blue lights, and open a brisk cannonade with ten-second shells. "Keep this up for half an hour, firing rapidly. . . . The object is merely to make the rebels think that we are about to make an attack. They are prepared to sink their gunboats at the first sign of one. Understand perfectly what I want done. . . . It is not necessary for any one of the monitors to make any changes in their positions. The only object is to make a noise." [27]

The President's demonstration, from 12:30 to 1:30 A.M. on April 2, anticipated the evacuation of Richmond and the self-destruction of the long-hoarded Confederate flotilla by about thirty hours. At 7:30 on the morning of the third, Captain H. A. Adams, Jr., came on board the *Malvern* to report that Richmond was evacuated and two hours later the heavy explosions of the Confederate flotilla were heard.

Porter accompanied the restless President on visits to Petersburg and Richmond. When Stanton learned of Lincoln's projected trip to Petersburg, he admonished sharply:

"Commanding generals are in the line of their duty in running such risks; but is the political head of a nation in the same condition?" "Thanks for your caution," responded Lincoln, "but I have already been to Petersburg. Staid with Grant an hour and a half and returned here. It is certain now that Richmond is in our hands, and I think I will go there to-morrow. I will take care of myself." [28] At 10:45 A.M. on the fourth, as soon as Porter's boats had cleared the torpedoes from the James River, Porter headed upstream in the *Malvern,* followed by the President in the *River Queen,* which had returned from Washington. The *Malvern,* having grounded a short distance below Richmond, Porter took the President in his barge, and, accompanied by a tug with a file of twenty-four marines, continued on to Richmond. Through streets crowded with rejoicing Negroes, Lincoln walked to General Weitzel's headquarters at the Confederate White House. At times Porter had to protect his charge from the jubilant mobs by threatening to use the bayonets of his marines. Federal troops who had been fighting fires in the central part of the city at length appeared on the scene to give added protection to Mr. Lincoln. "It was a gala day," Admiral Porter later recalled, "and no man was ever accorded a warmer welcome. The heat of the weather was suffocating; the President towered a head and shoulders above the crowd, fanning himself with his hat, and looking as if he would give the Presidency for a glass of water." [29]

After a night on the *Malvern* anchored at the Rockets, Lincoln spent a second day at Richmond before returning to Washington.

The electrifying news of the surrender at Appomattox Court House rang down the curtain on the story of Mr. Lincoln's Navy. Through four years it had grown in numbers from a handful of 23 to 641 ships of all types. Many of these were converted merchantmen, ferryboats, and whaling schooners. Soon after they had fired their victory salutes they would find their way to auction block or wrecker's hammer. But others were more permanent, like the double-turreted, seagoing monitors. The U.S. monitor *Miantonomah* would soon cross the Atlantic to return a ceremonial visit to the Russians. The U.S. monitor *Monadnock* would soon sail around Cape Horn to become the first modern American warship to enter the Pacific.

The work of Mr. Lincoln's Navy, as it had been blocked out by Gideon Welles near the beginning of the struggle—splitting the Confederacy in two along the line of the Mississippi River, establishing the greatest blockade in history, defeating enemy raiders on the high seas, and, in conjunction with the Army, seizing key positions along the coast—was work that Mr. Lincoln and the entire country felt had been well done.

Indeed, in Lincoln's words, "Uncle Sam's web feet" had been present "at all the watery margins . . . on the deep sea, the broad bay, and the rapid river . . . up the narrow, muddy bayou, and wherever the ground was a little damp, they had been and made their tracks. Thanks to all." [30]

BIBLIOGRAPHICAL REFERENCES

Bibliographical References

Abbreviations Used in Bibliographical References

Battles and Leaders = *Battles and Leaders of the Civil War* (4 vols., New York: The Century Co., 1887).

Fox, *Corr.* = R. M. Thompson and R. Wainwright (eds.), *Confidential Correspondence of Gustavus Vasa Fox, Assistant Secretary of the Navy, 1861-1865* (2 vols., New York: Naval History Society, 1918-1919).

O.R.N. = *Official Records of the Union and Confederate Navies in the War of the Rebellion* (30 vols., Washington, D. C.: Government Printing Office, 1894-1922). Unless otherwise noted all references are to Series I.

Reb. Rec. = Frank Moore (ed.), *The Rebellion Record:* A Diary of American Events, with Documents, Narratives, Illustrative Anecdotes, Poetry, etc. (11 vols., New York: G. P. Putnam, 1861-1864).

Report = *Report of the Joint Committee on the Conduct of the War* at the Second Session of the Thirty-Eighth Congress (Washington, D. C.: Government Printing Office, 1865), II, III. Vol. II contains hearings on the Red River and Fort Fisher campaigns, and Vol. III the investigation of the light-draft monitors.

Scharf, *Confed. Navy* = J. T. Scharf, *History of the Confederate States Navy* (New York: Rogers & Sherwood, 1887).

W.R. = *The War of the Rebellion: A Compilation of the Official Records of the Union and Confederate Armies* (128 vols., Washington, D. C.: Government Printing Office, 1880-1902). Unless otherwise noted all references are to Series I.

Welles, *Diary* = *Diary of Gideon Welles.* (3 vols., Boston: Houghton Company, 1911).

West, *Second Admiral* = Richard S. West, Jr., *The Second Admiral: a Life of David Dixon Porter, 1813-1891* (New York: Coward-McCann, Inc., 1937).

West, *Welles* = Richard S. West, Jr., *Gideon Welles: Lincoln's Navy Department* (Indianapolis: The Bobbs-Merrill Company, 1943).

CHAPTER 1. THE OVERT ACTS

1. *Reb. Rec.,* I, Diary, 4.
2. *Ibid.,* p. 3.
3. *W.R.,* I, 100.
4. *Ibid.,* p. 103.
5. *Reb. Rec.,* I, Diary, 7.
6. *W.R.,* I, 114.
7. *O.R.N.,* IV, 220.
8. *W.R.,* I, 334-35; *O.R.N.,* I, xv.
9. *O.R.N.,* IV, 48-53.
10. *Ibid.,* p. 61.
11. *Ibid.,* pp. 41, 56.
12. *Ibid.,* p. 63.
13. *Ibid.,* p. 71.
14. *Ibid.,* p. 89.
15. *Reb. Rec.,* I, Documents, No. 43.

CHAPTER 2. FORT SUMTER AND FORT PICKENS

1. *Reb. Rec.,* I, Document No. 46, p. 42.
2. *Ibid.,* Diary, p. 16.
3. N. Y. *Herald,* Nov. 28, 1861, p. 2.
4. *W.R.,* I, 196.
5. West, *Welles,* p. 99.
6. Fox, *Corr.,* I, 9.
7. *W.R.,* I, 292.
8. *O.R.N.,* IV, 227.
9. *W.R.,* I, 230.
10. *Ibid.,* p. 235.
11. *Ibid.,* p. 291.
12. *O.R.N.,* IV, 136.
13. West, *Second Admiral,* Chs. 8, 9.
14. D. D. Porter, *Incidents and Anecdotes of the Civil War* (New York: D. Appleton and Co., 1885), pp. 15-16.
15. West, *Welles,* p. 101.
16. *O.R.N.,* IV, 109.
17. *Ibid.,* p. 129.
18. *Ibid.,* p. 112.
19. West, *Welles,* p. 105.
20. Gideon Welles Papers, Library of Congress, 28891.
21. *W.R.,* I, 285.
22. *Ibid.,* p. 301.
23. Fox, *Corr.,* I, 32-33.
24. *W.R.,* I, 378.

CHAPTER 3. LOSS OF THE NORFOLK NAVY YARD

1. Welles, *Diary,* I, 40.
2. *Reb. Rec.,* I, Document 54, p. 61.
3. *W.R.,* II, 771.
4. Scharf, *Confed. Navy,* p. 132.
5. *O.R.N.,* IV, 291-92.
6. *W.R.,* II, 23.
7. *O.R.N.,* IV, 274.
8. *Ibid.,* pp. 277-78.
9. Sen. Rept. No. 37, 37th Cong., 2d Sess., p. 26.
10. *O.R.N.,* IV, 279.
11. *Ibid.,* p. 281.
12. Welles, *Diary,* I, 44.
13. *Ibid.,* p. 45.
14. *Reb. Rec.,* I, Documents, 120.
15. *O.R.N.,* IV, 290.
16. Sen. Rept. No. 37, 37th Cong., 2d Sess., p. 52.
17. *O.R.N.,* IV, 291.
18. *Ibid.,* p. 295.
19. *Reb. Rec.,* I, Documents, 100.
20. Sen. Rept., No. 37, 37th Cong., 2d Sess., p. 19.

CHAPTER 4. GIDEON WELLES FORMS A PLAN

1. *O.R.N.,* IV, 156, 340.
2. Welles, manuscript diary, Library of Congress.
3. *Ibid.*
4. Rept. of Sec. Navy, Dec. 2, 1861, pp. 18-19.
5. Fox, *Corr.,* I, pp. 44, 45.
6. R. S. West., Jr., "Private and Confidential—My Dear Fox," U. S. Naval Institute *Proceedings,* May, 1937.
7. *O.R.N.,* XII, 195-206.
8. Ex. Doc. No. 1, 2d Sess., 37th Cong., Vol. III. Rept. of Sec. Navy, July 4, 1861.
9. West, *Welles,* p. 139 ff.; and R. S. West, Jr., "The Morgan Purchases," U. S. Naval Institute *Proceedings,* Jan., 1940.
10. Welles Papers, Library of Congress, 28536.
11. Rept. of Sec. Navy, Dec. 2, 1861, p. 3.

CHAPTER 5. BEGINNING THE BLOCKADE

1. *O.R.N.,* V, 620-22.
2. *Reb. Rec.,* I, Diary, p. 10.
3. C. R. Boynton, *The History of the Navy during the Rebellion* (2 vols., New York: D. Appleton and Co., 1867) I, 317.

4. *O.R.N.*, V, 788.
5. *Ibid.*, p. 702.
6. *Ibid.*, pp. 732, 641.
7. *Reb. Rec.*, II, Diary, 37.
8. *Ibid.*, p. 51.
9. *O.R.N.*, XVI, 551.
10. *O.R.N.*, IV, 125.
11. Welles, *Diary*, I, 76.
12. *Reb. Rec.*, I, Diary, 77.
13. *O.R.N.*, XVI, 527.
14. *Ibid.*, p. 574.
15. *Ibid.*, p. 543.
16. *Ibid.*, p. 571.
17. Fox, *Corr.*, II, 73.
18. *O.R.N.*, XVI, 572.
19. Fox, *Corr.*, II, 74.
20. *O.R.N.*, XVI, 160-61.

CHAPTER 6. EARLY AMPHIBIAN OPERATIONS ON THE COAST

1. *O.R.N.*, XII, 195.
2. *Ibid.*, p. 207.
3. *W.R.*, VI, 171.
4. *O.R.N.*, V, 688.
5. *Private and Official Correspondence of Gen. Benjamin F. Butler* (5 vols., Norwood, Mass.: Privately issued, copyright 1917, by Jessie Ames Marshall), I, 213. Hereafter cited as "Butler, *Corr.*"
6. *O.R.N.*, VI, 120.
7. *Reb. Rec.*, III, Documents, 17.
8. Butler, *Corr.*, I, 227-28.
9. *O.R.N.*, VI, 124.
10. *Ibid.*, p. 217.
11. *Ibid.*, p. 234.
12. *Ibid.*, pp. 220, 215.
13. *O.R.N.*, XII, 262.
14. *Reb. Rec.*, III, Documents, 307.
15. *Ibid.*, p. 313.
16. *O.R.N.*, XII, 291.

CHAPTER 7. WILKES AND THE *Trent* AFFAIR

1. *Reb. Rec.*, III, Diary, 60.
2. *O.R.N.*, I, 169.
3. *Ibid.*, pp. 143-44.
4. *Ibid.*, p. 132.
5. *Ibid.*, p. 135.

6. *Ibid.*, p. 158.
7. N. Y. *Times,* Dec. 6, 1861, p. 4; *Reb. Rec.*, III, Documents, 333.
8. *O.R.N.*, I, 148.
9. G. Welles, *Lincoln and Seward* (New York: Sheldon and Co., 1874), p. 186.
10. West, *Welles,* p. 131.
11. T. L. Harris, *The* Trent *Affair* (Indianapolis: The Bowen-Merrill Company, 1896), p. 119.
12. *Ibid.*, p. 124.
13. *Reb. Rec.*, III, Documents, 473.
14. N. Y. *Times,* Nov. 21, 1861, p. 4.
15. *Ibid.*, Nov. 20, 1861, p. 4.
16. *O.R.N.*, XII, 833.
17. West, *Welles,* p. 137.
18. N. Y. *Times,* Dec. 20, 1861, p. 2.
19. *Reb. Rec.*, IV, Diary, 1.

CHAPTER 8. THE *Merrimack* THREAT

1. West, *Welles,* p. 148 ff.
2. *Battles and Leaders,* I, 717.
3. Rept. of Sec. Navy, July 4, 1861; J. P. Baxter, *The Introduction of the Ironclad Warship* (Cambridge, Mass.: Harvard University Press, 1933), p. 245.
4. Rept. of Sec. Navy, Dec. 2, 1861, p. 152.
5. Baxter, *op. cit.*, p. 246.
6. Rept. of Sec. Navy, Dec. 2, 1861, p. 152.
7. *Ibid.*, p. 153.
8. W. C. Church, *The Life of John Ericsson* (2 vols., New York: Charles Scribners' Sons, 1906), I, pp. 246-47.
9. *Battles and Leaders,* I, 749, 748.
10. *Reb. Rec.*, IV, Documents, 58.
11. *Battles and Leaders,* I, 731.
12. Church, *op. cit.*, II, 2.
13. *Reb. Rec.*, IV, Documents, 57-58.
14. P. Benjamin, *The United States Naval Academy* (New York: G. P. Putnam's Sons, 1900), p. 203.
15. H. C. Baird, "Narrative of Rear Admiral Goldsborough, U. S. Navy," U. S. Naval Institute *Proceedings,* July, 1933, p. 1023 ff.
16. A. T. Mahan, *From Sail to Steam* (New York: Harper & Brothers Publishers, 1907), p. 192.
17. *O.R.N.*, VI, 682.
18. *Battles and Leaders,* I, pp. 720-21.
19. *O.R.N.*, VII, 69.
20. *Ibid.*, p. 44.

CHAPTER 9. THE *Monitor* AND THE *Merrimack*

1. T. Dennett (ed.), *Lincoln and the Civil War in the Diaries and Letters of John Hay* (New York: Dodd, Mead & Company, 1939), p. 36.
2. Welles, *Diary,* I, 63.
3. *W.R.,* IX, 20.
4. *Ibid.,* p. 19.
5. *Ibid.,* p. 53.
6. *O.R.N.,* VII, 11.
7. *Battles and Leaders,* I, 725.
8. *O.R.N.,* VII, 11-12.
9. *Battles and Leaders,* I, 727.
10. *O.R.N.,* VII, 59.
11. *Ibid.,* p. 6.
12. *Ibid.,* p. 220.
13. *Ibid.,* p. 751.
14. *Ibid.,* p. 326.
15. N. Y. *Herald,* May 13, 1862, p. 7.
16. *Ibid.,* May 11, p. 4; May 12, p. 5; May 13, p. 7; May 15, p. 4.
17. Welles, *Diary,* I, 67.

CHAPTER 10. LAUNCHING THE NEW ORLEANS CAMPAIGN

1. *O.R.N.,* XVI, 627.
2. *Ibid.*
3. *Ibid.,* pp. 675-76.
4. *Ibid.,* p. 680.
5. West, *Second Admiral,* Ch. 12.
6. G. Welles, "Admiral Farragut and New Orleans," *The Galaxy,* November, 1871, p. 677; C. L. Lewis, *David Glasgow Farragut, Our First Admiral* (Annapolis: U. S. Naval Institute, 1943), Ch. 1.
7. Welles, *Diary,* I, 60.
8. Welles, "Admiral Farragut and New Orleans," *The Galaxy,* November, 1871, p. 674.
9. Welles, *Diary,* II, 117.
10. R. S. West, Jr., "Admiral Farragut and General Butler," U. S. Naval Institute *Proceedings,* June, 1956, pp. 635-43.
11. L. Farragut, *The Life of David Glasgow Farragut, First Admiral of the U. S. Navy* (New York: D. Appleton & Co., 1879), p. 208.
12. *O.R.N.,* XVIII, 5.
13. *W.R.,* VI, 678.
14. Butler, *Corr.,* I, 372-74.
15. *O.R.N.,* XVIII, 14-15.
16. Fox, *Corr.,* II, 90.

17. J. Parton, *General Butler in New Orleans* (New York: Mason Brothers, 1864), p. 209.
18. *O.R.N.*, XVIII, 48-49.

CHAPTER 11. THE SEIZURE OF NEW ORLEANS

1. A. T. Mahan, *The Gulf and Inland Waters* (New York: Charles Scribners' Sons, 1883), pp. 58-59.
2. J. T. Durkin, *Stephen R. Mallory, Confederate Navy Chief* (Chapel Hill, N.C.: University of North Carolina Press, 1954). A good general picture of Confederate difficulties in shipbuilding.
3. N. Y. *Times*, April 2, 1862.
4. West, *Second Admiral*, pp. 124-26.
5. *W.R.*, VI, 525.
6. *O.R.N.*, XVIII, 365.
7. Scharf, *Confed. Navy*, p. 294.
8. *O.R.N.*, XVIII, 164.
9. *Ibid.*, p. 361 ff.
10. *Ibid.*, p. 769.
11. *Autobiography of George Dewey* (New York: Charles Scribners' Sons, 1913), p. 65; R. S. West, Jr., *Admirals of American Empire* (Indianapolis: The Bobbs-Merrill Co., 1948), p. 71.
12. *O.R.N.*, XVIII, 182.
13. *Ibid.*, p. 142.
14. *Ibid.*, p. 158.
15. *Ibid.*, p. 154.
16. *Ibid.*, p. 158.
17. N. Y. *Herald*, May 10, 1862, p. 5.
18. *O.R.N.*, XVIII, 229.
19. N. Y. *Herald*, May 2, 1862, p. 1.
20. West, *Second Admiral*, p. 140.
21. Fox, *Corr.*, II, 107.

CHAPTER 12. EARLY OPERATIONS ON THE "INLAND SEA"

1. Scharf, *Confed. Navy*, p. 239.
2. *O.R.N.*, XXII, 278.
3. *Ibid.*, p. 284.
4. *Ibid.*, p. 307.
5. Fox, *Corr.*, II, 25.
6. *Ibid.*, p. 23.
7. *Ibid.*, p. 36.
8. *O.R.N.*, XXII, 516.
9. *Ibid.*, p. 523.
10. *Ibid.*, p. 537.
11. *Ibid.*, p. 546.

12. *Ibid.*, p. 549.
13. *Battles and Leaders,* I, 342-45.
14. *O.R.N.*, XXII, 585.
15. *Ibid.*, p. 652.
16. J. M. Hoppin, *Life of Andrew Hull Foote* (New York: Harper and Bros., 1874), p. 252.
17. *O.R.N.*, XXII, 636.
18. *Ibid.*, p. 527.
19. H. Walke, *Naval Scenes and Reminiscences of the Civil War* (New York: F. R. Reed & Co., 1877), p. 124.
20. N. Y. *Herald,* April 15, 1862, p. 1.
21. *O.R.N.*, XXIII, p. 14 ff.
22. *Ibid.*, p. 73.

CHAPTER 13. FARRAGUT ON THE RIVER

1. *O.R.N.*, XVIII, 8.
2. Ibid., p. 466.
3. *W.R.*, XV, 13.
4. *O.R.N.*, XVIII, 700.
5. *Ibid.*, p. 518.
6. *Ibid.*, p. 519.
7. *W.R.*, XV, 23.
8. *O.R.N.*, XVIII, 509.
9. *Ibid.*, p. 706.
10. N. Y. *Herald,* May 15, 1862, p. 1.
11. *O.R.N.*, XVIII, 499.
12. *Ibid.*, p. 498.
13. *Ibid.*, p. 499.
14. *Ibid.*, p. 521.
15. Butler, *Corr.*, I, 562.
16. *O.R.N.*, XVIII, 710.
17. *Ibid.*, p. 587.
18. *Ibid.*, p. 586.
19. *Ibid.*, p. 600.
20. *Ibid.*, p. 713.
21. *Ibid.*
22. *Ibid.*, pp. 638-43.
23. West, *Second Admiral,* p. 156.
24. *O.R.N.*, XVIII, 589-90.
25. *Ibid.*, p. 590.
26. *Ibid.*, p. 641.
27. *O.R.N.*, XXIII, 267.
28. *Ibid.*, p. 236.

CHAPTER 14. COMBINED ATTACKS ON VICKSBURG AND PORT HUDSON (Part One)

1. Welles, *Diary,* I, 157-58.
2. *W.R.,* XVII, Pt. II, 502.
3. *W.R.,* XXIV, Pt. I, 14.
4. *O.R.N.,* XXIII, 469.
5. West, *Second Admiral,* Ch. 18.
6. *O.R.N.,* XXIII, 512.
7. *Ibid.,* p. 508.
8. *Ibid.,* p. 421.
9. *Ibid.,* p. 529.
10. *Ibid.,* p. 508.
11. *W.R.,* XVII, Pt. II, 420.
12. *Ibid.,* p. 425.
13. N. Y. *Times,* Jan. 19, 1863, p. 1.
14. *O.R.N.,* XXIII, 573.
15. West, *Second Admiral,* p. 190.
16. *O.R.N.,* XXIII, 602.

CHAPTER 15. COMBINED ATTACKS ON VICKSBURG AND PORT HUDSON (Part Two)

1. *O.R.N.,* XXIV, 99 ff.; *W.R.,* XVII, Pt. II, 537.
2. West, *Second Admiral,* p. 196.
3. *O.R.N.,* XXIV, 108.
4. *Reb. Rec.,* VI, Documents, 365; W. T. Sherman, *Memoirs* (2 vols., New York: D. Appleton and Co., 1875), I, 331.
5. *W.R.,* XVII, Pt. II, 553-54.
6. *Ibid.,* p. 555.
7. *Ibid.,* p. 566.
8. *W.R.,* XXIV, Pt. I, 8.
9. *Ibid.,* p. 11.
10. *O.R.N.,* XXIV, 181.
11. *W.R.,* XXIV, Pt. I, 394.
12. *Ibid.,* p. 373.
13. West, *Second Admiral,* p. 215.
14. *Ibid.,* p. 218.
15. *O.R.N.,* XXIV, 493-94.
16. *Ibid.,* p. 495.
17. *O.R.N.,* XIX, 668.
18. *O.R.N.,* XXIV, 553-54.
19. *Ibid.,* p. 556.
20. West, *Second Admiral,* p. 223; Fox, *Corr.,* II, 170.
21. *O.R.N.,* XIII, 804.

22. *O.R.N.*, XXIV, 610.
23. *W.R.*, XXIV, Pt. I, 93.
24. West, *Second Admiral*, p. 237; Welles, *Diary*, I, 364.

CHAPTER 16. DU PONT AND DAHLGREN AT CHARLESTON

1. M. V. Dahlgren, *Memoir of John A. Dahlgren* (Boston: James R. Osgood and Co., 1882), contains extensive excerpts from the admiral's diary.
2. West, *Welles*, p. 218.
3. G. Hoyt (ed.), *Naval Letters of Captain Percival Drayton*, 1861-1865, from MSS in N. Y. Public Library, New York, 1906, p. 21. Cited hereafter as "Drayton, *Letters*."
4. *O.R.N.*, XIII, 324.
5. *Ibid.*, p. 423.
6. *Ibid.*, p. 550.
7. *Ibid.*, p. 556.
8. *Ibid.*, p. 579.
9. *W.R.*, XIV, 436.
10. Fox, *Corr.*, I, 197.
11. *O.R.N.*, XIV, 5.
12. H. Greeley, *The American Conflict* (2 vols., Chicago: G. and C. W. Sherwood, 1866), II, 466.
13. *O.R.N.*, XIV, 25.
14. *Ibid.*, p. 28.
15. *Ibid.*, p. 18.
16. T. Dennett (ed.), *Lincoln and the Civil War in the Diaries and Letters of John Hay* (New York: Dodd, Mead & Company, 1939), p. 59.
17. Welles, *Diary*, I, 268-69.
18. *O.R.N.*, XIV, 132.
19. *Ibid.*, pp. 132-33.
20. *Ibid.*, pp. 212-13.
21. *Ibid.*, p. 567.
22. Welles, *Diary*, I, 475.

CHAPTER 17. THE RED RIVER CAMPAIGN

1. Welles, *Diary*, I, 390-91.
2. *Ibid.*, p. 391.
3. *Report*, II, 102-03.
4. *Ibid.*, p. 103.
5. *Ibid.*, p. xviii.
6. *Ibid.*, p. xix.
7. *Ibid.*, p. xxi.
8. *Ibid.*, p. 114.

9. *O.R.N.*, XXV, 633.
10. West, *Second Admiral,* p. 245; *O.R.N.*, XXVI, 29.
11. *Report,* II, 303.
12. *Ibid.*, p. 18.
13. *Ibid.*, pp. 383-84.
14. *O.R.N.*, XXVI, 61; *Report,* II, 204.
15. West, *Second Admiral,* p. 255; *O.R.N.*, XXVI, 56.
16. *O.R.N.*, XXVI, 47.
17. *W.R.*, LXXII, 25.
18. *O.R.N.*, XXVI, 86.
19. *Ibid.*, p. 92.
20. *Ibid.*, p. 130.
21. *Ibid.*, p. 131.
22. *Ibid.*, p. 132.

CHAPTER 18. MOBILE BAY

1. West, *Second Admiral,* p. 148.
2. *O.R.N.*, XIX, 103.
3. *Ibid.*, p. 185.
4. *Ibid.*, pp. 646, 807.
5. *O.R.N.*, XXI, 547.
6. *Report,* III, "Light-Draft Monitors," i-iv.
7. *O.R.N.*, XXI, p. 89.
8. *Ibid.*, p. 53.
9. *Ibid.*, p. 219.
10. *Ibid.*, p. 416.
11. *Battles and Leaders,* IV, 388.
12. *O.R.N.*, XXI, 445.
13. A. T. Mahan, *Admiral Farragut* (New York: D. Appleton and Co., 1883), p. 277.
14. *O.R.N.*, XXI, 417.
15. *Ibid.*, pp. 406-13; *Battles and Leaders,* IV, 403.
16. *O.R.N.*, XXI, 440.
17. Welles, *Diary,* II, 100.

CHAPTER 19. WAR ON THE HIGH SEAS

1. *O.R.N.*, I, 34.
2. R. Semmes *et al., The Cruise of the Alabama and the Sumter* (1st vol., New York: Carlston, 1864), p. 49.
3. *O.R.N.*, I, p. 685.
4. Issue for May 3, 1862.
5. Issue for April 12, 1862.
6. West, *Welles,* p. 201.
7. *Reb. Rec.*, IV, Documents, 216.

8. J. D. Bulloch, *The Secret Service of the Confederate States in Europe* (2 vols., New York: G. P. Putnam's Sons, 1884), I, 57-58.
9. *Ibid.*, p. 162.
10. *O.R.N.*, I, 470.
11. Welles, *Diary*, I, 179, 191, 207.
12. *O.R.N.*, I, p. 779.
13. West, *Welles*, p. 252.
14. *O.R.N.*, II, 19.
15. *Ibid.*, p. 61.
16. Welles, *Diary*, I, 309.
17. *Ibid.*, pp. 304-05.
18. *O.R.N.*, II, 634-37.
19. *Ibid.*, p. 276.
20. *O.R.N.*, III, 677-81.
21. *Ibid.*, p. 648.
22. *Ibid.*, p. 677.
23. *Reb. Rec.*, IX, Documents, 236.
24. *O.R.N.*, III, 59.
25. *Ibid.*, p. 665.
26. Welles, *Diary*, II, 71.
27. *O.R.N.*, III, 257.
28. Welles, *Diary*, II, 186.
29. Compiled from Scharf, *Confed. Navy*, pp. 814-18.

CHAPTER 20. THE FINISH AT WILMINGTON

1. *Cambridge Modern History*, VII, 557.
2. *O.R.N.*, VIII, 526.
3. *Ibid.*, pp. 313-14.
4. *Ibid.*, p. 834.
5. Welles, *Diary*, II, 146-47.
6. *Ibid.*, p. 148.
7. *Ibid.*, p. 146.
8. *O.R.N.*, XI, 75-76.
9. *O.R.N.*, X, 594.
10. *Ibid.*, p. 618.
11. *O.R.N.*, XI, 3.
12. *Report*, II, "Fort Fisher Campaign," 216.
13. *Ibid.*, p. 95.
14. *Ibid.*, p. 69.
15. *Ibid.*, p. 15.
16. *Ibid.*, p. 26.
17. Welles, *Diary*, II, 215.
18. *Report*, p. 102.
19. *O.R.N.*, XI, chart opposite p. 425.

20. West, *Second Admiral,* p. 285.
21. Drayton, *Letters,* p. 78.
22. *Ibid.,* p. 75.
23. D. D. Porter, *The Naval History of the Civil War* (New York: The Sherman Publishing Company, 1886), p. 794.
24. West, *Second Admiral,* p. 293.
25. D. D. Porter, *Incidents and Anecdotes of the Civil War* (New York: D. Appleton and Co., 1891), p. 285.
26. Porter, *Naval History,* p. 796.
27. *O.R.N.,* XII, 95.
28. *W.R.,* XLVI, Pt. III, 509.
29. Porter, *Naval History,* p. 798.
30. C. O. Paullin, "President Lincoln and the Navy," *American Historical Review,* XIV, 285.

INDEX

Index